ALBANIA AND THE ALBANIANS

ALBANIA
AND THE
ALBANIANS

by

RAMADAN MARMULLAKU

translated from the Serbo-Croatian by
MARGOT and BOŠKO MILOSAVLJEVIĆ

ARCHON BOOKS
1975

First published 1975 in the United Kingdom
by C. Hurst & Co. (Publishers) Ltd., London
and in the United States of America as an
Archon Book, an imprint of the Shoe String Press, Inc.,
Hamden, Connecticut 06514

ISBN 0-208-01558-2

Printed in Great Britain

CONTENTS

Contents

PART TWO

PART THREE

viii   *Contents*

AUTHOR'S NOTE

Albania and the Albanians was commissioned by the British publisher, Mr. Christopher Hurst.

I have been studying Balkan affairs and in particular the Albanian question in depth since 1967. This manuscript has taken over a year to write. Perhaps there is an advantage in the fact that I have begun studying these questions relatively recently, for it has allowed me to take an unprejudiced view of the subject-matter discussed in this book. Too many people still hold conceptions about Albania that were formed during the cold war. At that time Albania was fully integrated, economically and politically, into the socialist camp and was a member in good standing of the Council for Mutual Economic Assistance and the Warsaw Treaty Organization. Albania was uncritically acclaimed by one side, and maliciously condemned or ignored by the other.

After it fell out with the Soviet Union in 1961, Albania distanced itself from the 'socialist community', and after the invasion of Czechoslovakia in 1968 it left the Warsaw Pact *de jure*.

In recent years Albania has taken an independent line, both within the country and in foreign affairs, and has overcome pressures to join either of the military and economic blocs. It has continued its propaganda attacks in the realm of ideology and foreign affairs against both the west and the east, and against the super-powers, the United States and the U.S.S.R. in particular. In its period of self-imposed isolation Albania's only window on the world was the People's Republic of China.

Albania began to re-emerge in world affairs after 1970, establishing contacts mostly with small and medium-sized states. The détente between the great powers is viewed by Albania with alarm, and their policy is attacked as a bid to establish a condominium over all other nations in the world. In Albania's eyes, all socialist countries – with the exception of itself and the People's Republic of China – have become revisionist, and the U.S.S.R. has become the leading social-imperialist power.

I have tried to give an all-round picture of Albania and the Albanians. A review of Albanian history has been provided to give readers, especially those in the west, the background for a better understanding of Albania at the present time.

I have added a chapter on Albanians in Yugoslavia, with a summary of their historical, economic and social development. I considered this necessary because much has been written on the subject, but very little by

Albanians themselves. The texts have often been superficial or down-right fallacious, and I thought it would be both interesting and useful to put forward my views as an Albanian.

The Albanians are a small nation undergoing radical transformations and changes which are interesting and instructive. Unfortunately, Albania has been closed to scholars from both the west and the east wishing to do research.

In writing this book I received invaluable assistance from contacts with friends who are scholars or figures active in political life. I would like to thank Velja Stojnić, who was head of the military mission of the National Liberation Army of Yugoslavia in Albania from August 1944 and later Yugoslav ambassador in Albania until October 1945, and at present a member of the Council of the Federation, for open and exhaustive talks about events in Albania of which he was an eye-witness. Thanks are also due for much useful information to my friend, Ambassador Arsa Mila-tović, who has served as Yugoslav ambassador in almost all the Balkan countries. Also useful were the remarks and suggestions of Dr. Duško Pirec, independent researcher at the Centre for Social Research under the L.C.Y. Presidency, who gave many suggestions for the chapter on the social and economic development of Albania.

I am grateful to the library personnel in the Institute of International Politics and Economics in Belgrade, who patiently satisfied my requests for rare books and documentary material on Albania, and to my school friend Mehmet Grguri at the National and University Library in Prishtinë, who gave his unselfish help in finding rare books. I should add that the form of this manuscript owes much to my friend Dr. Ranko Petković, editor of *Medjunarodna politika*.

In moments when I despaired of ever finishing this manuscript, my wife gave me much-needed encouragement and support.

As the author I am ultimately accountable for any mistakes and short-comings that might appear in the text. The period of gestation for this work was a long one, and at last the work is complete.

If this book helps the reader in the west to have a better understanding of Albania and Albanians and of the special political and spiritual environment in which they live, then my purpose will have been achieved.

Belgrade, 1975   RAMADAN MARMULLAKU

PART ONE

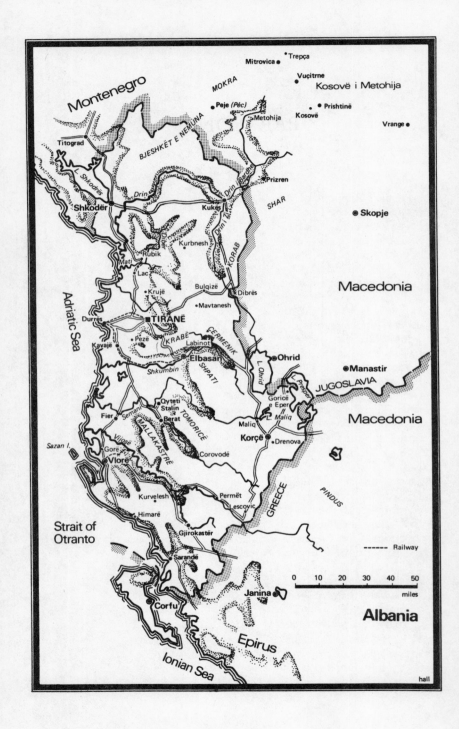

Mitrovica • Trepça
Vuçitrne •
Kosovë i Metohija
MOKRA
Peje (Péc) •
Metohija
Prishtinë •
Kosovë •
Vrange •
Montenegro
Titograd •
BJESHKËT E NEMUNA
L. Shkodrës
Drin
Shkodër •
Kukës
Prizren •
SHAR
Skopje •
Drini Zi
Drin i Bardhë
Kurbnesh •
KORAB
Rubik •
Dibër
Lac •
Mati
Bulqizë •
Dibrës •
Krujë •
Macedonia
• Mavtanesh
Durrës •
TIRANË
KRABË
ÇERMENIK
Kavajë •
• Pezë
Labinot
L. Ohrid
Elbasan •
Ohrid •
Shkumbin
SHPATI
L. Prespar
Manastir •
JUGOSLAVIA
Adriatic Sea
Qyteti
Stalin
Goricë
e Eper
Macedonia
Fier •
Seman
Berat •
TOMORICË
L. Maliq
Maliq •
Vjosë
Korçë •
Drenova •
Sazan I.
Goricë •
Corovodë •
Vlorë •
PINDUS
Kurvelesh •
Permët •
GREECE
Himarë •
Lescovic •
Strait of
Otranto
Gjirokastër •
------ Railway
Sarandë •
0   10   20   30   40   50
miles
Janina •
Corfu •
Albania
Epirus
Ionian Sea
hall

I

INTRODUCTION

(i) *The Country*

The People's Republic of Albania (Republika Popullore e Shqipërisë) consists of territory of 11,100 square miles, half-way down the western coast of the Balkan peninsula, bounded to the north and east by Yugoslavia and to the south and south-east by Greece. It faces Italy across the strategically important Strait of Otranto, with the Adriatic Sea to the north and the Ionian Sea to the south.

Two-thirds of Albania is mountainous, with forests and high plateaux, and a continental climate. In the north is Bjeshkët e Nemuna (Prokletije), part of the Dinaric range, and on the south-west lie the Shar and Pindus mountains. Korabi i Madhë (9,066 ft.) is on the Yugoslav–Albanian border; it is Albania's highest peak and Yugoslavia's second highest. In the southern part of the country, mountains stretch from the Greek and Yugoslav borders to the coast. The highest mountains are in the frontier regions, but there is also a mountain range with peaks between 5,000 and 6,000 ft. high in central Albania. There is a gradual westward slope giving way to the coastal plains, which are Mediterranean in climate and vegetation, and which comprise one-third of the national territory.

Arable land and orchards account for 510,700 hectares or 17·8 per cent of the total land surface; 719,400 hectares (25·0 per cent) are given over to meadows and pastureland; forests cover 1,253,500 hectares (43·6 per cent); 391,200 hectares (31·6 per cent) is uncultivated or infertile. The principal crops are maize, grown on 160,000 hectares, with yields of 165,000 tons, and wheat grown on 13,000 hectares, with yields of 115,000 tons. Rice, rye, barley, grapes and olive oil are other important agricultural commodities, while citrus fruit and tobacco are cultivated in small quantities. Albania is well endowed with mineral resources.

The population of Albania is 2,226,000, of which 95 per cent are ethnically Albanian. At the time of the 1961 census it included 40,000 Greeks (2·4 per cent), 15,000 Macedonians and Montenegrins (0·9 per cent), 10,000 Vlachs (0·6 per cent) and approximately 10,000 gypsies; but many Albanians live outside their homeland. A very large number of Albanians (1,309,523) live in Yugoslavia. Some 50,000 live in Greece, 80,000 in Italy and 15,000 in Turkey, not to mention those in North America.

The Albanians are divided into two dialect groups: the Tosks in the south and the Ghegs in the north. Their language belongs to the Indo-European group, but forms a sub-group of its own. A congress held at Manastir (Bitola) in 1908 introduced the orthography which is still used today. In 1972 a congress on the orthography of the Albanian language was held in Tiranë, and phonetic rules of spelling were adopted.

Economically, Albania is a developing country passing through the process of industrialization. Before the liberation in 1944, its economy was extremely backward; industrialization had hardly begun and agriculture was still primitive and at subsistence level. However, there has been a heavy emphasis on industrialization since the revolution, a factor which has held the standard of living at a rather low level. Leading industries include oil extraction and the mining of chrome, copper, nickel and bitumen. Electrical power production is undergoing rapid growth. In 1971 Albania completed its programme of bringing electrification to all communities, and the rate of production of electrical power was expected to double in the 1971–5 plan period. The metal and chemical industries are also growing quickly. The *per capita* national income is around US $400 (as estimated by the International Bank for Reconstruction and Development).

Albania maintains trade relations with over fifty countries. Its principal exports are the raw materials and agricultural products mentioned above, while industrial machinery and equipment, vehicles, paper and textile products are imported.

Albania is a people's republic in which the unicameral People's Assembly is invested with supreme political sovereignty. Deputies to the Assembly are elected every four years, and there is one deputy for every 8,000 voters: the present Assembly is composed of 264 deputies. The People's Assembly elects a thirteen-member Presidium and appoints the government, which is responsible to it. When the Assembly is not in session, the government is responsible to the Presidium. Since 1953 the Presidium Chairman and head of state has been Haxhi Lleshi.[1]

Albania has been a member of the United Nations since 1955. In 1961 all diplomatic, political and economic relations and indeed all forms of co-operation with the U.S.S.R. were broken off. Albania stopped participating in Comecon meetings in 1961, and on 13 September 1968 made its withdrawal from the Warsaw Pact official. After this break Albania embarked on a course of friendship and co-operation with the People's Republic of China, which is today the country's major ally and trading partner, and the main source of loans financing its development.

(ii) *Who are the Albanians?*

The Albanians are probably descendants of the ancient Illyrians. Over the centuries they have been called by different names. The Albanians (*Arbanasi* in Serbian, or *Arnauti* in Turkish) or *Shqipëtarë*,[2] as they call themselves, were named after an Illyrian tribe, the Albanoi; later this name was used to refer to all the Illyrian tribes in this region. The Albanian language belongs to the Indo-European group of languages, and it is generally agreed to be the modern descendant of the Illyrian language, although this claim is disputed. The Albanian language was mentioned in 1285 in Dubrovnik manuscripts as *lingua albanesesca*.

The name of Albania is to be found in thirteenth-century Latin dictionaries, and its Byzantine name was similar: Albanon. The geographical region between the city of Durrës and the Drin river is called Arbanon (Arber) in Byzantine sources, and is also mentioned in Greek sources of the second century A.D. Ptolemy states that it is inhabited by the Illyrian tribe, the Albanoi. In the middle ages, Albanians called their country Arbën-Arbër and themselves Arbënesh-Arbërësh. This name is preserved even to this day by Albanians who migrated from their country during and before the Turkish invasions. Fleeing before the invading Turks to other Christian states, they formed small colonies there,[3] and there are still Albanian colonies in southern Italy, Sicily, Morea (Greece) and Arbereshi near Zadar in Yugoslavia. In the Middle Ages the names used by other people for Albanians were based on the *arb* and *alb* stems (Byzantine Arbanon and Albanon, Latin Arbanum and Albanum, and Slavonic Arbanas and Raban).

The Illyrians were an Indo-European people who settled the western portion of the Balkan peninsula around 1000 B.C. The Greek logographer Hecataeus of Miletus mentions them as inhabiting the eastern Adriatic coast around 500 B.C. A century and a half later, Pseudo-Scilac enumerated some Illyrian tribes and placed their settlements on the coastal strip from the Krka river in Slovenia to Vlorë in Albania. It would seem that at first only those Illyrians living near the border of Epirus were actually known by that name. The most important Illyrian tribes from north to south were the Liburni, Dalmatae, Ardaei, Dardani, Albani, Tanlantii, Labeati, Orestes, Molossi, Chaones and Thesproti.

Ancient writers such as Herodotus, Livy, Pliny and Strabo give information on the physical qualities and life of the Illyrians, who are said to have been tall and well built, good fighters, fond of drinking and not much concerned with cleanliness. They lived in patriarchal communities and every eight years redivided their land. They were politically disunited, quarrelled with each other and waged wars against Greek colonists and Macedonians, and later even against the Romans. Some groups lived within fortifications and their main occupations were agriculture, hunting and sea piracy. After the incursion of the Celts into the Balkan peninsula, some Illyrian tribes mixed with them. According to Strabo, the *Iapodi* were an Illyrian people mixed with Celts. Hence, some tribes described as Illyrian by ancient writers were already an Illyrian-Celtic mixture.

Only once did the Illyrians succeed in setting up a kingdom of any size. In the third century B.C., the Ardaei controlled several Illyrian tribes and organized a state under King Agron, whose territory extended from the Krka river in Slovenia to present-day Albania. Illyrian piracy threatened trade in the Adriatic, and conflicts with Rome ensued. The Liburni, for example, had fast galleys and in their frequent clashes with the Romans they were invariably the victors. However, the Romans copied the design of these ships, which they called *liburnae*. In a war in 229 B.C. the Romans defeated the Illyrians, whose kingdom was reduced to a narrow strip between Dubrovnik and the area of Lezhe, and formed the protectorate of Illyricum over the Greek colonies on the eastern Adriatic coast and their hinterland. In a military campaign against the Illyrian King Genthius in 167 B.C., Rome was again victorious and brought his kingdom under its rule. New conquests expanded the concept of Illyria: in the second half of the first century B.C., the Roman province of Illyricum stretched from the river Rosa in Istria to the river Mat in Albania. In 27 B.C. it became a senatorial province, administratively attached to the territory of Pannonia. The Illyrian tribes were overwhelmingly crushed in a war from A.D. 6 to 9.[4] Thus began their gradual Romanization which, however, was intensive only around administrative centres, garrisons, military strongholds and staging posts along the main routes.

From that time Illyrians began to enter the Roman army and administrative bodies. Some, like Aurelian, Diocletian and Probus, even became emperors. The names Illyria and Illyrians were preserved in tradition even after the settlement of the Slavs in the Balkan peninsula. It is certain that the Illyrians were not Slavonic; the Slavs entered the Balkans several centuries later than the Illyrians.[5]

As we have seen, there has been much speculation through the centuries on the origin and evolution of the Illyrians. Today there are two main schools of thought: first that the Illyrians migrated to the Balkan peninsula, and secondly, that they were an autochthonous people in the Balkans. Modern investigations in Albania and the Balkans have convinced archaeologists, ethnologists and linguists that the second hypothesis is the correct one. Be that as it may, there is no dispute over the fact that the Illyrians lived in the area now inhabited by Albanians and elsewhere in the Balkan peninsula.[6]

The Illyrians were primarily agriculturalists and livestock breeders, the latter exclusively in the mountainous regions and among the luxuriant upland pastures. Tools for cultivation included the wooden plough, the iron axe and a bronze or iron sickle. The Illyrian lands were also rich in mineral wealth: iron, copper, gold and silver.

Bronze implements predominate in archaeological finds on Illyrian sites of the first millenium B.C. up to the sixth century, when iron was used to make tools and weapons. This has been established by the excavations at Sanski Most in Yugoslavia and in Albania. The most recent excavations at Novo mesto in Yugoslavia in 1967 and 1968, carried out by the Archaeology Department of the University of Ljubljana and the Dolenjski Museum of Novo mesto, are the richest and most significant finds of the Hallstatt culture left by the Illyrians tribes who lived in the north-western Balkans. Some of the vessels, graves, implements and ornaments are considered among the finest from any ancient culture.

Of particular importance are the sixth-century *situlae* – bronze vessels decorated with reliefs depicting deities, athletic contests, animals, etc.[7]

Modern knowledge of the Illyrian language is largely based on epigraphic remains. The language belonged to the Indo–European group of languages; some of its features relate it to the languages of the Celts, Germanic tribes, Italic peoples, Greeks and Thracians, with whom the Illyrians had come into contact during their migrations: it is also akin to Messapic and Venetic. Gustav Meyer and other German scholars laid the foundations of Albanian Studies in the last century: according to him, the present-day Albanian language represents the latest phase of the old Illyrian language or, more precisely, of an Illyrian dialect. He also expressed the opinion that those who accept the origin of the Albanian as Illyrian need not try to prove it; the burden of proof lay rather on those who deny it.[8]

The migrations of barbarian tribes, which dealt the death blow to the western Roman empire, also shook the foundations of the Byzantine empire. Hordes of Huns, Avars, Celts, Goths and other tribes swept through and ravaged the Byzantine provinces in the Balkans, but stayed only a short time and then passed on. The Illyrian tribes south of the Sava and Danube rivers managed to remain in the areas where they had settled.

The great migration of Slavs, who poured across the northern boundaries of the Balkan peninsula in the first decades of the seventh century put an end to the Byzantine authority over a large area from the northern end of the Peloponnese in the south to the Sava and Danube rivers in the north. Constantinople retained power in only a few places on the edges of this vast territory, mainly in cities on the coast. It is difficult to determine the details and chronology of this Slavonic invasion, but the Slavonic tribes are known to have penetrated into all parts of the Balkan peninsula. The Romanized Illyrian population withdrew before the advance into the coastal towns and into the mountains of the interior:

thus in northern Albania there grew up an extensive settlement of old inhabitants.[9]

The arrival of the Slavs marked the end of the civilization that had flourished in the area for centuries. The Slavonic tribes, a synonym for good herders and farmers, also put an end to the slavery which the Romans, and even the Romanized Illyrian rulers, had established in the Balkans. The process of Romanization of Illyrian tribes was thereby ended, but those tribes which remained in the lowlands adjacent to the more powerful Slavonic tribes began to fall under Slavonic influence. However, the Illyrian mountain tribes which had less contact with the Slavonic tribes maintained their order and social system intact.

The incursion of the Slavs into the Balkans caused a severe crisis in the Byzantine empire which found itself in a vice between the Muslim world on one side and the Avars and Slavs on the other. Many parts of the Balkans were taken over by the Slavs, but they still did not have their own state organization. Surrounded by enemies, the empire responded by creating a new system of military administration known as *themes* or military provinces; the first such province in the Balkans was created at the end of the seventh century. The *strategia* of Thrace was established around 680, when the Bulgars crossed the Danube.

The importance of Durrës (ancient Dyrrachium) as one of the bulwarks of the Byzantine empire dictated the creation of an important *theme* there, at the beginning of the ninth century. Although the *themes* at first had the character of military corps, they had a great impact on the subsequent socio-economic and political development of the regions which were less subject to Slavic influence. In the *theme* of Durrës the Albanian tribes caused the region to develop a special character.[10] Early feudalism among the Albanians, with peculiar local features, arose under the influence of Byzantium, and later under the influence of the South Slavs and the Normans from the West.[11]

Charles I of Naples (1227–85), who had designs on the eastern shores of the Adriatic Sea, formed the Kingdom of Arberie (Regnum Albanai), and proclaimed himself 'king of Albania'. Undoubtedly, the main attraction of this region was again Durrës, which had well-developed commercial ties with other Adriatic cities and states and was a stage along the famous Via Egnatia, which linked Constantinople with the west. Until the Ottoman empire penetrated to the Balkans, some of the Albanian tribes, and at times the whole of Albania, came under the rule of neighbours such as Bulgarians, Serbs, Normans and Venetians. When the Turkish power actually began to threaten the Balkans, the Albanians at last began to play a notable role of their own in political events.

Introduction

NOTES

1 For biographical note, see below p. 100.
2 The national name Shqipëtarë is said to be derived from *shqipe* meaning 'eagle', and thus signifying a mountain people. Other explanations have it that the word *shqip, shqipëtarë* derives from the Albanian verb *më shqiptue* meaning 'to speak'. Thus the name would signify people who spoke the same language.
3 *Historia e popullit Shqiptar: I.* (2nd imp.), Prishtinë, 1969, p. 159.
4 Illyricum was now divided into the provinces of *Pannonia Superior* and *Provincia Illyricum*, later Dalmatia. Diocletian's reform later made Illyricum one of the four prefectures of the Roman empire, and as such it embraced almost the entire Balkan peninsula. This prefecture, to which Constantine the Great attached Epirus, Achaea and Macedonia, was split into three smaller provinces – Dalmatia, Proevalitana and Epirus Nova – and these administrative divisions remained largely intact until the coming of the Slavs to the Balkan peninsula.
5 Lovett F. Edwards, *Yugoslavia*, London, p. 33.
6 Zef Miridita, 'Iliri i etnogeneza Albanaca', lecture printed in *Istorija Albanaca*, Beograd, 1969, p. 9.
7 Tone Knez, 'Nove situlske umetnine', *Kronika XX*, 1972, and 'Novo mesto v davnini', *Obzorje*, Maribor, 1972.
8 Eqrem Qabej, *Hyrje në historinë e gjuhës shqipe* (2nd imp.), Prishtinë, 1970, p. 31.
9 Dr. Božidar Ferjančić, 'Albanija do XII veka', *Istorija Albanaca*, Beograd, 1969, p. 29.
10 Jadran Ferluga, 'Sur la date de la création du thème de Dyrrachium', *Extrait des Actes du XII Congrès International des Etudes Byzantines*, Vol. 2, Beograd, 1964, pp. 83–92.
11 Mirdita, op. cit., p. 10.

2

UNDER TURKISH RULE

(i) The Turkish Conquest of the Balkans

The old tribal organization of Albanian society was deep-rooted, and the people lived for centuries within small communities of blood relations. These were left intact by the ruling power, which only demanded taxes and formal allegiance, but did not interfere in the Albanians' internal affairs. It is undoubtedly this lack of unity which accounts for the fact that the Albanians became a politically organized force rather late, in the fifteenth century only, when they began their long struggle against the Turks. Since pastoral life predominated, the Albanians were always in search of better pastures and were a very mobile people, which accounts for their expansion into Hercegovina, Zeta, Serbia, Macedonia, Epirus and Thessaly.[1]

In the early Middle Ages some feudal families managed to form independent principalities. The tribe of Thopia had one of the strongest Albanian principalities – Principate e Arberisë, ruled by Karel Thopia. The tribe of Balshajt in the north was a powerful rival to the Thopia tribe in Albanian political life. As was the case among other feudal Balkan tribes, there was often war between them. The most important tribes in the political and social life of Albania, and particularly in the wars against the Turks, were the Dukagjin, Balshajt, Shpata, Muzaki, Komneni, Ariani, Thopia and Kastrioti. The Kastrioti tribe produced Albania's greatest national hero in the struggles against the Turks, Gjergj Kastrioti-Skenderbeg. The Ottoman conquest of Europe began with the invasion of 1352; in 1354 the Turks captured Gallipoli, which became their first stronghold on European soil. Another decisive battle was fought at the Maritsa river in 1371 when the Bulgarian tsar was forced to declare himself a vassal of the Sultan – which did not stop him from waging further battles against the Turks. Both Sofia and Niš were taken by 1386, but in 1389 the Serbian states were definitively crushed at the Battle of Kosovo. The victory of the Turks over Krujë in 1478 was the crucial battle in Albania.[2]

The Turks were constantly faced with fierce resistance from the peoples they were invading, and their advance into the Balkans was only gradual. They were filling the vacuum caused by the disintegration of the Byzantine empire. However, their success was also aided by the fact that the Balkan feudal lords were all preoccupied with wars among themselves, and were willing to recognize the sovereignty of the Turkish Sultan in order to preserve their economic privileges. The defeat of the Bulgarians at Maritsa in 1371 and the defeat of the Serbs at Kosovë in 1389 marked the collapse of Serbia, Bulgaria and Albania, which then came under Turkish rule.

In the occupied Balkan territories, the Turks established a military and feudal system which became the cornerstone of the entire Ottoman empire. According to Ottoman law, all land was owned by the state. The Sultan granted fiefs to deserving members of his feudal cavalry, known as *spahi*. In return for their fiefs (or *timars*), the *spahis* were obliged to take part in military campaigns, with a force in proportion to the size of their fief. Although the *timars* were not hereditary, a *spahi*'s son could inherit his father's land if he was fit for military service. A *spahi* could lose his fief if he failed to respond to a summons to battle, if he were disloyal to the Sultan, or if he were convicted of a crime. Thus the feudal class structure of the Ottoman empire was based on a system of military land grants. Regional military and political units were called *sanjaks*, whose rulers were usually of the high feudal Turkish aristocracy. As a reward for loyal service, the Sultan gave them entire villages, whose inhabitants (the *raya*) worked for them. There were units smaller than the *sanjaks*, known as *vilayets*, headed by a *subasha*. In the *sanjak* and *vilayet* respectively, the *sanjakbey* and *subasha* were representatives of the supreme civil and legislative authority; but the highest authorities of all were the heads of the *sheriat* courts, the *kadis*. *Sheriat* law is the Islamic religious law based on the Prophets teachings and religious practice. It reflected the social, economic, political and religious conditions in Arabia and encouraged the feudalization of society. It was also applied in the Ottoman empire. Some sections of *sheriat* law were in force for Muslims in Albania and Yugoslavia up to 1941 and even throughout the Second World War, only being superseded when those states became socialist.

The Turks created the province of Rumelia from occupied Balkan territories and annexed some Albanian lands to it. In the year 1431 two *sanjaks* were created: the Albanian and the Dibrës. The Kastrioti and Balshajt feudal tribes, who had acknowledged Turkish sovereignty in return for autonomy as vassals, were not annexed to this administrative unit.[3]

The force of the Turkish army rested on the feudal *spahi* (landlord) system; the *spahi* cavalry were the basic army unit. The infantry was also of high military calibre and was composed of janissaries, soldiers who as children had been forcibly taken from their homes as tribute from the enslaved Christian lands and sent to Turkey, where their names and faith were changed and they were educated and trained to be good soldiers in the service of the Sultan. The janissaries excelled in the wars of conquest and earned a high position for themselves in the Turkish hierarchy, often becoming wealthy men.[4] Such advancement was a great incentive for the soldiers to conquer as much new territory as possible. Indeed, it was largely thanks to them that the Ottoman empire succeeded in expanding into three continents. There were many Albanians serving as janissaries in the Turkish army and administration, some of whom later became well-known officers in the Turkish army, grand viziers and important officials, at the court of the Turkish Sultan.[5] During nearly five centuries of Turkish rule, twenty-seven grand viziers (the equivalent of prime minister) were of Albanian origin.[6]

(ii) *Skenderbeg – National Hero*

One of the many Albanians groomed for high position in the Turkish hierarchy was Skenderbeg, who became the shining light in the Albanian national fight against the Turks. Skenderbeg was born in 1405 in the Kastrioti clan in Northern Albania, and given the Christian name Gjergj. His parents were compelled to hand him over as tribute to the Turks in order to maintain their vassalage and rule over the villages of Northern Albania.[7] At the age of seven Gjergj Kastrioti was taken to the court of Sultan Murad II, where he was trained in the military arts, converted to Islam, and given the name Skenderbeg, after Iskender (Alexander the Great), whom the Turks regarded as a hero. After twenty years of training at the Sultan's court, Skenderbeg became a soldier and soon showed brilliance as a strategist. He was highly respected at court, yet he never broke off ties with his homeland and his own people.

Frequent Turkish attacks, plundering and devastation aroused Albanian resistance against the invaders. In 1430 the Skopje governor Isak invaded Albania, and seized part of the possessions of Ivan Kastrioti. It thus became clear to the Albanian feudal lords that reliance on the Turks was futile. In 1433 an uprising began against the Turks in the entire area from Shkodër to Vlorë under the leadership of Arijanit Shpata, and with the help of leading Albanian families such as Thopia and Muzaki.[8] Three Turkish armies were defeated between 1434 and 1436, but Isak finally quelled the rebellion in the autumn of 1436.

Not many years were to pass before Albania again rebelled, this time with much greater success. In 1443 the Turks, with Skenderbeg's participation, clashed with the Hungarians near the town of Niš. At first, thanks to Skenderbeg's strategy, the Turks were successful and managed to stop the Hungarians before the town. In the meantime, Skenderbeg had decided to return with his 300 Albanian comrades-in-arms to his homeland, leaving the Turkish army. On 28 November 1442 he entered Krujë and proclaimed the independence of the principality of Kastrioti.[9]

Taking down the Turkish flag, he raised the red Kastrioti flag with a black eagle in the centre – which has been the flag of all Albanian tribes ever since, and became the national flag. After liberating Krujë, Skenderbeg reverted to Christianity. At this time the Turks were occupied in wars with neighbouring peoples and at first could not send reinforcements against the Albanians. Skenderbeg took advantage of the situation and expanded the territory of his state, driving out the Turks from almost the whole of Albania in a series of battles. However, as a military strategist he realized that his army alone, which was drawn from various clans that were often at war with each other, would be no match for the Turks, and he proposed an alliance with the Albanian feudal lords, which was concluded in Lezhë in 1444.[10] The feudal land-owners who joined the alliance promised financial and military support for Skenderbeg. It was decided to recuit 'one soldier from every household' thus uniting all the separate armed bands of the feudal lords into a single Albanian army that could thus offer effective resistance to the Turks.[11] After this alliance had been created, the Turks attacked Skenderbeg in Krujë many times, but without success.

From the time of his return to Albania, Skenderbeg had also had difficulties with the Venetians, who held a number of Albanian towns, several of which Skenderbeg sought to annex to his own state. His decisive actions in the vicinity of Shkodër and Durrës aroused the Venetians and a battle ensued. In this struggle Skenderbeg co-ordinated his actions with the Serbian despot, Djuradj Branković, who was vying with the Venetians for some Adriatic coastal towns, and maintained friendly ties with him.[12] He also wanted to co-ordinate his moves with the campaign of the Hungarian army which, under the command of János Hunyadi, had penetrated Serbia in the direction of Kosovë, but could not do so, since Hunyadi was halted by the Turks in his southward drive and forced to retreat. In order to have a free hand in the struggle against the Turks, Skenderbeg concluded a peace treaty with Venice in 1448.[13]

The long-anticipated large-scale Turkish attack came in 1450, and it was led by Sultan Murad himself. Krujë was besieged for five months with the most modern weapons of the day, but Skenderbeg was victorious, and his feat was acclaimed throughout Christendom and especially in Italy. Since an appeal for aid to King Alfonso I of Naples in 1451 yielded some food and 200 muskets, Skenderbeg felt encouraged to press for a firmer commitment, and in a treaty signed at Gaeta on 16 March 1451 he pledged vassalage to the Neapolitan king, promising that as soon as the Turkish danger had passed he would go to Italy personally and pay homage. However, the very small assistance which Naples sent to Albania was of little help in the defence of the country.[14]

With the accession to the Ottoman throne of Mohammed II, 'The

Conqueror' (1451–81) a time of uninterrupted struggle against the
Turks began for Skenderbeg. Mohammed II was determined to subdue all the Balkan states. He occupied Constantinople in 1453, the Serbian despotate in 1459, the remnants of the Greek state in the Peloponnese in 1460, and Bosnia in 1463. Ottoman victories in the Balkans
greatly alarmed Christian Europe, but as the Balkan states toppled one
by one, Skenderbeg consistently repulsed the enormous Turkish army.[15]
During these years Skenderbeg made great efforts to organize an alliance of the Balkan and other Christian states to halt the further penetration of the Turks into Europe. He envisaged a kind of crusade of the
European Christian countries against the Turks. Pope Pius II was enthu-
siastic about this plan and promised support for Skenderbeg, who was
then called the 'Champion of Christianity'. Preoccupied with their own
affairs, the European states never responded to this appeal for an alliance,
and with the death of Pius II in 1464 all such plans were abandoned.[16]
In 1455 Skenderbeg attacked the Turks at Berat but did not succeed in
taking the town, and suffered the loss of more than 6,000 men. In the
summer of 1457 the Turks attacked Skenderbeg with an army of 60,000,
conquered almost all the Albanian lowlands and prepared for an all-out
attack on Krujë. Skenderbeg withdrew to the mountains, since in the
meantime the Turks had managed to breach the fortifications at Krujë,
but shortly afterwards, in 1458, he forced the Ottoman army to withdraw from Albania, even though his own forces had been weakened by
the desertion to the Turks of Lekë Dukagjini.[17]

The Turks reacted with fury to their failure to subdue Albania, and in
1466 Sultan Mohammed II personally took command of his army and
set out to vanquish the country. He succeeded in taking almost the whole
of it, but like his father sixteen years earlier, he too failed to occupy
Krujë, despite a siege of almost two years. During that time, Skenderbeg travelled to Rome to beg the Pope for help: he was received in
Rome with the highest honours and the Pope presented him with a
sword and cap, but aid was not forthcoming. Soon afterwards Skenderbeg returned to Albania and tried to withstand the Turkish onslaught
with his own forces. In 1468 once again he obtained the support of
Albanian leaders, but he fell ill with fever and died at Lezhë on 17
January 1468.[18]

After his death the Albanian people continued to resist the Turks, but
after a two-year siege and blockade, Krujë was forced to capitulate.
Later, in 1479, Shkodër also fell. The rest of Albania was soon brought
into submission, except for some mountain strongholds. Durrës was the
last town to be taken, in 1501.

The Albanian people and feudal lords looked upon Skenderbeg's
death as a great national tragedy, and their sorrow was shared by neighbouring countries. Writers and poets of many countries have celebrated

the exploits of this hero over the centuries. But the Albanian people in particular have kept alive the memory of this great military leader and statesman as one of their greatest heroes. Although Skenderbeg's small army was in the end no match for the enormous might of the Ottoman empire, he was the initiator and organizer of a collective armed struggle against the Turks, who had previously conquered the disunited Albanian feudal lords one by one. Skenderbeg rallied and united all these lords in a holy war. But because he could neither win a final victory over the Turks nor even stem the Turkish tide into Albania, he could only postpone the inevitable conquest of his country and the entire Balkan peninsula. Albania and the other Balkan countries now entered a new period of their history, the period of direct Turkish rule.[19]

(iii) *Consolidation of Turkish Rule*

Having re-established their authority in Albania, after the fall of Skenderbeg, the Turks carried out a new administrative subdivision. Dividing the entire region into *sanjaks* and annexing them into Rumelia, they established the *spahi* system of feudal landownership, which was open to the feudal lords of Albania, provided they espoused Islam. Since property ownership and power were the privilege of a small class, the majority of the people were heavily burdened with high taxes and levies. As Albanians were welcomed into the Turkish army, these ex-soldiers were later to form the feudal class in Albania. The Albanians were good soldiers and much preferred an adventurous life to the drudgery of work. Since religion was of little concern to them, they were quite willing to fulfil the condition of becoming Muslim. It was one of the features of the Ottoman empire that all nationalities could rise to high posts in government, provide they fulfilled this condition. The large participation of Albanians in the political life of the Ottoman empire caused the Albanians to link their fate with that of the Turkish empire for five centuries.

In the interior, where the *spahi* landlord system had been only formally introduced, if at all, the mountain people remained organized in their clans, although these were in the process of disintegration. The Turks did not succeed in imposing their landownership system on the mountain tribes and finally granted them tribal autonomy on the basis of traditional legal norms (the canons) and payment of a tax.[20] The first so to benefit were the Himari, in 1492.

Isolated from the rest of the world and with their own social and legal system and subsistence economy, the Albanians withdrew within their tribal boundaries, so that there appeared to be a revival of the tribal system, even though it was declining. Matters of interest for all members were settled at tribal meetings, though these meetings had only a limited competence, in particular when people outside the clan were involved. The head of the clan was selected from families which had traditionally provided tribal chieftains, and an army comprising members from each household was led by a *voivode*. The body of customary norms had several names – the 'Old Canons' and the 'Canons of Lek Dukagjin,' of 'Skenderbeg', of 'the Mountains' and of 'Father Zhulia'. These semi-autonomous tribal regions, particularly in the first years of Turkish rule, were the cradle of Albanian resistance to the Turks.[21]

The hard life and poverty of the mountain regions caused many to turn to brigandage and leave their native villages, while many mountain clansmen, with their reputation of being good soldiers, joined the Turkish army. Several Albanians became the highest military commanders in Ottoman wars in Europe, Asia and North Africa. We need mention only the campaigns against Yemen and Egypt, where Albanian commanders won battles for their Ottoman rulers. Sinan Pasha (The Great), an Albanian by birth, won renown as the 'Victor of Yemen'. In the words of the modern Turkish historian Alia, 'Sinan Pasha was one of those stubborn Albanians who, once they got an idea into their heads, never let go of it.'[22] Sinan Pasha also led the assault on La Gulete in Tunisia in 1574, razing it to the ground and driving out the Italians and the Spanish. Albanians sought their fortunes throughout the length and breadth of the Ottoman empire as traders or artisans, or even as manual labourers in the Balkan towns. This tradition lasted in Albania up till the Second World War and still persists today among the Albanians living in Yugoslavia.

In the sixteenth century almost every part of Albania was Christian, the Orothodox Church being dominant in the south, and the Roman Catholic Church in the north. At first, only a small number of town clans became converted to Islam, in order to maintain their economic position and privileges.

In the seventeenth century the Turks began a policy of Islamization of the population at large to ensure peace in the Albanian lands, and to win the allegiance of this nation of warriors to the Ottoman empire:[23] the propagation of Islam was the best means of pacifying the Albanians. They also used economic incentives to convert the people. Those who adopted Islam received land, and had their taxes lowered, whereas the *raya* in subjugated Balkan countries worked the land without the right of ownership. The Albanian *raya* at first put up rather strong resistance to Islamization, as can be inferred from the length of time needed to convert most of the population. However, in the eighteenth and nineteenth centuries Islam became predominant, and its adherents far outnumbered the Roman Catholics and Orthodox. Among the Muslims the Bektashi sect began to win adherents, and later played a key role in the Albanian national renaissance.[23]

After the Turkish occupation, the Albanian economy not only stagnated but was ruined by the devastations of many years of war. In the fifteenth and sixteenth centuries, the cities became flourishing trade centres linking the Ottoman empire and neighbouring states. However, the introduction of new agricultural crops and increased agricultural output provided the basis for growing artisan and other urban classes, which in turn led to the creation of a local market. Some regions began to specialize in certain goods. Goldsmiths, silversmiths and gunsmiths reached a high level of skill, and centres of carpenters and woodcarvers, and tailors making national costumes, were formed.[25]

The religion of Islam brought Muslim culture in its wake. In the seventeenth century, religious schools (*medrese*) began to be established in the towns. One of the most important centres of oriental culture was Berat, with many *medrese*, where at the beginning of the eighteenth century there flourished an intellectual élite and circle of poets who imitated Arab and Persian writers. The literature of that time was secular and written in the Turkish–Arabic script, with many orientalisms. It dealt with social themes and everyday life. The Orthodox clergy in the towns and monasteries taught in Greek: they were mostly educated on Mount Athos, and their teachings were Hellenistic.

It was only in the Roman Catholic Schools, in northern Albania, that the Albanian language was maintained at this time. Franciscan missionaries began in 1632 to found elementary schools in the villages of northern Albania. The first writers to use the Albanian vernacular were Catholic priests. In 1555 John Buzuku published the first book in the Albanian language – *Meshari*, a book of prayers – which is preserved in the Vatican library. Pjeter Budi translated into Albanian a book on Christian doctrine and in 1621 published an original work, *A Company of Saints*. Another exponent of this religious and didactic literature, which had little original thought in it, was Pjeter Bogdani. Frang Bardhi published the first Latin–Albanian dictionary in 1635, and Andre Bogdani wrote the first Latin–Albanian grammar. The Council of Albanian Bishops, convened by Pope Clement XI, resolved to propagate religious literature in the Albanian language, but the decision was never put into effect, since the number of Roman Catholics was greatly reduced in the course of the seventeenth century, and foreigners came to hold the highest positions in the Albanian Catholic hierarchy.[26]

Vernacular folklore, folk literature and tradition were nurtured and jealously preserved by the people. Songs, legends and epics commemorating the struggles of the Albanian people against outsiders were passed orally from one generation to the next.

In the eighteenth century and early in the nineteenth, the *spahi* gradually decayed, and with it the empire's administration. The ownership of land gained a new significance: military posts could now be bought and sold, so that those who held them considered the estates and fiefs that went with them to be their inviolable freeholds. The previous system of military fiefs, which had been granted for life to distinguished soldiers, who were then obliged in turn to serve the Sultan faithfully and go to war with an armed retinue whenever summoned to do so, was thus undermined, and it received its death blow when the feudal lords began to turn the land of the state (*merat*) into private feudal estates – known as *chitluk*.[27] The *chitluk* land was rented to the Muslim peasantry by the feudal lord, who was known as the *chitluk-sahibija*; the peasant working a *chitluk* was known as a *chivchija*.

These *chitluks* were small at first, and held by individual owners. Later, they passed into the control of small clans. In this general rush of the landowners to acquire wealth, antagonisms were engendered which led to anarchy. The lot of the peasants became ever more unbearable. Feudal rents were raised: instead of one-tenth of his crops, the peasant now had to give a quarter, or sometimes as much as half to the lord of the *chitluk*. Peasant dissatisfaction grew, and led to uprisings.

In the confused economic conditions which had arisen in Albania, the strongest feudal lords began to increase their economic and political power and to assert their independence from the Porte by creating independent *pashaluks*. These lords were not at first interested in breaking away completely from Turkish rule, since they protected their own interests through the Ottoman state and the Sultan's power. The *pashaluks* were the largest administrative territorial units in the Ottoman empire, and their rulers, *pashas*, were directly subject to the Porte. The Shkodër and Janina *pashaluks* were perhaps the best known,[28] and the latter, under its notorious ruler for over thirty years, Ali Pasha Tepelena, was especially powerful.

Ali Pasha Tepelena was born in 1744 at Tepelen, in southern Albania, and in his youth was the leader of a band of brigands. Later he entered the service of the Sultan and managed to achieve his ambitions: he created the largest *pashaluk* in the Ottoman empire. His ambitions were to amass a great fortune, to avenge himself on his private enemies, and to become the independent ruler of Albania and part of Greece. Ali Pasha established and maintained contacts with all the great powers of Europe at that time. He maintained contacts with Napoleon Bonaparte, the English Admiral Nelson and the Russian Tsar. He also gave support to the Greek struggle for liberation from Turkish rule. His *pashaluks* harboured organizations dedicated to winning independence for Greece. He would also have liked to secede from the Ottoman empire.

Ali Pasha's ruthlessness, cunning and diplomatic skills earned him the title 'The Lion of Janina', and his court was visited by many eminent Europeans, including in 1809 Lord Byron, who was thus inspired to devote a canto of *Childe Harold* to Albania and the Albanians.

Rival feudal lords, both Albanian and Turkish, whom Ali Pasha had ousted from their holdings in Albania, Epirus and Thessaly, as well as the Greek patriots fighting for their own liberation, put pressure upon the Porte to get rid of Ali Pasha. Turkish forces attacked Janina, and Ali Pasha found himself deserted by his sons and allies. He fought to the bitter end and was killed in 1822. His head was sent to Constantinople and publicly displayed.

Ali Pasha was a member of the Bektashi sect. His head was buried by an Albanian dervish beside the graves of his sons. The inscription on his tombstone reads: 'Here lies the head of the renowned Ali Pasha Tepelena, a former statesman of Janina, who independently ruled over Albania for more then 30 years.'

Under Ali Pasha, Janina was the most advanced centre in the Western Ottoman empire. Although the great powers did not recognize the Janina and Shkodër *pashaluks* as independent principalities, they treated them as separate states as relations with the Porte deteriorated.

The great *pashaluks* created the conditions for a faster economic development of the Albanian regions. Also important was the fact that power was concentrated in the hands of a single feudal lord, and instead of squabbling among themselves the Albanian lords were not united against the Turkish authorities.

At the end of the nineteenth and the beginning of the twentieth centuries, the Ottoman empire entered a new phase of decline. Its downfall came from within and not from without, through the successful struggle of the subjugated peoples in the European part of the empire – a struggle in which the Albanians played a prominent part. As early as the first decades of the nineteenth century, but especially after the new centralist reforms of the *tanzimat*[29] which were introduced to save the empire, a strong national independence movement took root in Albania, which was not satisfied with concessions such as the creation of semi-autonomous *pashaluks*, but which demanded full national and cultural rights. It soon became a well-organized movement.

NOTES

1 Momčilo Spremić, *Iz istorije Albanaca* (Excerpts from Albanian History), Beograd, 1969, p. 36.
2 *Historia e popullit shqiptar*, op. cit., p. 220.
3 Op. cit., p. 235.
4 Ibid., p. 236.
5 Radovan Samardžić, *Mehmed Sokolović*, Beograd, 1971.
6 M. Frashëri, *Liga e Prizrenit edhe efektet dipllomatike të saj* (The Prizren League and its Diplomatic Effects), Tiranë, 1927, p. 8.
7 *Historia e popullit shqiptar*, pp. 249–66.
8 M. Spremić, op. cit., p. 40.
9 Fan Noli, op. cit., p. 25.

10 *Historia e popullit shqiptar*, p. 255.
11 Ibid., p. 256.
12 M. Spremić, op. cit., p. 41.
13 Fan Noli, op. cit., pp. 69–92.
14 *Historia e popullit shqiptar*, pp. 270–4.
15 M. Spremić, op. cit., p. 42.
16 Ibid.
17 Lekë Dukagjini came from a strong tribe in Albania. In the last years of his life he helped Skenderbeg, although at one point, as mentioned above, he betrayed him and went over to the Turkish side. After Skenderbeg's death, his possessions being threatened, Lekë led the struggle against the Turks.
   The body of customary law formed since that time to the present among the Albanian tribes has been called the 'Kanuni i Lekës' or 'Kanuni i Lekë Dukagjinit' (in English known as the Canon of Lek). The Turkish authorities had to recognize or at least tolerate the existence of these laws as governing relationships among the mountain people, just as they had to acknowledge, tacitly or publicly, their tribal autonomy.
18 J. G. Senkevich and N. D. Smirnova, *Histori e shkurtë e Shqiperisë* (Short History of Albania, translated from Russian), Prishtinë, 1967, p. 34.
19 M. Spremić, op. cit., p. 44.
20 *Historia e popullit shqiptar*, p. 325. The size of the tax depended on how wealthy the tribe was, and what its wealth consisted of. It was sometimes collected only at very long intervals.
21 Dr. Bogumil Hrabak, *Iz istorije Albanaca*, op. cit., p. 51.
22 Quoted by R. Samardžić, op. cit., p. 338.
23 Ibid., p. 59.
24 *Histori e popullit shqiptar*, p. 342.
25 B. Hrabak, op. cit., pp. 61–4.
26 Ibid., p. 60.
27 Senkevich and Smirnova, op. cit., p. 47.
28 Ibid., pp. 61–81.
29 The *tanzimat* reforms. The unrest of the subject peoples of the Turkish empire finally made reforms in the administrative and social system imperative. For instance, the Albanian peasantry were constantly rising up in peasant rebellions against taxes and the obligatory seven or even twelve years' military service in the Turkish army. These rebellions lasted from the 1840s to the 1870s. The extensive reforms prepared by Mustafa Rashid and proclaimed by Abdul Mejid Sultan made all subjects of the Ottoman empire equal under law with safeguards for their lives and property; taxation was regulated, and military service was reduced to a limited number of years, which Christians could even exempt themselves from upon payment of a special tax.

3

THE INDEPENDENCE MOVEMENT AND THE FORMATION OF THE ALBANIAN STATE

(i) *The Ottoman Decline*

The formation of the Albanian state in 1912 was the direct outcome of the Albanian people's independence movement. The movement had several specific features which influenced the course of its development and the process of creating Albanian statehood. Some of these special features were occasioned by the attitude of the great powers and neighbouring states towards the Albanian national question and the formation of an Albanian state. Others had to do with social and political developments in Albania.

In the nineteenth century and the first decades of the twentieth, the Albanian struggle for national liberation entered a phase in which the achievement of political, economic and cultural independence was inevitable. After the Janina *pashaluk* of Ali Pasha Tepelena in the south and the Shkodër *pashaluk* in the north were crushed, peasant risings broke out in nearly every part of the Ottoman empire that was inhabited by Albanians and continued to do so spasmodically from the 1840s to the 1870s. The peasants from the mountains, who were predominantly Muslims, were the prime movers of the rebellions. Although the uprisings were mainly concerned with preserving the local autonomy which the peasants and feudal landowners had enjoyed under the old régime, they also had a broader national and Balkan importance, since they opposed the entire administrative system of the Ottoman empire: its taxes and levies, the seven- and twelve-year terms of army service, and so on, which had had a devastating economic effect in Albania and every country under Ottoman rule. The economic inequalities which the system engendered led to social antagonisms and strengthened national sentiment against the Ottoman rulers. The revolts of Albanian peasants dealt a heavy blow to the new centralist system introduced by the Turks to consolidate the lands they ruled. In order to create an alliance for the struggle against the Turks, political organizations and governments of the neighbouring countries seeking liberation from the Ottoman empire established contacts with the Albanian leaders. Albanians participated in the Greek and Rumanian revolutions.[1] The Albanian bourgeoisie, which could have given the rebels a unified political programme, was unable to do so, since it was economically weak at that time, and was not prepared to let the peasant revolts grow into a national liberation struggle. However, the other revolutions and independence movements in the Balkans, as well as the ideas of European bourgeois revolutions, had their effect in inspiring the Albanian bourgeoisie – both inside and outside the country.

The political programme offered by the young Albanian bourgeoisie did not seek to alter the country's existing status within the Ottoman empire. The influence of Islam and Christianity, both Roman Catholic and Orthodox, was strong and, more than any other nation in the Balkans, Albania was under the conservative influence of the Porte and the Greek Patriarchate, which sought, respectively, to islamize or hellenize the Albanian people by language and faith. In the 1860s the programme for the renaissance of the Albanian people emphasized the teaching and use of the Albanian language. The leading proponents of the renaissance movement wished to overcome religious divisions and to do this, awareness of Albanian nationhood was to be fostered. These leaders were Naum Veçilhadxhi and Zef Jubani. Albanians living abroad, particularly in Rumania, Bulgaria and metropolitan Turkey, formed patriotic societies propagating the idea of Albanian independence. The national renaissance fostered political thinking among the Albanians and inspired a rich literature.

In the complex international situation of that time, Turkey was undergoing a deep economic, social and political crisis. A rudimentary but growing capitalism was clashing with the still strong feudal forces. In addition, Turkey was threatened with disintegration, particularly at the hands of Russia which, with the other great powers, or in spite of them, wished to settle the 'Eastern Question' in its own favour. Under the guise of protecting Christians and pacifying the Balkans, Austria-Hungary and Russia were intent on establishing their own dominion in the Balkans. Britain and Italy were also interested. The Rastatt Treaty of 8 July 1876 envisaged, among other things, that in the event of a complete disintegration of European Turkey, independent principalities would be formed in Bulgaria, Rumelia and Albania, and the Russo-Austrian Convention of 15 January 1877 concluded in Budapest provided for the creation of independent states in those territories.[2]

The manoeuvres of Russia and Austria to gain influence in the Balkans were viewed with alarm by the Albanians. In Albania, Austria vied with Italy for influence. Having recently achieved its own unification, Italy sought to portray itself as the father of Albania's independence movement. The neighbouring countries, Greece, Serbia and Montenegro, were also interested in how the Albanian question would be settled within the larger context of the Balkan question. The bourgeoisie and leading circles in these countries and in Bulgaria raised unjustified territorial claims on Albania.[3]

When Russia went to war against Turkey on 24 April 1877, the crisis in the area entered an even more acute phase. The great powers were spurred to even more intense activity in seeking to solve this question. Italy made soundings to find out if it would gain anything in this melée, and received the answer from Bismarck that if Austria-Hungary received Bosnia, then Italy could receive Albania or some other Balkan country. Britain approved the award of Albania to Italy, but Austria-Hungary opposed it, fearing Italy's growing power, and ambition to dominate the eastern Adriatic. In March 1878, after a Russian victory in the war, the San Stefano peace treaty was concluded, and among its provisions was the creation of Greater Bulgaria which would include some Albanian territory.[4]

Thus Russia sought to maintain its dominance in the Balkans, but the other great powers were opposed to the San Stefano Treaty, and Russia was compelled to agree at the Berlin Congress that its provisions should be revised. Between the San Stefano Treaty and the Congress of Berlin, the great powers waged a fierce diplomatic struggle, which had the side-effect of stirring up political hopes in Albania. The question of the further existence of European Turkey became paramount. The San Stefano Treaty caused a strong reaction in Albania, and there were local uprisings.[5] It was in this situation that one of the guiding lights of the Albanian movement for independence came into being – the League of Prizren.

(ii) *The League of Prizren*

The League of Prizren was the fruit of ripening internal conditions as well as contemporary international events. The League owed its existence chiefly to the beys, who held the dominant economic and political positions in Albania. Also influential were Albanian emigrés – wealthy men, politicians and intellectuals – as well as intellectuals within the country. These had their societies, which disseminated educational and national propaganda; some even had committees for the liberation of Albania. The Albanian emigrants in Istanbul, many of whom held responsible political positions, were chiefly responsible for the formation of the League of Prizren.

An external factor which precipitated the formation of the League was the unfriendly attitude taken by the Serbian government towards the Albanians in Southern Serbia, which had been annexed to Serbia after the Serbo-Turkish war of 1876–8. The region in which these Albanians were settled stretched from Leskovac and Vranje to Niš. The Serbian government had promised that it would take no action against the Albanians so long as they were loyal in the war of 1876–8. The Albanians in these regions kept their side of the bargain and maintained a loyal attitude. However, the Serbian government did not keep its promise: it gave instructions to its troops that they would be helping their fatherland if, when penetrating Southern Serbia, they took strong action against the Albanians and expelled them from these regions. The Serbian troops carried out their orders, causing great distress not only to the Albanians in these parts but also to others, especially since the Albanian population in this region was predominantly driven into the Kosovë region. Relations between the Albanians and Serbs living there became very strained after this.[6] Finally, the announcement that the Congress of Berlin would soon be held, to revise the provisions of the San Stefano Treaty, gave the immediate impetus for the formation of the League of Prizren to make Albania's demands known to the world, i.e. to oppose the cession of territories which it considered Albanian. The reaction of the more prominent Albanians to San Stefano was a feeling that they were between the devil and the deep blue sea – between the tutelage of Turkey on the one hand and the predatory designs of the Balkan states, which wished to dismember Albania, on the other.[7]

Thus the Albanian movement against Turkey and Albania's predatory neighbours was brought under the leadership of a single Albanian political organization. On 20 June 1878 the constituent assembly was held in Prizren, attended by over 300 delegates, representing the Albanian middle class, who arrived from all areas inhabited by Albanians, the majority from Kosovë and the Dukagjin Plain and from Western Macedonia. The delegates from southern and central Albania sought complete autonomy, while those from Kosovë and the Dukagjin Plain and Western Macedonia wanted government to be in the hands of the local inhabitants, and refused the cession of any land settled by Albanians.

The latter idea prevailed. However, in the later phases of the Prizren League's activities, the struggle for autonomy and independence became all-important. As Tucović says in *Srbija i Albanija*, Southern and Central Albania were the 'spearheads of the modern movement for autonomy'.[8]

Faced with new difficulties during the holding of the Berlin Congress, because it had to draw frontiers with Montenegro and Greece, Turkey at first allowed the League to function, especially as the majority of Albanians were violently incensed over the cession of Ulcinj, Plavë and Gusinje to Montenegro and of the southern regions of the country to Greece. After settling its border questions, Turkey turned to the problem of establishing peace and order, but the Albanian movement had begun using its right of autonomy to agitate for independence.[9] Since the Porte could no longer tolerate the League, which had collected the local taxes

for two and a half years in northern Albania, it also could not take a
phlegmatic attitude towards the movement for autonomy and independence, which it decided to crush, concentrating all its forces in the effort.

To do this, Turkey used an armed force of 20,000 men. The operation
against the Albanians was led by Dervish Pasha, who brought heavy
artillery into action against the insurgents. He was met at Kosovë by a
force of 6,000 Albanians. In the fighting at Kaçanik and Shtimlje, many
thousands of Albanians were killed. Dervish Pasha succeeded in crushing
the independence movement and entered Prizren in 1881 without resistance. Here he rounded up most of the leaders of the autonomy movement and sent them into exile to Rhodes or Asia Minor. Adherents to the
movement were sent for trial. In Prishtinë alone, over 4,000 Albanians
and 200 Serbs, who had helped the Albanians in their struggle, were tried
and sentenced to terms of imprisonment. Trials of members and leaders
of the movement and the League were also held in other provincial
capitals – Shkodër, Manastir and Janina. About 1,000 men and several
hundred familes from Southern and Central Albania were deported to
Asia Minor and the Black Sea, where they were interned in camp and
served sentences.

This reign of terror, the arrests, trials and persecution of the movement of sympathizers, activists and leaders, increased the antagonism
between the now awakened people and the oppressive Turkish government, and this disaffection was of prime importance for the further
growth of the Albanian independence movement. The League of Prizren aroused the national sentiments of the Albanian people. It was a
powerful weapon, the first organization to lead a movement for the
autonomy and national independence of Albanians on any notable scale
in political and military action. As such, it was a milestone in the Albanian national rebirth.[10]

(iii) *The Young Turks, the Balkan Wars and the new Albanian State*
The suppression of the League of Prizren dealt a heavy blow to the Albanian independence movement. However, the desire for national independence was fully aroused among the population at large, and the years
up to 1908 were filled with Albanian revolts and uprisings. A large number of societies carried on lively political and cultural activity; some
thirty newspapers and journals were published, both in Albania and
abroad. A large number of schools using the Albanian language were
opened in Elbasan, Vlorë, Tiranë and other towns and villages, not only
in Albania proper but also in Kosovë and western Macedonia. An outstanding cultural event of that time was the Congress held at Manastir in
1909, at which representatives of the Albanian intelligentsia from all
lands inhabited by Albanians and delegates from societies abroad

adopted a unified Albanian alphabet to replace the several scripts that had been used previously.

Fresh political developments in Turkey were giving impetus to Albanian political and cultural activity. The revolution of the Young Turks occurred in 1908 and was assisted by Albanians in return for promises that they would be relieved of taxes and given constitutional rights. Sultan Abdul Hamid had enacted the Constitution of 1876 under pressure of the revolutionary ferment at that time, but the Young Turks did not follow his example and, after consolidating their political power, they reneged on the programme that had been proclaimed during the revolution. The Albanian societies and schools were soon closed down, and publication of newspapers and periodicals in the Albanian language was forbidden.

The chauvinistic policy of the Young Turks provoked a large-scale revolt of thousands of Albanians in 1909, and in 1910 the insurgents managed to take Prishtinë and Vuçitrnë. Turkey responded by sending an army of more than 20,000 men to stamp out the uprising in Kosovë and northern Albania. The main battle was fought at Kaçanik near Skopje. The greatly out numbered Albanians were defeated, and the Turkish army took Prishtinë and Gjakovë and continued towards Shkodër, which in August 1910 it managed to conquer, together with Dibër, Elbasan and Tiranë. The Albanian insurgents stored their weapons against the day when a new revolt would be timely. At this time the Albanian committee charged with organizing and leading the future armed uprising had its headquarters at Podgorica – to-day Titograd – in neighbouring Montenegro. The uprising in northern Albania began in March 1911. Some 8,000 took up arms against the Turks. In the summer of 1911 the uprising spread to Kosovë, southern Albania and Western Macedonia. Sultan Mehmed Reshad went to Kosovë to try to placate the rebels, but without success. In June the leaders of the uprising held a meeting in Montenegro at which they adopted a twelve-point memorandum, which they sent to all the European powers as well as the Turkish government. Among the rebels' demands were the following: that the existence of the Albanian nation be recognized, that Albania be granted self-government, that no unconstitutional action should be taken against the Albanians, that free elections should be guaranteed, that Albanian schools should be free to operate, that the Albanian language should be freely used, that Albanians should be employed in the government administration, that Albanians should serve in the army in their own territories, that a major portion of the state revenues from these territories should be used for their economic and cultural advancement, that confiscated weapons should be returned to the people and that a general amnesty should be declared.[11] The Turkish government rejected the conditions in the memorandum, but made counter proposals. Although the latter contained some of the demands made in the memorandum, the demand for autonomy was rejected. Some of the rebels accepted the Turkish proposals and ceased fighting, but the rest continued their struggle.

In 1908, elections followed the proclamation of the Constitution which ended the absolutist regime, and over twenty Albanians, led by Ismail Qemal Vlora, became deputies in the Turkish parliament. Ismail Qemal was a politician and diplomat of renown not only within the Ottoman empire but internationally. In the first Turkish parliament he became leader of the liberal opposition Ahrar Party. The party programme advocated by Ismail Qemal called for decentralization of the empire and its institutions, and autonomy for the national regions. Prominent Albanians at home and throughout the Turkish hierarchy realized that the empire's days were numbered, and began intensive diplomatic activity to win the sympathies and practical help of the European powers for the formation and proclamation of an Albanian state. The powers – particularly Austria-Hungary, which was keenly interested in the outcome of the Albanian question – at first advised against a revolt, arguing that the Albanians could achieve their national aspirations within the empire; however, it later championed an independent Albania and encouraged Albanian patriots, since it realized that the Ottoman empire could no longer hold the Balkan nations, including Albania, in subjugation, nor could a policy of the great powers favouring the artificial maintenance of the Ottoman empire be successful in view of the increasing frequency of uprisings and social unrest.

In the spring of 1912, an uprising began in all Albanian lands and soon took on broad dimensions. Albanian patriots sought to form alliances with democratic forces in neighbouring Balkan states; however, the governments of these states (in particular Serbia, Greece and Montenegro) – were themselves ambitious to acquire Albanian territory, and tried to prevent the formation of an Albanian state. Similarly, it was Italy's dream to control the entire Adriatic and the Strait of Otranto, a corollary of which was the control of Albania. Indeed, the governments of the neighbouring states were fiercely divided in their rivalry for territorial gains. Because of its interest in the area, Austria-Hungary could not afford to let Italy or Serbia expand too much and upset the Balkan balance of power; so, to counter the expansion of these two states, Austria-Hungary supported the demands of the Albanian people for their own independent state.

By the beginning of 1912 the situation in Turkey had deteriorated still further. Seeing their chance, the insurgent committees, particularly the General Insurgent Committee of Kosovë, called the Albanians to an armed uprising. The revolt spread like wildfire to all the regions inhabited by Albanians. In Kosovë alone, there were 30,000 armed rebels. By

July 1912 the rebels had freed all the towns in Kosovë as well as Skopje, which forced the resignation of the Turkish government. The new government which replaced it sent a delegation to Prishtinë to negotiate with the leaders of the uprising, Hasan Prishtinë and Isa Buletini. The insurgents submitted a memorandum containing fourteen points, similar to those demanded in 1911 by the rebels of northern Albania. Turkey accepted most of the proposals with the exception of the demand for autonomy. The leaders of the uprising were informed of the Turkish reply on 18 August 1912, and accepted it, probably influenced by internal events and because of the reluctance of the powers to see the Turkish empire dismembered.

In the autumn of 1912 the Balkan states of Serbia, Bulgaria, Greece and Montenegro formed an alliance against Turkey. Montenegro declared war on 8 October 1912, the other states following on 17 October. In one month the Turkish empire in Europe had been overthrown, and on 3 November Turkey sought the mediation of the great powers. A truce was signed on 3 December 1912. At first the great powers wanted to maintain the *status quo* in the Balkans, but after the collapse of the Turkish empire in Europe, they had to recognize the true situation. At that time the armies of Serbia, Greece and Montenegro had penetrated deep into Albanian territory, as part of their plan to divide up Albania among themselves.

To Albanian patriots at home and in societies and organizations which were actively working for Albanian independence in the European capitals and in the United States, the impending fate of the European part of the Turkish empire was clear. They knew that the time had come to make their bid for independence. For this purpose, a meeting of Albanian societies, organizations and individuals from the homeland and abroad was held at Bucharest in November 1912. They decided to hold a national congress in Durrës to proclaim Albanian independence and elect a provisional government. They also sent out a plea to the great powers for recognition. Austria-Hungary and Italy gave diplomatic support to the demands of the Albanian patriots; the independence movement had taken on such momentum that it could no longer be stopped.

After the necessary preparations, delegates from all over Albania met at the congress in Vlorë. The congress, presided over by Ismail Qemal Vlora, the experienced Albanian politician and diplomat, proclaimed Albania an independent state on 28 November 1912. A provisional government was elected, and Ismail Qemal became head of the government and minister of foreign affairs. The Albanian people had at long last achieved their dream of a free state.

NOTES

1 Stefanaç Pollo, Ndreçi Plasari, 'The Role of the Albanian People in Recent History', paper delivered at the International Congress of Balkan and Southeast European Studies, Sofia, 1 September 1966. Published in the journal *Historical Studies*, in the Albanian language, Tiranë, No. 1, 1967.

2 Ali Hadri, 'Istorija Prizrenske lige i albanskog pokreta za autonomiju' ('History of the Prizren League and the Albanian Movement for Autonomy'), *Perparimi*, a journal of science and culture, selection of articles in Serbo-Croatian, Prishtinë No. I, 1967, p. 31.

3 Hadri, op. cit., p. 32.

4 Dimitrije Tucović, *Srbija i Albanija*, Beograd, 1945, p. 61. Article 6 of the San Stefano Treaty called for the borders of Bulgaria to extend to Korçë in Albania, including part of Albanian territory and Pogradec. (By the 1860s plans were afoot for a greater Greece, which would include Constantinople. There was also Garašanin's plan for a greater Serbia, including almost the whole of Macedonia and Albania.)

5 *Besa*, special issue, Shkodër, 1938, Nos. 10–12, p. 450.

6 Hadri, op. cit., p. 34.

7 Tucović, op. cit., p. 61.

8 Ibid., p. 66.

9 *Historia e Shqipërisë*, Tiranë, 1967, Vol. II, pp. 181–201.

10 Ali Hadri, *Iz istorije Albanaca*, op. cit., p. 143.

11 Ibid., p. 149.

4

ALBANIA BETWEEN THE TWO WORLD WARS

The independence of Albania which had been proclaimed at Vlorë on 28 November 1912 was confirmed by the Conference of Ambassadors of five great powers held in London on 20 December 1912. The Conference of Ambassadors held on 29 July 1913 decided to guarantee Albania's independence as a sovereign principality and select a ruler. The frontiers of the new state were drawn, but border disputes with neighbouring countries continued, since the foreign armies had still not withdrawn from the regions they had occupied.

(i) *How the Frontiers of Albania were formed*
The Conference of Ambassadors was presented with two different proposals by Austria-Hungary and Russia. Agreement could not be reached, so the conference set up two international commissions, one charged with the task of drawing the frontiers of Albania with Serbia and Montenegro, and the other the frontier with Greece. The borders of Albania today, with the exception of a few minor corrections, are the same as those fixed by the international commissions. The fairness of these frontiers can be judged from a speech by Sir Edward Grey, the British foreign secretary, to the House of Commons on 12 August 1913, in which he openly stated that the basic objective of the agreement on the borders was to satisfy the great powers, but that many criticisms could be raised by anyone who really knew Albania and viewed the issue from the standpoint of that country's existence.

After long debate, Prince Wilhelm of Wied was proposed by Austria-Hungary as the ruler of the new state. His appointment was the signal for a renewed outbreak of hostilities between different political groups in Albania. Prince Wilhelm arrived in Durrës on 7 March 1914, but just seven months later opposition forced him to leave the country. Italy in particular feared that his presence would create a stronger Austro-Hungarian influence in Albania. The Prince had formed a government composed of Albanian feudal lords, which caused great dissatisfaction among the peasantry, who had expected to gain their freedom after centuries of feudal bondage. However, not even the landlords were satisfied with Prince Wilhelm, they had wanted a Muslim ruler, and were even willing to accept a Turkish or Egyptian prince. Essad Pasha Top-tani[1] had himself attempted to seize power in Albania and was particularly active in intrigues against Prince Wilhelm, who took action against him in May 1914, forcing him to seek refuge in Italy. However, a rebellion broke out in Durrës three days later, and rapidly spread to the entire country. The government and the Prince controlled only Durrës, while the rest of the country was under the control of many local tribal armed groups. Serbia, Greece and Italy assisted these movements in order to foment internal dissension as a prelude to stepping in themselves. The Prince cherished the hope that the powers which had appointed him would come to his aid, but on 3 November 1914 he left Albania for good.[2]

The struggle over Albania flared up again during the First World War, during which time the country had no effective central government. The population of northern Albania petitioned Austria-Hungary for support against Serbian and Montenegrin territorial aspirations, while the southern Albanians had to defend themselves against the Greeks.

The attitude taken by the warring powers towards the Albanian question was determined by the efforts of both camps to win over Italy and Greece, which did not join in the conflict immediately. Hence the Entente powers gave Greece permission to occupy southern Albania, provided the occupation was temporary, i.e. that Greece would withdraw when the Entente powers so decided, and they allowed Italy to occupy Vlorë.[3] The Greek army moved into southern Albania, taking the towns of Korçë and Gjirokastër, and soon afterwards declared these Albanian districts to be formally annexed to Greece. Italy responded by sending its fleet to the port of Vlorë at the end of October 1914. After Italy had occupied Vlorë and the island of Saseno, Greece occupied Sarandë.

In the secret Treaty of London of 26 April 1915, the Entente powers and Italy reached an agreement to satisfy Italian aspirations for Albanian territory. The same powers which in 1913 had proclaimed Albanian independence and sovereignty were willing to sacrifice it two years later, and to dismember the Albanian state. By the provisions of the secret Treaty, all Albanian territory from the river Vijosë in the north and east to the region of Himarë in the south, including the town of Vlorë, would belong to Italy. Italy for its part undertook not to oppose the partition of northern Albania and the rest of southern Albania between Serbia, Montenegro and Greece, or the drawing of a common Serbo-Greek frontier west of Lake Ohrid. A small autonomous state would be created from the rest of the country (central Albania), which Italy would represent in foreign affairs. In 1916, immediately after entering the war on the side of the Entente, Italy began carrying out the provisions of the secret

Treaty concerning Albania. The north of the country was occupied by
Serbia and Montenegro, without the consent of the Entente: Montenegro
occupied Shkodër, and the Serbian army moved into parts of northern
and central Albania, including Elbasan and Tiranë. However, in February 1916 the Serbian army withdrew, and Austro-Hungarian troops
entered northern Albania, occupying all the territory up to the line
formed by the river Vijosë, the town of Berat, and Lake Maliq. When
the monarchy was overthrown in Greece in 1916, the Allies forced the
Greek government to withdraw its troops from southern Albania. Italy
rapidly stepped into the vacuum to occupy Gjirokastër and even Janina.
The French army from the Salonika front occupied the rest of southern
Albania, all the way to Korçë.

On 3 June 1917 the Italian military commander in Albania, General
Ferrero, proclaimed the creation of a unified and independent Albanian
state under the protection of Italy, which thus clearly revealed its intention
of ruling Albania itself. France responded by proclaiming the Korçë
Republic, which lasted for three months. Albanian patriots had asked the
French to expel the Greeks from this area and to establish a French
administration. The expulsion of the Greeks from Korçë, to which they
had a justified claim, was an important event which strengthened the
Albanian independence movement. In September 1918 the Austrian
army was forced to abandon Albania, and the Serbian army re-entered
the north of the country, occupying all the territory along the river
Drini i Bardhë. France retained parts of southern Albania. The Allies
decided that Albania should remain occupied until its fate was decided
at the Peace Conference.[4]

Italy tried to maintain its foothold in Albania. It formed the government of Turkhan Pasha in Durrës, the members of which were all pro-
Italian, and which even sent its delegation to the peace conference in
Paris to back Italy's special strategical interests in Albania. The Durrës
government was willing to accept a prince of the House of Savoy for
the Albanian throne. However, Italian pretensions in Albania were con-
tested by the new Kingdom of the Serbs, Croats and Slovenes, as well as
by Greece. At this time Italy was going through its own internal difficulties, caused by the growing strength of the revolutionary workers'
movement, and was not able to withstand both the south Slav and
Greek pressures. Unable to use force, Italy opted for diplomacy and
sought to win Greece over to its plans. A secret agreement was signed by
the Italian foreign minister Tommaso Tittoni and the Greek prime minister Eleftherios Venizelos on 29 July 1919, whereby the Italian government undertook to support Greek claims to southern Albania, while the
Greek government would recognize Italian sovereignty over Vlorë and
its mandate over the rest of Albania. In mid-January 1920, Lloyd
George, Clemenceau and Nitti agreed that Italy should be given the

whole of Istria and Rijeka from Yugoslavia, and that in return Yugoslavia would be given northern Albania, while the rest of the country would be partitioned according to the provisions of the Tittoni-Venizelos treaty.[5]

At the Versailles peace conference, Albanian autonomy was a moot point. Plans to repartition the country were vigorously opposed by the Albanian delegates. In this they had the support of the U.S. President, Woodrow Wilson, who in principle advocated the self-determination of nations and accordingly backed Albanian interests. The British delegation also spoke on behalf of Albanian interests, and for a time even Yugoslavia, represented by its foreign minister, Dr. Trumbič, favoured Albanian independence and autonomy. British policy on the Albanian question at the peace conference was described by one of the Albanian participants, Nikollë Ivanaj, as follows:

At that time the policy of Great Britain on this question seemed enigmatic, for whereas Prime Minister Lloyd George appeared to be against the national programme of the Albanian people, other British delegates at the Paris peace conference took a different attitude in their advice to Albanian delegates. But the time has still not come to write about this . . .

While a diplomatic battle was thus being fought over Albania in France, the country was occupied by Italian troops – a fact deeply resented by the Albanian people. In 1918 a movement to expel the Italians took on many adherents. A national congress was convened in Lushnjë on 28 January 1920, which unanimously decided to fight against foreign domination in order to achieve the final liberation of the country and establish the sovereign rights of the Albanian state. The congress sent an energetic protest to the Peace Conference and to the Italian parliament against plans for the partitioning of Albania between Yugoslavia, Italy and Greece, and refused to accept any country's protectorate or mandate. It passed a decision to strip Turkhan Pasha of all government prerogatives and to set up a new government headed by Sulejman Delvina. It was also decided to elect a four-man regency council (one Muslim Bektash, one Muslim Sunnite, one Roman Catholic and one Albanian Orthodox) to govern the country, pending its final liberation. The government moved to Tiranë, which was chosen as the capital, and in April 1920 its troops liberated Durrës. At the same time, a committee of national defence was formed to prepare a campaign to expel the Italians. At the beginning of June this committee sent an ultimatum to the Italian army in Vlorë, ordering it to withdraw within twenty-four hours. The ultimatum was rejected, and, virtually unarmed, the people of southern Albania and Vlorë forced 20,000 Italian troops to withdraw; the Italian government could not send reinforcements, since a general strike was threatened by Italian workers if it tried to do so. The political and diplomatic success scored by the Albanian uprising was described by Benito Mussolini as follows: 'Several thousand Albanians, without artillery, ejected us by force from Valona, and to escape being thrown into the sea, we began negotiations, but to no avail.'[7]

The Italians subsequently sought to negotiate with the government in
Tiranë, and on 20 August 1920 the Tiranë Treaty between the two countries was signed, under which the Italian government recognized
Albania's territorial integrity and its sovereignty over Vlorë. In compliance with the treaty, it undertook to withdraw its troops from Vlorë
and other parts of Albania, except for the island of Sazan (Saseno).

The Congress in Lushnjë and especially the uprising in Vlorë showed
the world clearly that the Albanian would never accept, even from the
great powers, any decision on the partition of Albania. By expelling the
Italian troops, Albania had for all practical purposes already won its independence. According to the protocol, signed in Tiranë, Rome lost all
right to seek recognition at the Peace Conference for any territorial
claims in Albania. Having lost its own foothold in Albania, the Italian
government no longer had anything to gain by allowing Greek and
Yugoslav territorial claims in the country to be recognized. Albania
was admitted to the League of Nations on 17 December 1920, despite
objections by Yugoslavia and Greece that the country was not a specific
political entity – a standpoint also held by France. However, Britain was
in favour of Albania's admission, and these protests were overruled. The
plans of the Yugoslav bourgeoisie to create a buffer state – the so-called
Miridit Republic – were also thwarted. The conference of ambassadors of
the victorious states agreed on 9 November 1921 to recognize Albanian
independence, but this decision also recognized the 'special interests' of
Italy in the preservation of Albanian independence. This was a great
concession to Italy, which thus gained official international approval for
interfering in Albania's internal affairs – which it did under every possible
pretext in the years between the two world wars.[8]

The present-day borders of Albania were drawn by the 1921 conference of Ambassadors and, as already mentioned, these were nearly the
same as those drawn by the London conference of 1913. However, a
document on the Albanian–Yugoslav frontier was only signed in 1926 in
Paris.

Relations between Albania and its neighbours between the wars
underwent great vicissitudes, marked by attempts on the part of the
neighbouring states to acquire political influence within Albania. Interference by Yugoslavia and Italy in Albanian affairs was particularly
blatant. In 1924 Yugoslavia was instrumental in restoring to power
Ahmet Zogu, later King Zog, whom a democratic government had
otherthrown a few months earlier.

However, Zogu soon forgot his debt to Yugoslavia and increasingly
aligned himself with Italy; the Tiranë Treaty of 1926 strengthened Italian
political and economic influence in Albania.

Albania's struggle for national independence has been long and painful and the neighbouring states made no secret throughout this period of their desire to enlarge their own territory at Albania's expense. Almost all the great European powers were interested in directly or indirectly influencing developments in Albania and its relations with neighbouring countries; and it was their opinion that the Albanian people, who were undergoing a national awakening, were incapable of organizing a state and government administration, and that therefore the country should be partitioned among the neighbouring countries or made a protectorate of a foreign power. New traumas were to be added after the Second World War.

Thus deep scars were left on the national psyche, some of which still fester to this day. This perhaps explains the suspicion with which the Albanian leaders of today view their neighbours.

(ii) *Political, Economic and Social Conditions*

In the years immediately after Albanian independence had been won and recognized, numerous social difficulties and antagonisms came to a head and were even further exacerbated by economic backwardness, a semi-feudal society and the fact that power was the exclusive monopoly of the landowners. The burning issue of the day, agrarian reform, began to polarize society.

The first National Assembly was convened in March 1920. Elections were held in 1921, and the political groups eventually developed into political parties of the Western type – the Democratic Party, the Popular Party, the Progressives (who mainly comprised feudal landowners) and several factions of Independents. Ahmet beg Zogu, a member of one of the leading families of central Albania, who at first was a member of the Democratic Party led by Fan Noli, was also a member of the first government, a coalition, which was formed at the Congress in Lushnjë in 1920. At this time he played an important role in normalizing conditions and stabilizing the internal situation. However, he took advantage of his office as minister of internal affairs and the gendarmerie to ingratiate himself with the landowners and the Progressive Party of Shevchet beg Vrlaci, and their support enabled him to become prime minister in 1922.

The Democratic Party, whose credo was social reform, left the coalition and formed an opposition bloc, which rallied many groups opposed to Zogu's government. Popular dissatisfaction with Zogu's government was manifested in the elections for the national assembly held in December 1923. The opposition, led by Fan Noli, won thirty-five out of ninety-five seats in parliament, whereas Zogu managed to carry forty seats; considering the intimidation and corruption used it was surprising he did not carry more. After the 1923 elections, a new government was formed by Shevçet beg Vrlaci. However, the impoverished peasants found themselves in a difficult position; a crop failure the preceding year had even threatened famine. Revolutionary ferment began in the country, and dissatisfaction with the government burst into an armed uprising. The insurgents were joined by some military units, and inevitably the government fell.

The bourgeois democratic revolution of 10 June 1924 unseated the landowning aristocracy from their positions of power, and Ahmet Zogu fled to Yugoslavia. The democratic government under Fan Noli was formed, and announced a number of ambitious social reforms, the most important being the agrarian reform. The government also established diplomatic relations with the Soviet Union, and had a positive programme of co-operation with neighbouring countries. However, the neighbouring countries and great powers viewed these changes with suspicion. The government of Fan Noli did not have sufficiently strong support within the country, not was it energetic enough in carrying out its programme; thus its days were numbered. Towards the end of 1924, direct foreign intervention – from Yugoslavia – overthrew Fan Noli's government and returned Ahmed Zogu to power. This was the end of parliamentary government in Albania. The return of Zogu meant the restoration of the power of the landowners, and the banning of political parties. A republic was established in Albania in January 1925 with Ahmet Zogu as president, and in 1928, having consolidated his power, he proclaimed Albania a 'parliamentary and hereditary monarchy' with himself as 'King of the Albanians', with the title of Zog I.

In his foreign policy Zogu very soon turned to Italy. By means of a number of treaties, an open-door policy and tariff preferences for Italian goods, he undercut attempts to develop domestic industry, as well as co-operation with other countries. Loans and other financial transactions, concessions to Italian firms for exploitation of mineral and other natural resources, as well as the employment of Italian experts in key posts in the administration, in education, and even in the army and police, put Albania into a semi-dependent position *vis-à-vis* Italy. With the Italian-Albanian pact of 27 November 1926, signed in Tiranë, Zogu put Albania into complete subservience to Italy; and when, in 1939, he refused to renew it, the Italians occupied the country.

King Zog's rule was characterized by a semi-feudal society, with poverty and misery the lot of the majority of the population. On the eve of the Second World War, 88 per cent of the population lived in the country, but 53 per cent of the peasants were landless; large landowners and 3 per cent of the total of peasant families held more than 40 per cent of the total of the cultivable land. The entire income from concessions and mining and from taxes for meadowland and forests was spent by the royal court. King Zog's rule meant exploitation of the masses, a complete absence of political freedom, persecution of liberal elements and permanent social dissension. King Zog was accurately characterized in Europe as an oriental potentate.

Agriculture was the mainspring of the economy, accounting for 90 per cent of the total national income. However, only between 7 and 9 per cent of the land was under cultivation. A large proportion of it was unsuitable for farming because of unregulated rivers and marshland along the coast. The production of grain, particularly maize, could only meet the needs of the population if there was a bumper crop. Tobacco and olives were cultivated, although production of olive oil was very primitive, and the plantations were neglected. Livestock breeding held an important place as the main supplier of Albanian export products. Of the 14·7 million gold francs which constituted the total value of exports in 1928, 9·6 million were earned from the products of livestock breeding. Industry was in its infancy, and all industrial goods had to be imported. Artisan crafts could only satisfy the needs of the rural population. The result was a very adverse balance of trade. Between 1926 and 1928, imports amounted to 103 million gold francs, while exports only earned 55 millions.[9] But Albania had already come completely under the sway of Italy, both economically and politically, and its deficit was offset by Italian loans.

The low level of economic development of Albania was also evident in its very small national income. No figures are available for national income in the first years after the war, but figures for 1927 and 1928 show just how backward Albania was. In 1927 the *per capita* annual national income was just U.S. $40.07 (Yugoslavia had $76.93, Rumania $77.74, Bulgaria $67.57 and Greece $75.75). The backwardness of the Albanian market is clear from the fact that in 1928 the value of transactions per head of the population was only $2.42, compared with $6.42 in Bulgaria, $6.48 in Rumania, $7.89 in Yugoslavia and $10.9 in Greece.[10]

Zog's undemocratic regime, his policy of submitting the country to Italian influence in order to finance the organization of his state and military apparatus and so consolidate his power, went with economic stagnation. The credits provided by Italy all contained provisos of political concessions, and they were spent to build strategic roads, which Italy was later to use for its own purposes. The fertile lowlands and plateaux were taken over for Italian agricultural estates, which were quite free of any control by the Albanian government and were an important factor in the spread of Italian influence.

The life of the peasants was hard. The law on agricultural reform which Zog promulgated in 1930 remained a dead letter, and was completely evaded by the beys and landowning class, to which Zog himself belonged. Farming remained at a very primitive level (in 1938 there were just thirty-two tractors in the entire country), since the semi-

feudal system, cheap labour and the poverty of small freeholders pre-
cluded any advance. Agricultural production was very low, and large
quantities of grain had to be imported to feed the population. In 1938, for
instance, 39,000 tons of wheat were harvested,[11] and wheat yields per
hectare were 860 kilos – eloquent proof of the state of Albanian
agriculture between the wars.

Industry was in equally bad shape. Between the wars the only plants
to speak of were small factories for the processing of agricultural products, while absolutely nothing was done in mining or the generation of
hydro-electric power. In 1938 industry accounted for only 9·8 per cent of
total production. The *per capita* output of principal industrial products
was the lowest in Europe. In that same year production per head of population was only 8·95 kilowatt hours of electrical power, 8·65 kg. of
cement, 0·43 kg. of sugar, etc.[12] The balance of trade was permanently
in deficit. In 1938 exports offset only 42·2 per cent of the value of
imports.[13]

Italy was of course Albania's principal trading partner, and its aim
was to control Albania's economy completely and to keep out the
political and economic influence of other countries. In 1937, 73 per cent
of the foreign capital in Albania was Italian, and by 1938 the proportion
had risen to 77 per cent. Until the Second World War, there was not a
single bank with domestic capital. The Albanian National Bank,
founded in 1925, was completely dominated by Italian capital. The
Agrarian Bank, founded in 1937, was under the control of the Banco di
Napoli. Attempts were made to found a commercial bank with domestic capital, but Italy nipped this plan in the bud, and until the occupation
its monopoly in this area was maintained.[14] It was not in Italy's interests
for Albania to have a bank which would control capital and be a potential
economic and financial rival to Italian banks, which were then draining
off all profits earned in Albania.

This ruthless exploitation had disastrous effects on the life of the
country. Even by Balkan criteria, the Albanian people had very low
living standards: poor hygiene and nutrition and the total lack of preven-
tive medicine left the door open to the ravages of epidemics and disease,
particularly malaria in the lowland and marshy areas. There was no such
thing as social security. Between 1927 and 1932 the budget of the
General Directorate for Public Health varied between 519,000 and
594,000 gold francs a year. There were no medical schools, and the number of doctors and nurses was very small. In 1938 Albania had just 155
doctors, forty-four dentists, twenty-nine pharmacists and twenty-nine
midwives, with a total of eleven hospitals, only three of which had
modern equipment. The mortality rate in 1938 was 17·8 per thousand of
population, the birth rate was 34·7 and thus the rate of population increase was 16·9 per thousand.[15] The absolute growth of the population

was rather slow, considering that the Albanian people have one of the highest birth rates not only in Europe but in the entire world. Of course, disease took its toll, but there was also a high rate of emigration because of the difficult economic conditions, particularly from southern Albania, to the United States and other countries.

Education and culture were also at a very low level. On the eve of the Second World War, over 80 per cent of the population were illiterate. There were no universities or colleges, and anyone seeking a higher education had to go abroad, the majority of students choosing Italy, Austria or France. In 1937 there were 428 Albanian students studying abroad. In 1938 there were eighteen secondary schools, with a total enrolment of 5,677. Only 36·7 per cent of school-age children received an elementary education.

The semi-colonial dependence on Italy, the difficult economic, social and cultural conditions and the political autocracy of King Zog all caused popular dissatisfaction. Hatred of the regime was rife, and there were strikes and protests against the foreign domination. Anti-Zog and anti-fascist movements began to operate, and in the national liberation struggle of the 1940s against Italian and German occupying forces, these were to have a very important role.

After the German-Austrian *Anschluss*, Albania's international position entered a state of crisis. Italy feared German penetration into the Adriatic, and in consequence Count Ciano, the Italian foreign minister, advised Mussolini as early as May 1938 to make the necessary preparations for annexing Albania to Italy. New threats to Albanian independence appeared during the Sudeten crisis and the Munich conference in the autumn of 1938. However, Albania's fate was sealed on 15 March 1939, when Germany occupied Czechoslovakia. Mussolini and Ciano now ordered all steps to be taken to foment internal disorder in Albania. As Ciano wrote in his diaries, the directive was to 'muddy the waters so much that no one can perceive our true intentions'. On 25 March 1939 Zog was handed an Italian proposal for an 'agreement' under which Albania would voluntarily become an Italian protectorate. On this occasion Zog sought the protection of Great Britain and Yugoslavia. On 5 April Italy, counting on the indifference of the European powers, delivered its ultimatum, which expired at noon on 6 April. Since no reply was received, the Italian fleet, with air support, sailed into Albanian harbours and began a landing the next day. On the same day, the King and government fled to Greece.[16] The Italian troops met very little resistance, except in the coastal towns and at Shkodër, and within three days had occupied the whole of Albania. A new chapter thus opened in the history of the Albanian people, in which they began a new struggle for national independence – this time from fascism – and for a democratic society.

NOTES

1 Essad Pasha (1864–1920), member of a wealthy family from Tiranë, became Albanian deputy to the Turkish parliament under the Young Turks. The Porte put him in charge of the army at Shkodër, then under attack by Montenegro. In a secret deal with Montenegro, he allowed himself and the town to be captured. He was immediately released and went to Durrës to serve as minister of the interior and of war under Prince Wilhelm. He intrigued with the Italians, Greeks and Serbs immediately prior to and during the First World War in order to achieve his ambition of becoming the ruler of central Albania. In 1920 he was assassinated in France by an Albanian patriot, Avni Rustem.

2 Živko Avramovski, *Iz istorije Albanaca*, op. cit., p. 155.
3 Ibid., p. 155.
4 Ibid., p. 157.
5 Ibid.
6 Nikollë Ivanaj, *Historija e Shqipërisë së Re* (History of Modern Albania), Shkodër, 1937.
7 *Historia e popullit shqiptar*, p. 485.
8 Avramovski, op. cit., p. 159.
9 *Historia e popullit shqiptar*, p. 547.
10 Avramovski, op. cit., p. 161.
11 Stavro Skendi, *Albania*, New York, 1958, 2nd ed., p. 167.
12 Avramovski, op. cit., p. 181.
13 Hans-Joachim Pernack, *Probleme der wirtschaftlichen Entwicklung Albaniens*, Munich, 1972, p. 167.
14 Avramovski, op. cit., p. 183.
15 *Vjetari statistikor i RPSH 1967 dhe 1968*, Tiranë, 1968, p. 33.
16 From there he went to Egypt, and eventually took up residence in England. He was forbidden to return to Albania after the war, and died in exile.

5

THE ALBANIAN
SOCIALIST REVOLUTION

(i) *Albania invaded and under Fascism*

The small Albanian nation was among the first victims of fascism in the Balkans. Its fate warned the other Balkan countries of what awaited them. However, from the very outset the Balkan nations, particularly the Albanians, Yugoslavs and Greeks, put up a resistance against Italy and Germany and created strong resistance movements, which led eventually to liberation and socialist revolutions.

Albania and Yugoslavia are examples of countries which underwent autonomous socialist revolutions. They fought for national liberation by revolutionary means, and progressive and patriotic forces destroyed the old order and established a socialist society, thanks to the fighting spirit and the political consciousness of the people, who were led and organized by the Communist Party. It should be emphasized that these autochthonous revolutions were not imported at gun point – hence their strength and the fact that they could never later be stamped out by pressure of any kind. We do not want to underestimate the importance of the Atlantic Pact countries in the struggle against the Axis powers, nor of the Soviet Union which, as a socialist country, gave special inspiration to the national liberation forces in the Balkans. Yet the burden of organizing the uprising and revolutionary struggle was borne by the national Communist Parties, led by people for whom the interests of their own nation and national revolution were paramount. This fact was reflected in the specific features of the Albanian revolution, which we will discuss later.

Forty thousand Italian troops invaded Albania, backed by air and artillery support. The Albanian strength was 14,000 men. After its capitulation, Albania was governed by Italian occupation authorities until Italy itself capitulated in September 1943. Albania was then held by German troops until the end of November 1944, when the national liberation army succeeded with its own forces in driving the last German soldier out of Albania.

Immediately after occupying the country, Italy tried to obscure its true intentions by announcing the union of Albania and Italy as free states. By 12 April 1939, 120 representatives from all ten Albanian pre-

fectures met in Tiranë at a 'constituent assembly', which abrogated the
Albanian Constitution and promulgated a 'constitution' which had been
drawn up in Rome. The Albanian throne was offered to the Italian king,[1]
and a quisling puppet government, headed by Shevçet beg Vrlaci,
was formed. On 16 April 1939 a government delegation, headed by
Shevçet beg, officially handed over the crown to the Italian king. On
3 June Victor Emmanuel III 'granted' Albania a new constitution, according to which a monarchy of the House of Savoy was introduced there.
The king was to exercise legislative power in conjunction with the
supreme fascist corporative council; executive power belonged to the
king, in whose name all administration was carried out.[2]

This 'constitution' allowed Albania its own government to administer
domestic affairs; however, it was a puppet government, serving the
interests of Italian fascism. The government of Shevçetbeg Vrlaci
signed a list of agreements, giving Italians and Albanians equal civil rights
in both countries; it also agreed to a convention on a customs and monetary union, whereby Albania was included in the Italian economic and
customs systems and was denied the right to maintain trade relations
with foreign countries.[3] The Albanian foreign trade ministry was
abolished.

For all practical purposes, Albania had been incorporated into the
Italian state. Victor Emmanuel III became king of Albania, but this was
not a legitimate confluence of two thrones in the person of a single heir;
it was the symbol of an unconstitutional and coercive occupation. Later
Albanian diplomatic representation abroad and the country's ministry of
foreign affairs were abolished, all diplomatic and consular services being
taken over by the Italian foreign ministry. An agreement was signed
uniting the Albanian and Italian armies and police forces. The Italian
fascists set up the Fascist Party of Albania, proclaiming its statute on
2 June 1939.

Thus Albania was completely stripped of its sovereign powers, while
the creation of a personal union, solely through the person of a common
head of state, was a constitutional farce.

The military forces which Italy maintained in Albania were relatively
large: its Ninth Army and special units of the air force, navy, fascist
militia, carabinieri and customs service totalled 100,000 men. During the
invasion of Greece, the number rose to more than 150,000. These forces
were making large-scale preparations for a deeper penetration into the
Balkans towards Greece and Yugoslavia, and for this purpose strategic
roads, airports and military installations were built throughout Albania.
Tens of thousands of Italian citizens were also resettled to colonize
Albania. Between April 1940 and September 1941, 51,623 Italian workers entered Albania, and there were plans for more than 4,000,000
Italians to colonize the country.

In the political and ideological domain, the Italian fascists announced a far-fetched plan to set themselves up as the 'liberators' of the Albanians, promising to annex to the Albanian heartland parts of Yugoslavia, like Kosovë, settled by Albanians and the Greek province of Çamëria (Tsamouria), which was also predominantly Albanian. Albanian patriots, particularly the communists, saw these promises for what they were, namely attempts by the Italian fascists to disguise their true agressive intentions against Yugoslavia and Greece. The Italians also tried to mobilize the Albanian people against their neighbours, but they had no success, since the Albanians had no desire to fight on behalf of others. Ever since the formation of their national state in 1912, they had had bitter experience with propaganda from various sources promising their 'liberation'. The Albanian people not only refused to join the Italian army, but organized a national liberation front of their own against the Italians. During the Italian invasion of Greece, which began on 28 October 1940, the Albanians showed their solidarity with the struggle of the Greeks and gave them assistance against the Italian invaders. The Albanian soldiers who were forced to go to the front in the 'Tomori' and 'Taraboshi' battalions deserted sooner than fight, some of them joining up with the Greeks. Others were disarmed by the Italians and sent to concentration camps.[4]

The anti-fascist sentiments and patriotism of the Albanian people were manifested in 1939 and 1940 through a series of demonstrations, strikes, acts of sabotage and attacks on the police. The ruthless exploitation by the Italians caused great discontent among the workers. Even by the end of 1939, over fifteen strikes had been organized for political as well as economic purposes. Mass anti-fascist demonstrations were oganized on 28 November 1939, the anniversary of Albanian independence, in Tiranë, Shkodër, Korçë, Vlorë and other towns. On 11 April 1940 the Italian occupation authorities issued an order prohibiting demonstrations, strikes and meetings. The Italians tried to crush the anti-fascist movemement by terror and repression: in May 1941 alone, 1,130 houses were searched, 21,131 Albanians were proclaimed enemies, and 5,270 patriots and anti-fascists were taken for internment to camps in Italy. All these measures served to inflame the hatred of the Albanian people for their Italian occupiers.[5]

In the spring of 1941 the situation in the Balkans had become even more critical. After the disastrous failure of the Italian invasion of Greece, Mussolini asked for German assistance. The Germans agreed to come to their rescue, taking the opportunity of this offer for carrying out their plans to occupy Yugoslavia and Greece before embarking on 'Operation Barbarossa' against the Soviet Union. They found an excuse to attack Yugoslavia after the pro-German Yugoslav government was overthrown on 27 March 1941. The German troops, assisted by Italians and

Hungarians, attacked Yugoslavia and Greece from Bulgaria. The Italian troops were thus able to recover their positions on the Albanian-Greek border and to advance into Greece.

The German attack on the Soviet Union on 22 June 1941 precipitated revolutionary activity in Albania, Yugoslavia and Greece. In Albania, the strikes, demonstrations and assassination attempts which had characterized the two years of Italian occupation now gave way to a higher and more organized form of resistance. Since the beginning of 1940, the band of patriots led by Muslim Peza had made armed attacks against the Italian fascists and used guerrilla warfare.[6] On 18 May 1941 a worker named Vasil Laçi tried to assassinate the king of Italy in the centre of Tiranë. Almost all the acts of resistance in Albania were led by members of communist groups, workers and patriots, and especially the youth. The former felt that the time was ripe to unite into a single party which would lead an organized armed struggle of the Albanian people, and at a conference of the representatives of the three main communist groups held from 4 to 8 November 1941 the Communist Party of Albania was created. It became known as the Albanian Party of Labour in 1948.

(ii) *The Albanian Party of Labour*

Although the Communist Party of Albania was only formed in 1941, the workers' movement in Albania was of much earlier origin. The first workers' strikes had broken out in 1921 at Korçë, Gjirokastër and other towns; Avni Rustemi, an important personality in the Albanian independence and democratic movement, formed the *Bashkimi* (Unity) association in 1922, which had democratic and socialistic ideals, although it was heterogeneous in composition and had no clearly defined programme. In 1924 Bashkimi deputies compelled the Albanian parliament, despite its landowner majority, to commemorate the death of Lenin, and it was the only parliament in Europe to do so. The growth of the progressive movement was greatly spurred by the revolutionary and communist groups abroad and at home which were gradually being formed and gaining new members.

After the fall of Fan Noli's liberal democratic government, its members with a more revolutionary orientation formed a National Revolutionary Committee in Vienna in 1925, which had a very progressive programme. In 1928 the committee purged its ranks and reorganized itself with the name 'National Liberation'; this new committee associated itself with the Comintern and its Balkan section. Albanian communists living in France were particularly active in Grenoble and Lyons, and even published their own paper, *Populli* (The People). Most important, perhaps, was the formation of an Albanian communist group in Moscow in 1927. This group consisted of intellectuals and workers, left-wing forces of the earlier Bashkimi organization and Fan Noli's movement, who had emigrated after the failure of the bourgeois-democratic revolution of 1924. The objective of this group was to form a nucleus for propagating the communist movement in Albania and among the Albanian emigrants. The most outstanding personality of this group in Moscow was certainly Ali Kelmendi, born in Pejë (Kosovë), who died in France in 1939.

The first communist cells appeared in Albania in 1927. Although they were poorly organized, they were very active among the artisan class and assisted the formation of labour and professional organizations. Later, in 1931, the communist cells in Korçë acquired a more organized form and became the first and leading communist group in Albania, thereafter known as the Korçë group or simply *Puna* (labour).

The communist movement in Albania was given a great boost by the return of various communist emigrants, particularly that of Ali Kelmendi as representative of the Comintern. In 1933-5, Ali Kelmendi was instrumental in the organizational and ideological strengthening of the communist group in Korçë. Later, in 1936-8, another communist group came into being at Shkodër, consisting largely of high school students and intellectuals. In 1940 the so-called 'Young' communist group was formed; this was a splinter from the Korçë group.

The communist groups numbered a great many loyal cadres, who promoted the workers' movement and took a leading role in the popular struggle against Zogu's government and later against fascism. However, they suffered from many weaknesses, such as localism and factionalism, not to mention those of organization and ideology. Nevertheless, disunity and the lack of a single party were the principal faults of the communist movement; the revolutionary situation which arose after the Italian occupation made unification an urgent priority. The first direct contacts between groups failed to bear fruit, with the temporary exception of a 'central committee' and later of an 'arbitration commission', which were formed. The Albanian communists then turned for assistance to the Communist Party of Yugoslavia, with whom their first contacts had taken place in 1939, being maintained later by communists of Albanian nationality in Kosovë, who had joined communist groups in Albania, and who later became the nucleus of the uprising in Kosovë. The Communist Party of Yugoslavia was largely responsible for uniting the communist groups and creating a unified communist party in Albania. It had been instructed to do so by the Comintern, but it also considered this help to the Albanian comrades as its internationalist duty.

On 4 November 1941 a joint meeting began in Tiranë of three communist groups: 'Korçë', 'Shkodër', and the 'Youth' group. The meeting lasted for four days and culminated in a decision to unite the communist groups and to create the Communist Party of Albania. The meeting elected a provisional Central Committee, which included none of the previous group leaders, who had engaged in factional in-fighting. Enver Hoxha (whose part in the Albanian revolution and in building socialism is described in more detail on pp. 67 ff.) was elected head of the provisional Central Committee.

The Communist Party of Albania immediately set about consolidating its organization and preparing for a general armed liberation struggle. The Organization of Communist Youth of Albania was set up soon after, and a year later the National Liberation Front was formed. The basic purpose established in the resolution adopted by the communist groups of Albania at their meeting which founded the C.P.A. was first to fight for the national liberation of the Albanian people and secondly, to fight for a popular and democratic government in an Albania liberated from fascism.[7]

The uprising of the Albanian people in the second half of 1941, and particularly after the creation of the Communist Party of Albania, soon took on a nation-wide proportion. Partisan and other patriotic groups made armed attacks on Italian units, military barracks, convoys, ammunition dumps, the airport in Tiranë – where they destroyed various installations – and telephone lines, which they cut over the entire country. The Italian fascists soon realized the extent of the uprising in Albania, and responded with severe repression, burning villages and hanging patriots and sympathizers of the 'communist bandits'. Armed resistance spread to all parts of the country, and the people gave full support to the partisan companies. At the end of 1941 and the beginning of 1942 the following were the main organized partisan units which were taking part in military engagements: Çeta e Kurveleshit, çeta e Gorës, Skraparit, Mokrës, Devollit, Dibrës, Pezës, Kollonjës. The company of Muslim Peza, which had been striking at the Italians since the first days of the occupation, became a partisan company in August 1941. The partisan companies offered a more sophisticated form of armed resistance, compared with the earlier acts of sabotage and unorganized harassment of the enemy. Not only did they engage in pitched battles, but they actually managed to drive the enemy forces out of various entire regions of Albania and turned these liberated territories into strongholds of the future national government. The partisan companies liberated Gorë, Opar, Skrapar, and part of the Mokë and Dibër area. The Skrapar company carried out successful actions against a unit of the fascist militia and the Çorovodë garrison, and on this occasion Çorovodë was liberated. These remarkable successes of the partisan companies and the fighting spirit of the people convinced the leadership of the Albanian Communist Party that the time had come to create an anti-fascist national liberation front.

(iii) The Anti-Fascist Front

The conference at which the Anti-Fascist National Liberation Front of Albania was created took place at Pezë on 16 September 1942. The idea of creating the front was mooted at the first consultation of the Albanian Communist Party in April 1942. The conference, which was attended by communists and patriots from all parts of Albania, adopted important decisions on the further course of the armed struggle of the people. All patriotic forces in the country, regardless of class, political, religious or regional affiliation, were called upon to engage in an armed struggle against the fascist occupiers.[8]

The Front was not a coalition of political parties, but rather a voluntary unification of the broad popular masses under the leadership of the General Committee of National Liberation of Albania, which was elected at the conference.[9] It was decided to set up national liberation committees in liberated and enemy-held territory, to serve as organs of future governmental authority and as bodies to unify and mobilize the Albanian people in the struggle. These decisions laid the foundations of the future government. Decisions were also taken to reinforce the partisan detachments and create larger military units.

The conference in Pezë struck a responsive chord throughout the country. The partisan movement grew in strength and scope; fighting against the Italians became fiercer and by the end of 1942, new territories had been liberated: Pezë, Skrapar, Tomoricë, Kurvelesh, Mavtanesh, Gora e Epërme, Opar, Mesaplik, part of Çermenik, Mallakastër, Devoli, Deshnicë, Shpati, and part of the region above Shkodër. The national liberation committees were established in liberated territory to take the place of the old government.[10] After the conference in Pezë, the partisan companies swelled into battalions, which were formed in the regions of Korçë, Gjirokastër, Mallakastër, Vlorë, Pezë, Mat, Dibër and Shkodër. The battalions carried out large-scale attacks on the enemy forces.

The Italian occupying forces were greatly perturbed by the spread of the national liberation movement, and particularly by the success of the partisan companies in liberating some of the regions of southern Albania. The fascist troops attacked Pezë and burned hundreds of homes to the ground, carried out mass executions of the civilian population, and seized all their livestock. However, they did not succeed in destroying the partisan units or the fighting spirit of the people of this region, who had joined the liberation struggle in large numbers from the very first days of armed resistance. Punitive expeditions and operations were launched against the partisan units in other parts of Albania as well, one of the largest being that against the free territory of Vlorë in December 1942. Two infantry regiments and over 1,500 well-armed police with air and tank support took part in this expedition,[11] which had the object of annihilating the partisan forces, disarming the population, burning down the houses of peasants who sheltered resistance forces, and putting their families into concentration camps. As in 1920, the people of this region were totally on the side of the insurgents, and the enemy suffered a heavy defeat. A pitched battle between the partisan units and the Italian army took place on the mountain of Gjormë on 1 January 1943. The Italian troops were defeated, and on this occasion the Italians even lost the commandant of the punitive expedition, Clementis. The battle won by the Albanian partisans with the support of the people in the Vlorë region has become known as the 'Valona epic'. It revived memories of 1920, when the Albanian people were faced with extinction, but ejected the Italians from their country unaided.

During 1942, and in the beginning of 1943, the National Liberation Front of Albania, led by the communists, united the forces of the Albanian people on a broad political front against the Italian fascists. Politically, but most of all militarily, the Albanian partisans had already achieved remarkable success. On 17 December 1942 the British foreign secretary said in the House of Commons that His Majesty's Government wished 'to see Albania freed from the Italian yoke and restored to her independence'.[12] On 12 December 1942 President Franklin D. Roosevelt had the following to say on the same subject: '. . . Consistent with its well-established policy not to recognize territorial conquest by force, the Government of the United States has never recognized the annexation of Albania by the Italian crown. The restoration of a free Albania is inherent in that statement of principle.'[13] These official statements by the western allies were broadcast in the Albanian language. The Soviet foreign minister, Molotov, made a similar statement.

At that time the partisans had freed part of southern Albania. This success, combined with the advance of the Allied forces, both on the eastern front and in the west, increasingly alarmed the Italians and Albanians who served their interests. Within Albania a political polarization began to take place. At the end of 1942, reactionary forces formed a political organization called Balli Kombëtar (National Front), which tried to win the people away from the Anti-Fascist National Liberation Front. The leaders of Balli Kombëtar propagated their policies with such slogans as 'battle against the Italians when the time is ripe'. Some of these leaders had played a prominent part in the struggle for an Albanian state more than two decades earlier; now, however, they fell headlong into direct betrayal of the popular interest. Thus on 15 March 1943, in Tiranë, an agreement was signed between General Dalmazzo, commander of the Italian occupying forces in Albania, and Ali Kelcyra and Nuradin Vlora, representatives of Balli Kombëtar, who pledged to do all in their power to crush the national liberation movement in Albania, thus openly declaring their collaboration with the Italian enemy. After this agreement, armed groups belonging to Balli Kombëtar regularly took part in battles with partisan units on the Italian side.

In this complex political situation, the leaders of the Albanian Communist Party held a national conference in Labinot, near Elbasan, from 17 to 22 March 1943, which was attended by seventy delegates. The programme was to analyse the political situation caused by the creation of Balli Kombëtar and its open collaboration with the enemy. Organizational and political consolidation of the party, the armed struggle, and the setting up of national committees were treated as priorities. It was decided to begin forming the general staff and regular units of the National Liberation Army of Albania, and in consequence the general staff was created on 10 July 1943 with Spiro Mojsiu elected first commandant and Enver Hoxha political commissar. Later, Enver Hoxha also became the commandant of the general staff. In Vithkuq, on 15 August 1943, the first shock brigade of the National Liberation Army was formed under the command of Mehmet Shehu,[14] a commander of great renown in the people's national liberation struggle.

In the spring and summer of 1943 the partisan units, now doubled in strength, carried out a number of armed attacks on Italian units in Mallakastrë, Leskovik and other parts of the country. One of the more famous battles was that for the liberation of Leskovik from 17 to 19 May 1943, when this town was freed and the enemy suffered heavy losses – over 200 dead and 500 wounded. In June the same year, the Italians mustered a force of 14,000 to retake the liberated town of Pezë. A partisan unit of 200 fighters, with popular support, at first defeated sections of the enemy troops. Thanks to their numerical superiority the Italians managed to take Pezë, and then decimated the population, burning more than 300 houses. Wherever they passed, the Italian troops left behind burned villages and massacred populations, but in every skirmish with the partisan units, they suffered great losses. In Përmet, a five-day battle was waged, and the Italian army suffered heavy losses in men and equipment. The partisan battalion 'Tomori' attacked a German convoy on 6 July 1943 on the Korçë–Janina road and destroyed most of the vehicles, killing more than sixty men. The Germans retaliated by attacking the village of Borovë, burning all the houses and killing 107 people, including women and children. The partisan units also suffered losses, but they emerged from every fray with strengthened resolve.

Winston Churchill wrote in his war memoirs of the extraordinary resistance put up by partisans in Albania, Yugoslavia and later Greece, on which he possessed first-hand information received from British intelligence officers and later from the British military missions sent to the headquarters of the National Liberation Armies in Albania and Yugoslavia. After Mussolini's fall, Churchill considered it of the utmost importance for the Allies that Italian forces in the Balkans (Albania,

Yugoslavia and Greece) should either immediately withdraw or sur-
render.[15] According to his memoirs, Churchill prepared a report criticizing the incorrect planning of operations in the Mediterranean following the victory at Salerno: '... We have failed to give any real measure of
support to the Partisans and Patriots in Yugoslavia and Albania. These
guerrilla forces are containing as many [German] divisions as are the
British and American Armies put together. Hitherto they have been
nourished only by supplies dropped from the air. It is now more than two
months since we have had air and naval superiority in the mouth of the
Adriatic, yet no ships with supplies have entered the ports taken by the
Partisans.'[16]

In the summer of 1943, the Albanian popular struggle became fiercer,
and the communists organized in the National Liberation Front and the
nationalist group became even more polarized. In such a situation, the
leaders of the National Liberation Front decided on 9 July 1943 to make
a last effort to reach an agreement with the leaders of Balli Kombëtar
over mounting a joint offensive against the enemy. At the negotiations
Ymer Dishnica, Mustafa Gjinishi and Abaz Kupi represented the Front,
whose platform, according to official Albanian sources, was as follows:
(*a*) that Balli Kombëtar should enter the fight against the enemy; (*b*)
Balli Kombëtar should concentrate on fighting against fascism and not
on proclaiming independence; (*c*) a joint command should be formed
after the military action carried out by Balli Kombëtar; (*d*) unity must be
achieved through struggle and membership in national liberation councils and Balli Kombëtar should stop fighting the communists; (*e*) a joint
conference and congress should be held when all the above conditions
had been fulfilled.[17] However, the representatives of the Anti-Fascist
Council of the National Liberation Front did not carry out in full the
instructions given by the leaders of the General National Liberation
Committee, but falling under the influence of representatives of Balli
Kombëtar, formed instead a 'Council of National Salvation', with an
equal representation of Balli Kombëtar and the Anti-Fascist Council.
Hasan Dosti and other members of Balli Kombëtar refused to accept the
conditions of the General National Liberation Committee, and for propaganda reasons sought a proclamation of 'independence' and annul-
ment of the decisions of the 'constituent assembly' of 12 April 1939,
which, after the fact of the Italian occupation, had been convened to
make it look as though Albanian representatives had constitutionally
voted in favour of union with Italy. The representatives of Balli Kombëtar tried to gain an easy guarantee of participation in government with
the communists in post-war Albania, and even to take the leading role.

A second stumbling-block between the representatives of the Front
and Balli Kombëtar was the latter's proclaimed policy of an 'ethnic
Albania', that is, annexation of those regions which under the decisions

of the London Conference of Ambassadors in 1913 had not been awarded to Albania but were largely settled by Albanians. The representatives of Balli Kombëtar raised this question, wishing to ingratiate themselves with the Albanian people who, in their independence struggles before 1912 and even later, had sought unification within a single national state, including in particular the Albanian national minority in Yugoslavia. Between the two wars, as we shall see later,[18] the Albanian minority in Yugoslavia was disenfranchised in all respects – politically, economically and culturally – so that the irredentist movement was strong. The leaders of the Albanian Communist Party and the Anti-Fascist National Liberation Front of Albania considered the possibility of uniting all Albanians into a single major national and democratic state, but felt that in view of the complexity of this problem, both from the international aspect and from the standpoint of relations between the revolutionary movements of Albania and Yugoslavia – which, from the very outset, had found themselves on the same side of the barricades in the struggle against Italy and Germany – it would be impolitic. Dissension would arise between the Albanians and Yugoslavs, thus hindering their joint struggle against the enemy. The question of the regions with predominantly Albanian populations, and of relations between the resistance movements in Albania and Yugoslavia, would be discussed in more detail later. For this reason, the agreement which had been reached between the representatives of the Anti-Fascist Council of the National Liberation Front and Balli Kombëtar on 8 August 1943 put the former at a disadvantage, even though they were the only true voice of the Albanian people.

The Albanian Communist Party leaders and the National Liberation Front therefore condemned the agreement of Mukje.[19] In these trying times, a second National Liberation Conference was convened at Labinot on 4 September 1943, attended by delegates from all over Albania. It reviewed the successes of the national liberation movement since the first conference, and adopted decisions on the further course of the war, the reinforcement of troops in the field, and so on. Also the Mukje agreement was condemned and the programme and slogans of Balli Kombëtar were rejected as demagoguery.[20] The conference reaffirmed that national unity could only be achieved on the platform of the Peza conference, provided that the struggle against the German and Italian enemy continued and that the national liberation committees were recognized as the only democratic authority representing the Albanian people.[21]

As the second conference was winding up its work in Labinot, Italy capitulated on 8 September 1943. The population now began to join the national liberation struggle on a large scale, and partisan units managed to disarm part of the Italian troops in Albania, while some

Italian units joined in the fight against Germany, the strength of whose forces in Albania had been increased in August 1943 in preparation for a take-over from the Italians, and on the pretext of liberating Albania from Italian subjugation, claiming that Germany supported an independent Albania. Balli Kombëtar decided to collaborate with the Germans. Abaz Kupi, who had earlier joined the national liberation movement, left it at the end of 1943 and formed the Legality Party, which championed the restoration of King Zog.

In its first encounter with the Germans at Drashovicë on 14 September 1943, the National Liberation Army won a significant victory. Within the fortifications were 1,000 Germans and over 7,000 disarmed Italian soldiers. The Albanian units took the military barracks in Mavrovë and Drashovicë and set free all 7,000 Italian soldiers, many of whom joined the partisan units; the Germans lost over 3,000 men in this fight, with a large number of wounded. New partisan units were formed to operate throughout Albania. The German troops tried to secure their lines of communication, but partisan units attacked the Vlorë–Sarandë–Greece road and killed several hundred Germans. The enemy took Sarandë, but Gjirokastër and Kelcyra remained in the hands of the National Liberation Army units. Fighting occurred in Berat and Pogradec, and the first shock brigade in the Elbasan–Krob–Tiranë district carried out a number of actions against the Germans and quislings.

In the winter of 1943–4, the German occupying forces undertook an ambitious operation known as the winter offensive. The German command put the 15,000-strong quisling forces of Balli Kombëtar and the Legality Party into the fight against the partisan units. The enemy forces inflicted terror and repression on the population of southern and central Albania. Several hundred peasants were killed, and many more made homeless. Terror was also inflicted on the towns, and thousands of people were sent to camps in Prishtinë, Buchenwald and Mauthausen, whence the majority never returned. Together with the gendarmerie of the quisling government, the enemy killed eighty-five people in Tiranë with bayonets, including young boys and girls. However, despite this terror the morale of the National Liberation Army and of the people as a whole was growing, as can be seen from the fact that in these darkest hours of the struggle six new partisan brigades were formed. During the winter offensive, the Germans suffered great losses – over 3,000 dead and 2,000 taken prisoner. The National Liberation Army of Albania suffered the loss of about 1,000 dead and wounded or frozen to death.[22]

In February and March 1944, the National Liberation Army took the counter-offensive, and by the end of March had succeeded in regaining all the regions which had fallen into enemy hands during the winter offensive. In the spring of 1944 the National Liberation Army numbered over 20,000 armed fighters, organized in more than twelve brigades and a large number of detachments and partisan battalions. In Tiranë, Shkodër, Elbasan, Korçë and Vlorë, very strong diversionary and guerrilla groups were active, as well as the National Liberation Committees and anti-fascist organizations. The greater part of southern and central Albania was liberated by the partisan units. At this time the military strength of the partisan units numbered over 35,000 men; the partisan army had grown into a strong, organized force.

On the proposal of the Central Committee of the Communist Party of Albania, the leadership of the Anti-Fascist Council of the National Liberation Front decided at a meeting on 15 April to convene the First Congress of the Anti-Fascist Council of National Liberation of Albania as soon as possible.

(iv) *The First Congress of the Anti-Fascist Council of National Liberation*

When the First Congress of the Anti-Fascist Council of National Liberation of Albania was held the international and internal conditions were auspicious. Soviet troops had already entered Bessarabia and Bukovina; they had broken through to the Czechoslovak border and were massing to enter Rumania and Hungary. The western allies had achieved enormous successes in North Africa and Sicily. On 6 June 1944 the Second Front in the west was opened. In Albania, Yugoslavia and Greece partisan units had already liberated most of their countries. In fighting with the German units, the Albanian partisans had achieved outstanding military successes from August 1943 to May 1944. They were thus able to turn their attention to political and state affairs and set about consolidating the democratic and popular government, whose roots lay in the Albanian revolution and the wholehearted participation of the entire people in the fight against the enemy.

The congress met in the town of Përmet from 24 to 28 May 1944, with 186 delegates present from all parts of Albania. Enver Hoxha addressed the assembly, reviewing the course of the national liberation struggle and the international situation on behalf of the General National Liberation Committee and the general staff of the National Liberation Army. The congress elected the Anti-Fascist Council of National Liberation of Albania (KANÇ), which was invested with the highest executive and legislative power. The Anti-Fascist Council formed an anti-fascist committee of thirteen members as a provisional democratic government, with Enver Hoxha, General Secretary of the Albanian Communist Party, being elected as its president. In addition to setting up the provisional democratic government of Albania and elect-

ing the Anti-Fascist Council as the highest legislative and executive
organ, the congress of Përmet promulgated the following decisions:
(a) Albania was to have a democratic and popular government, according to the will of the Albanian people as expressed in the Anti-Fascist
Council of National Liberation (KANÇ), the sole national authority
to have arisen from the national liberation struggle; (b) King Zog was
forbidden to return to Albania; (c) The formation of any other government in Albania or abroad was not to be recognized; (d) All treaties
or agreements concluded by the Albanian government with other
countries before 1939 were declared null and void; (e) The struggle
against the enemy and domestic reactionaries was to continued until
Albania was finally liberated.

The Congress appointed Enver Hoxha supreme commander of
the armed forces. At the proposal of the General Staff, the ranks of
officer, commander and commissar were awarded. Larger military
units (divisions and corps) were formed, and these inflicted heavy
damage on the German units in the battle for the final liberation of
Albania. Enver Hoxha also reported to the congress on the activity of the
British military missions in Albania, which had been attached both
to the general staff of the National Liberation Army and to the Legality
Party and other Albanian groups since May 1943. The Congress charged
the general staff also to invite military missions from the United States
and the Soviet Union. These missions, as well as one from Yugoslavia,
arrived in the summer of 1944. The general staff later sent its own military mission to the general staff of the National Liberation Army of
Yugoslavia. The Albanian general staff had on several occasions in
1943 asked the British military mission for an Albanian military mission
to be represented at the supreme allied command for the Mediterranean
to co-ordinate the Albanian partisan action with that of the Allies.[23]
However, this request was not granted.

(v) The Summer Enemy Offensive

Immediately after the First Congress, the Germans attacked partisan
units with the aim of destroying the main force of the National Liberation Army and thereby disorienting the Albanian people, who had given
their loyalty largely to the partisans. At this time there were 35,000
armed fighters in the ranks of the National Liberation Army. The German forces, aided by mercenaries from Balli Kombëtar and the Legality
Party, attacked partisan units near Korçë, Elbasan, Berat and then
pressed on towards Gjirokastër and Vlorë. After long and bitter fighting,
the enemy, thanks to their superior numbers and armaments, managed
to take several of these towns. However, enemy casualties exceeded 3,000

while the National Liberation Army lost only 500 men. However, in mid-June 1944 the National Liberation Army launched a counter-offensive and compelled the enemy forces to withdraw from several of the larger towns.

At that time the general staff decided that the first division should move into central and northern Albania, to carry their campaign to regions where Balli Kombëtar and the Legality Party had their strong-holds. The enemy was taken by surprise by the strong attack of the partisan units. German units in central Albania and the forces of the Legality Party suffered a heavy defeat. The majority of towns in central and northern Albania were liberated. After the failure of the summer offensive, the Albanian people joined the partisan units in even greater numbers. The General Staff of the National Liberation Army had al-ready drawn up a plan of military action to liberate Tiranë and the entire country.

From then on the National Liberation Army remained constantly on the offensive, and battles were even fought in city streets. Southern Albania, except for the island of Sarandë, which had a strong German fortification controlling the Strait of Otranto, was entirely liberated. The Allied chief of staff in Italy, through Field-Marshal Alexander, sought permission from the Albanian general staff for a British para-chute brigade to take part in battles to break up the German fortifica-tions in Sarandë. The Albanian general staff decided to grant this per-mission on condition that the action should be jointly carried out by the National Liberation Army of Albania and the British parachute brigade under Brigadier T. B. L. Churchill, that the Albanian side should direct the entire operation, that all spoils of war should belong to the National Liberation Army and that on completion of its mission, the British brigade would return to its base in Italy. Field-Marshal Alexander accepted these conditions, and after the liberation of Sarandë the British brigade withdrew to Corfu. This was the first agreement of a military nature between the Albanian general staff and the allied staff in the Mediterranean.[24]

After these notable successes in the battlefield, the internal and inter-national military and political conditions had become ripe for the Second Session of the Anti-Fascist Council of the National Liberation of Albania.

(vi) *The Second Session of the Anti-Fascist Council of National Liberation*

The Second Session took place in Berat from 20 to 23 October 1944. A report on the fighting and the international situation was given by Enver Hoxha, and the provisional democratic government of Albania

was formed. The government elected Enver Hoxha national president
and commandant of the National Liberation Army. The democratic
government of Albania issued an eight-point declaration containing its
programme and orientation. Its actual words were:

1. The Democratic Government of Albania shall remain loyal to the
decisions of the Anti-Fascist Congress of National Liberation held in Përmet
and the Anti-Fascist Council of National Liberation of Albania. The government shall continue the policy of the Anti-Fascist Committee.
2. The Government proposes to continue and extend the struggle to achieve
the rapid and complete liberation of Albania and to preserve its independence.
3. The Democratic Government of Albania shall rally all the forces of the
Albanian people to the support of the National Liberation government and
shall strengthen the authority of the national liberation committees.
4. After the complete liberation of Albania and after the situation is stabilized,
the Democratic Government of Albania shall hold free elections on a democratic basis for a constituent assembly, which shall lay down the form of the state
and promulgate a constitution.
5. The Democratic Government shall review all the political, military,
and economic agreements concluded by the Zog regime with foreign states
and shall declare null and void those which are to the detriment of the people
and government of Albania.
6. The Democratic Government shall ensure and defend all the civil rights
of its citizens.
7. The Democratic Government of Albania shall try to promote co-
operation with the great allies, Great Britain, the Soviet Union and the United
States.
8. The Democratic Government of Albania shall seek recognition as the
sole government of Albania from the allied powers, Great Britain, the Soviet
Union and the United States, as well as from all other participants in the Anti-
Fascist Coalition.

After the Second Session of the Anti-Fascist Council of National
Liberation, the National Liberation Army entered the battle to free
Tiranë. The general staff entrusted this operation to Mehmet Shehu,
the leading partisan commander. The battle lasted twenty days. Well
armed and entrenched, the enemy put up a strong resistance. The partisan units had to capture each street and building one by one. After days
of constant attacks and assaults by Albanian partisans against enemy
tanks, Tiranë was at last completely liberated on 17 November. During
the fighting in the towns, the partisans were joined by citizens, the youth
and women. The enemy suffered over 2,000 casualties and great losses in
material, which was seized by the National Liberation Army.[25] The
battle of Tiranë again proved the strength of the resistance movement in
Albania.

The battle of Tiranë was among the factors which nipped in the bud
the ideas of the allied staff in the Mediterranean and its commander

General Sir Henry Maitland Wilson, which became clear in the note delivered to the Albanian general staff on 12 July 1944 via the liaison officer in the British military mission attached to it. According to Albanian sources, the note stated that General Wilson would not tolerate the Albanian partisans interfering with his strategic plans because of their civil war; the national liberation movement could not control the whole of Albania, or resist the Germans without allied assistance. The allied staff in the Mediterranean also invited the National Liberation Army of Albania to send representatives to Italy to negotiate on co-ordinating military action and ending the civil war.[26] In addition to this note, the British liaison officer informed the general staff verbally that if the National Liberation Army attacked Abaz Kupi, the representative of the Legality Party, which championed the monarchy and King Zog, all aid from the allies to the National Liberation movement would be cut off.[27]

The general staff of the National Liberation Army appointed a delegation to negotiate with the allied staff in the Mediterranean and answered General Wilson's note. It was led by Major-General Bedri Spahiu, and included Ramadan Çitaku-Baca and Nesti Kerenxhi. The delegation delivered Enver Hoxha's reply to the Allied Staff in the Mediterranean, and there were negotiations between them at Bari in August 1944. In his reply to the note, Enver Hoxha said, among other things: 'We are profoundly convinced that the struggle of the Albanian people, which has been taken up by the entire country, led by the Anti-Fascist National Liberation Front, both in the south and in the north does not hinder the strategy of the allies but rather helps them in the best possible way. On the other hand, we are aware that without the assistance of the allies, without the struggle of the great allied powers against Germany, our liberation movement would not be very strong. . . .'[28]

The note denied that there was a civil war in Albania and stated that the strategic positions of the allies had never been stronger than in this war, since the Albanian people, like few other nations, had been on the side of the allies from the very outset of the war. The material assistance provided by the allies was greatly appreciated, and it was sought that delegates of the Albanian general staff should be accredited to the allied staff for the Mediterranean at its headquarters in Italy. In the negotiations the Albanians refused to allow any interference by the allies in their internal affairs and in the national liberation movement. The two sides reached an agreement on the supply of war material to the Albanian partisans. This was the second agreement to be made with the allied staff in Italy.

Indeed, the successes of the National Liberation Army in the field, especially the decisive battle for the liberation of Tiranë, were the best justification of the Albanians' determination not to allow anyone to interfere in their internal affairs. The National Liberation Army had 70,000 men under arms. The leadership of the resistance movement greatly appreciated the allies' assistance and co-operation as articles and speeches of Enver Hoxha at that time make clear, but as the result of pressures applied to the Albanian democratic government by the British and American governments, diplomatic relations were never established.

Immediately after the liberation of Tiranë on 17 November 1944, the National Liberation Army moved on Shkodër, where there was a strong concentration of enemy forces. The second division liberated Shkodër on 29 November, marking the end of the National Liberation Army's efforts to free the country. The 28 and 29 November are national holidays commemorating the independence of the Albanian state, respectively known as 'Independence Day' and 'Flag Day'. On Independence Day 1944 – *Dita e flamurit shqiptar* – the Democratic Government of Albania led by Enver Hoxha entered Tiranë. At a great public meeting attended by over 50,000 of the city's inhabitants, Enver Hoxha for the first time directly addressed the Albanian people after the five-year-long war. He explained the programme of the new government and its foreign policy, emphasizing co-operation with the allies and with Yugoslavia and Greece on the basis of the decisions passed at the second session of the Anti-Fascist Council of National Liberation in Berat and the Congress in Përmet.

In November 1944 two Albanian divisions went to fight in Yugoslavia at the request of the Yugoslav National Liberation Army and Marshal Tito; this was later ratified when a delegation of the Albanian National Liberation Army staff and the democratic government visited Belgrade early in 1945. These two divisions fought with the Yugoslav partisans in Kosovë, Rrafshi i Dukagjinit (Metohija), Montenegro, Sandžak and Bosnia.

The national liberation war and the popular struggle against the enemy from 1939 to 1944 was a socialist revolution both in its character and in its objectives. The peasantry and working masses were the driving force and mainstay of the revolution, and they were led by the left and communist intelligentsia. The working class element was strong but the peasantry was the main force. The basis of a new democratic socialist government was laid, but from all points of view this revolution can be considered one of the great epics in the history of the Albanian people. The Albanians steadfastly defended their hill country and formed their national liberation army in the course of fierce combat. Freedom-loving nations will always respect the Albanian people, who held down several enemy divisions during the darkest hours of the war, when the Germans had reached the Volga and Rommel's Afrika Korps had pentrated the Nile valley; they thus deflected the striking force of the Axis war machine and at the same time gave strong moral support to other subjugated nations. It warmed the hearts of the Yugoslav fighters during the Fourth Offensive to hear of the continuous fighting and actions of their southern neighbours.[29]

The losses suffered by the Albanians in the Second World War were over 28,000 dead, 12,600 wounded and 10,000 arrested and interned. Material damage was great: over 52,000 houses were burned, and almost every bridge, port and mine, and much else was destroyed. The Italian occupying forces never numbered less than 100,000, and after Italy's capitulation the German forces were 70,000 strong. Over 26,000 enemy soldiers and officers died on Albanian soil, 21,245 were wounded and 20,000 were taken prisoner.

The spearheads of the Albanian revolution were the peasants and urban middle classes, the youth and anti-fascist intelligentsia, who were dissatisfied with the political, social and international position of the Albanian people and of Albania between the two wars. For this reason, young Albanians took the national liberation struggle to heart. The struggle succeeded because it was the expression of the vital national interests of the Albanian people. The revolution took its inspiration from the theory and practice of Soviet Russia, but creatively, not dogmatically. The idea of internationalism and solidarity was exceptionally strong throughout, especially in terms of co-operation between the resistance movements of Albania and Yugoslavia.

NOTES

1 Krystyna Marek, *Identity and Continuity of States in International Law*, Geneva, 1954, p. 330.
2 Ali Hadri, *Albanija*, 'Resistance Movements in Europe 1939–1945', Beograd, 1968, p. 18.
3 Avramovski, op. cit., p. 178.
4 *Historia e popullit shqiptar*, p. 672.
5 Ibid., p. 675.
6 Muslim Peza was an Albanian patriot and fighter who did not start out as a member of the Communist Party. He met Enver Hoxha in June 1941 and they discussed the strategy to be followed by Albanian patriots in their struggle against the enemy. Later Muslim Peza and his men joined a partisan group. He took part in all important meetings during the war and was a member of all the supreme anti-fascist bodies of the new government of Albania. Today he is vice-president of the Presidium of the People's Assembly.
7 *Dokumenta kryesore te PPSH*, Tiranë, 1960, Vol. I, pp. 22–3.
8 Ndreçi Plasari, 'Strategy and Tactics of the Albanian Party of Labour in the National Liberation War', Naim Frashëri, Tiranë, 1966, pp. 20–5.
9 Ibid., p. 25.
10 Ali Hadri, op. cit., p. 220.
11 Ibid., p. 220.
12 Quoted by R. Longer, *Seizure of Territory*, Princeton, 1947. *Albania – Basic Handbook*, Western Central District Office, 1943, II, 60.
13 Ibid.

14 Mehmet Shehu's career is discussed in more detail on pp. 71 ff.
15 Winston S. Churchill, *The Second World War*, Vol. V, 1952, p. 170.
16 Ibid., p. 292.
17 Enver Hoxha, *Collected Works*, Vol. I, Tiranë, 1968, p. 330. See Plasari, op. cit., p. 68.
18 See below, pp. 137–9 ff.
19 Ibid., pp. 330–41.
20 *Historia e popullit shqiptar*, p. 716.
21 Ibid.
22 Ibid., pp. 731–44. *See* Hadri, op. cit., pp. 224–6.
23 Enver Hoxha, op. cit., p. 223.
24 As told to the author by Veljo Stojnić, head of the military mission of the general staff of the National Liberation Army of Yugoslavia, which was in Albania from August 1944 to July 1945.
25 *Historia e popullit shqiptar*, p. 780.
26 Enver Hoxha, *Collected Works*, Vol. II, p. 273, contains the reply to the note of General Wilson, Commander of the General Staff in the Mediterranean, of 12 July 1944, which is paraphrased above. This reply was published for the first time in the works of Enver Hoxha, Tiranë, 1968.
27 Enver Hoxha, ibid., p. 273.
28 Ibid., p. 274.
29 Col. Velja Stojnić, head of the Yugoslav military missions to the general staff of the National Liberation Army of Albania from August 1944 to July 1945, described his experiences in *Borba*, No. 8, 8 January 1945.

PART TWO

PART TWO

6

REVOLUTIONARY ALBANIA

(i) *The Legal and Political System*

Under the Albanian Constitution, People's Councils and the People's Assembly are the sovereign political bodies. The People's Assembly is the supreme legislative organ, elected every four years by all citizens over the age of eighteen, according to the principle of one deputy to every 8,000 voters. The Assembly is unicameral. The Presidium of the People's Assembly performs the function of head of state as a collective body, presided over by the chairman of the Presidium.[1] The People's Assembly appoints the Government, which is the highest executive and administrative organ of authority.[2] The Government co-ordinates the work of the ministries, commissions and other institutions under its direct control.[3]

The principal organs of local authority are the People's Councils; each of the District People's Councils comprises several communal councils. The council members of the district and communal people's councils are elected for three-year periods by universal adult suffrage.

As is the practice for the People's Assembly, candidates for the councils are nominated by communal and district organizations of the Party of Labour, the Democratic Front, trade unions, the youth organization, the League of Women, and other organizations. These organizations, however, are a rubber stamp for the Party, which draws up a list of candidates in advance.

The People's Councils have executive committees composed of a chairman, his deputy, secretary and members.[4] The executive committee is responsible to the People's Council for its activities. Similarly, the executive committees are subordinate to higher executive organs of the state administration.[5]

On 11 January 1946 the Constituent Assembly proclaimed Albania to be a People's Republic and promulgated the Constitution. The Constitution was amended in July 1950, and minor changes were made later. It was formulated on the model of the Soviet constitution (the Stalin Constitution) of 1936.

The highest tribunal is the Supreme Court of the People's Republic of Albania. Other tribunals are district courts, people's courts and military tribunals. The law provides for the appointment of special courts to try specific cases.[6] The courts are independent in carrying out their duties and are separate from the administration in all cases. Verdicts handed down by judges can only be reversed by a higher competent court.[7] Even though the courts are nominally independent under the law, the judges are very much under the influence of the Party, which must approve the list of nominations for judgeships.

The Supreme Court judges are selected by the People's Assembly for a four-year term of office. The judges of district courts are appointed for three-year periods by district people's councils. The judges of lowest instance, i.e. those of the people's courts, are elected by citizens in the commune by direct secret ballot every three years.[8] The Supreme Court is a court of appeal which decides whether the decisions of all the lower courts are according to law.[9]

The attorney-general's office, an arm of the People's Assembly, has the duty of supervising law enforcement. The attorney-general of Albania and his assistants are nominated by the People's Assembly; other public prosecutors are appointed by him. The public prosecutors are independent of local organs of government, and are subordinate only to the attorney-general.[10]

(ii) *Political Organizations*

Political organizations, particularly the Albanian Party of Labour, play an important role in the country. Other organizations besides the Party of Labour are the Democratic Front and organizations of trade unions, of the youth and students, of women, of veterans from the national liberation struggle and of pioneers (children). All these organizations are united in the Democratic Front but each operates individually and has its own set-up and leadership and include the organization forms of political training in their programmes. However, they are subordinate to the Party of Labour and actually act as a mouthpiece for Party decisions.

The Constitution of the People's Republic of Albania defines the Party of Labour as the organized leader of the working class and the working masses in the struggle to build the foundations of socialism and as the leading unit of all other socio-political organizations and state institutions.[11] In fact, the provisions of the Albanian Constitution on the status and role of the Party are more or less similar to those in the Stalin Constitution of 1936 defining the status and role of the C.P.S.U. Therefore the claim by some left-wing authors in the west – advocates of permanent revolution and of equality among all members of Society, regardless of an individual's contribution in social affairs – that the Constitution contains innovations and special features must be regarded as false.[12]

The Stalinist model of Party unity is still dominant: this means that the Party is above all other forces in society, which are mouthpieces for the Party. Decisions taken by the Central Committee are put into effect without the possibility of any comment by the rank and file. No organ can take measures before the Party has decided on the relative policy. Perhaps this is the case more in theory than in practice these days, because since 1970 there have been attempts to increase internal democracy within both the Party and the party organizations and in general. Enver Hoxha himself announced such a policy at the Tenth Plenum of the Central Committee in 1970.[13] However, the democratization of the life of society and of the Party itself did not last long after the events in Czechoslovakia in 1968 – only up to the end of 1972.

It was Enver Hoxha himself who called publicly for the further democratization and evolution of the system in the 1970s. After the sixth congress (November 1971) and at the Fourth Plenum of the Central Committee of the Albanian Party of Labour (February 1973) Enver Hoxha reversed himself and clamped down on the process that he had initiated. The Party felt that things were going too fast and was afraid that it would not be able to keep the process of democratization under control. Democratization was thus postponed for another, more auspicious, time.

The freeze was heralded by slogans denouncing 'foreign influences' and 'liberal ideas'. The first to be attacked were some intellectuals, writers, musicians, artists and film workers. The first wave of criticism was also directed at university staff and members of the Writers' Association, in particular its president Dhimiter Shuteriqi. After the intelligentsia at the university and among the writers had been purged, the strongest blow of all was dealt, late in 1973, at the President of the People's Assembly, Fadil Paçrami, and Todo Lubonja, both members of the Central Committee of the Albanian Party of Labour. This would seem to have been the epicentre of the purge.

Fadil Paçrami had been a participant in the national liberation struggle from the very first actions against the Italians. Born in Shkodër in 1922, he studied medicine in Italy. Then during the war and immediately after liberation, he was head of the Albanian Anti-Fascist Youth League. A writer and journalist, speaking fluent French, Italian and Russian, Fadil Paçrami was for years editor-in-chief of the chief Party organ, *Zeri i popullit*. In 1973 his articles, in which he advocated greater freedom of literary and artistic creativity, came under attack. As a prolific writer himself, he was outspoken on the need to abandon dogmatic socialist realism in literature.

It would seem, however, that the Party leadership was only too aware of where all this would lead – namely to the breakdown of many values and dogmas in Albanian society. The campaign against Fadil Paçrami was first launched on television and later was taken up throughout the cultural and artistic world.

Fadil Paçrami was accused of having used his position 'as a springboard for achieving his hostile and counter-revolutionary ends' against the Party and people. In view of the serious charges levelled against him in this campaign, Fadil Paçrami and his followers may well be brought to court and charged with anti-state activities.

In this latest campaign, which became especially virulent after the 'mini-cultural revolution' of 1966 and which is aimed at religion and old patriarchal customs, the slogan is that the struggle against foreign ideologies must be permanent and long-term. The Party, it is said, must never relax its vigilance and its struggle against these weaknesses, lest they or other similar ideologies crop up again.[14] It is often reiterated that the ideological struggle in Albania is taking place 'under conditions of imperialist-revisionist encirclement'. This is actually an old slogan of Enver Hoxha's which he has resurrected in this stage of Albania's development. According to official statements by Albanian leaders, this imperialist-revisionist blockade is not just geographical, but preeminently military, ideological and economic. It is a real threat to the development of socialism and the independence and autonomy of Albania. At the Fourth Plenum of the Central Committee, Enver Hoxha stated that the objective of imperialist-revisionist pressure was to silence the only voice in Europe which was raised against aggressive and expansionist policy, the only bold attack on the demagogic smoke-screens of the super-powers, which are doing everything in their power to subvert the revolution.[15]

According to information presented at the VI Congress in November 1971, the Albanian Party of Labour had a membership of 86,985, of whom 18,217 were candidates.[16] In the period between the V and VI Congresses, the Party gained 20,628 new members.[17] The majority of new members are young, skilled workers and other skilled cadres – i.e. various technical personnel, doctors, dentists, teachers, etc. (One can only become a member at the age of eighteen, having first been a member of the pioneer organization and then the youth organization. Candidate members must show their fitness for membership by their acceptance and implementation of party assignments.)

(iii) *Political Leaders*

(a) ENVER HOXHA

Head of the Albanian Party of Labour and leader of the people, Enver Hoxha is the outstanding figure in the country and the only Albanian of world stature. Like Mao Tse-tung and Marshal Tito among leaders in the socialist countries, he personally led the national liberation war.[18]

Enver Hoxha exemplifies the spirit of his people in many ways. Oriental culture and civilization have influenced Albania over many centuries and Enver Hoxha possesses an oriental cunning and political shrewdness. However, he received a French education in the Lycée français in Korçë and at universities in France. He is an intellectual par excellence and it is noteworthy that in Albanian society intellectuals have played an outstanding role since the time of national renewal. They were in the vanguard of the struggle for national independence and the formation of a national state, whereas in other countries, this role has been performed by other social classes. Similarly, the Albanian intellectuals led the resistance movement during the Second World War.

Enver Hoxha was born on 16 October 1908 in Gjirokastër of an urban Muslim family. He received his primary education in his home town and at home, later studying at the Lycée français in Korçë. Gjirokastër and Shkodër were two of the oldest centres of Albanian nationalism. Dissatisfied with the situation within Albanian society, as well as with Albania's international status, he followed the example of many other young people in Albania between the two wars and joined the revolutionary workers' and communist movement in Korçë, which was the strongest revolutionary centre in the country.

By 1924, Enver Hoxha and his schoolmates from the Lycée in Korçë had organized the first protest demonstrations, and for the first and last time in his life, when he was just sixteen, he found himself in gaol. On completing the Lycée with brilliant success, he was awarded a scholarship by the Albanian government to study in France.[19]

In 1931, when he was twenty-three years old, he enrolled in the school of engineering at Montpellier. He also joined the Communist Party of France. When the Albanian authorities found out about this, they suspended his scholarship in February 1934, and he was forced to go to Paris to seek work. For some time he worked on the staff of *L'Humanité* and made friends with the editor-in-chief, Paul Vaillant-Couturier. In his articles, he attacked King Zog's regime for putting Albania into complete subservience to Italy.[20] In Paris Enver Hoxha enrolled in the second year of law and continued to write articles for *L'Humanité*; however, Zog's intelligence service found him out, and he had to change his job. During his stay in Paris he was in contact with the Albanian emigrants, particularly the communist group which was trying to form a 'democratic front' against the Zog regime, following the Comintern line. At that time he made the acquaintance of an Albanian diplomat in Brussels and until 1936 was the private secretary of the Albanian consul there. He continued his law studies, but never completed them.[21]

On the eve of the Second World War he returned home, believing that in those troubled times his place was among his own people. Soon afterwards, he became politically active. For a few months he taught in a high school in Tiranë and often, thanks to his knowledge of French, he was employed as a master at the French Lycée in Korçë, and used his position to propagate his ideas of the communist movement, appealing to his pupils' pro-democratic and anti-royalist sentiments. He was active in the political life and the trade union movement of Korçë, becoming a leading member of the communist group there and helping apprentices and workers from the small factories around town to organize trade unions.

During the Italian invasion, many Albanian communists demanded that the government should issue weapons so that they could fight the invaders. One of the participants in the demonstrations organized in Gjirokastër was Enver Hoxha. After the occupation, the fascist federation for Korçë forced Enver Hoxha out of his post at the Lycée after he had refused to join the fascist party. He then moved to Tiranë on a mission from the Korçë communist group and continued his work underground, working in a tobacconist's shop, which became a communist and anti-fascist headquarters. There he found new colleagues, in particular Qemal Stafa and Vasil Shantu from the Shkodër group, both of whom were killed during the war. His underground activities convinced him that the only course left open to the Albanian people was to wage a partisan and guerrilla war against the enemy.

In 1940 several bands of patriots and anti-fascists were already operating in the Albanian mountains. The group led by Muslim Peza was particularly prominent and later joined the National Liberation Front led by Enver Hoxha. At the time when ten guerrilla bands were already active in the mountains, Enver Hoxha was still in Tiranë and with other comrades was working on uniting the communist groups, which were torn by factional rivalries. However, conditions existed for these groups, particularly the three basic communist groups in Albania, to rise above their differences in the common interest. It is true that attempts had been made previously to unite the communist groups, but these attempts failed for three main reasons: first, the ban on political parties, and especially the Communist Party, enforced by King Zog – through his fear of being ejected from power; secondly, factional struggles between the groups; and thirdly, the negative attitude taken by the Comintern towards those foreign communist parties which were not under its direct control and influence. However, the situation after the Italian agression and the strongly felt need to organize armed resistance provided the catalyst for unification of the communist groups into the Communist Party of Albania in November 1941. As Enver Hoxha had held himself aloof from these internal squabbles, he was the natural choice of all the groups to be made secretary of the provisional Central

Committee, and he was later elected general secretary at the National Conference in 1943.[22]

The conference in Peza in September 1942 was of particular importance, since delegates from all Albania elected Enver Hoxha leader of the national liberation movement. In addition, he was the main theoretician and propagandist of the partisan movement. In August 1942 he founded and edited the paper *Zeri i Popullit*, for which he wrote editorials, reports and political commentaries under various pseudonyms, such as Taras, Selami, Malo, Valbona and Shpati, which have been republished in his selected works.

As leader of the partisan movement, he had to deal in 1942 with the factionalists Anastas Lulja and Sadik Premte and a year later with the representatives of Balli Kombëtar and the Legality Party, organizations which had rallied nationalist and royalist supporters. On both occasions, Enver Hoxha was successful. When the regular national liberation army was formed, he became commissar and later head of the general staff with the rank of colonel-general. At the congress in Përmet on 20 May 1944, he was elected president of the Anti-Fascist Committee of National Liberation, and at the second conference of the Anti-Fascist Council in Berat in October 1944, he was appointed head of the democratic government of Albania. In this capacity he entered Tiranë on 28 November 1944, and in an address to 50,000 citizens he set out the programme of the democratic government in domestic and foreign policy. Enver Hoxha is a speaker who can hold an audience spellbound.

As president of the Albanian government and first minister of foreign affairs after the war, Enver Hoxha conducted a very lively political and diplomatic campaign for the international recognition of Albania by the western allied powers. The peace conference in Paris, which began work on 29 July 1946, refused to recognize Albania, on the pretext that it had collaborated with Italy. At the insistence of the ministerial conference held in New York, Albania was permitted to take part in its work in order to conclude a peace treaty with Italy. As the representative of Albania, Enver Hoxha delivered a speech in the Palais du Luxembourg in Paris on 21 August 1946. Ten years after leaving Paris as a student, he had returned as a head of state. In his speech, which he delivered in French, he boldly and adroitly defended the interests of the small Albanian state, which had been done a great disservice by not being awarded the status of a member of the anti-fascist coalition. When he spoke, neither the American and British delegations nor the French premier, Bidault, were present but Enver Hoxha made a strong impression on the diplomats and ministers who were present, as Molotov later stated.[23]

When Churchill said that because Italy had used Albania as a springboard for its attack on Greece it could not be accepted as belonging to the anti-Hitlerite coalition, Enver Hoxha replied that according to that logic, France too could not be in the anti-Hitlerite coalition, since Hitler had used French territory as a springboard for its attack on England. But Enver Hoxha's wish to establish diplomatic and other relations with the western countries, primarily Britain, France and the United States, was never to be realized because of the attitude of those countries, which were exerting pressure against the Albanian leadership and Albania. British foreign policy was responsible for this attitude towards Albania, being influenced by the civil war in Greece, which had been assigned to the British sphere of influence at the Yalta Conference.

In his long report to the Youth Congress in April 1945, Enver Hoxha declared:

Think, comrades of the youth movement, what would have happened if the people of the great democracies – of Great Britain – had not been strong, those people who placed in the service of the anti-fascist war all their economic and military potential; if it were not for the great British and American armies which stormed the German fortress from the West; if it were not, in the first place, for Churchill, with his rare ability as a leader; if it were not for the great Roosevelt, whose death has grieved our people because we lost one of our great friends, and the progressive world one of the true defenders of democracy and freedom.[24]

I have quoted this speech according to the rendering in Skendi's book, since this part of the speech has been excised in the selected works of Enver Hoxha. Only that part where he spoke about Stalin and his role in the anti-fascist war was left intact. However, there is no doubt that Enver Hoxha was sincere and that this is what he meant and genuinely felt about the western allies. The problem was not that the western allies misunderstood him, but that they did not wish to understand him.

Immediately after the war, some of Enver Hoxha's associates in his own party and from some 'fraternal parties' labelled him a 'pro-western intellectual' and a 'bourgeois nationalist', and later as a 'Russian spy'; his own writings are the best refutation of all these epithets.

Enver Hoxha made a serious study of the position of a small country in the world community; he knew what it meant to be dependent on one's 'protectors'. For this reason, he endeavoured to strengthen his own position and his strategy for Albania's development, and even when Albania was in the 'fraternal community of socialist countries' before 1961, it had held an independent position *vis-à-vis* the Soviet Union. At the world conference of communist and workers' parties in Moscow in November 1960, Enver Hoxha publicly confronted Khruschev; he supported China in the Sino-Soviet dispute and ideological confrontation. Then and later Khrushchev tried to effect a reconciliation with him, but to no avail – Khrushchev remarked that it was easier to negotiate with Macmillan than with the Albanians. In 1961 all diplomatic and other relations between the Soviet Union and Albania were broken off.

Enver Hoxha had skilfully negotiated a tricky course. He managed to detach Albania from the Soviet Union at a time when the latter was building its modern naval fleet and had truly become a world naval power. However, it needed bases in warm waters, just as the Russian tsars had sought a foothold in the Mediterranean through the Balkans. As Enver Hoxha recalled at the celebration of the sixtieth anniversary of the independence of the Albanian state, on 28 November 1972, Khrushchev and his defence minister, Marshal Malinovsky, came to Albania in 1959 not to turn it into a 'flower garden' but rather into a strong naval base. In his speech Enver Hoxha said among other things: 'Vlorë will never be held by foreign hands'.[25] Since he took part in the world conference of communist and workers' parties in Moscow in 1960, he has not been outside the country.

In 1945 Enver Hoxha married a partisan girl, Nexhmija Xhangolli, born of a Muslim family in Dibër. She completed secondary school in Tiranë and was a member of the Communist Party from its inception and one of the leaders of the communist youth. They have three children – Ilir (born 1948), Sokol (born 1951), and Pranvera (born 1954). Nexhmija is a leading figure in the struggle to emancipate the Albanian woman. She has been a member of the Central Committee since 1948 and is at present director of its Institute of Marxism–Leninism.

The overriding goal of this skilful politician and pragmatist is to emancipate Albania and the Albanian people and to consolidate the country's independence. It is impossible to imagine either Albania's present or its probable future without his work.

(b) MEHMET SHEHU

The prime minister, Mehmet Shehu, is the legendary commandant of the national liberation war. At the time when the general staff headed by Enver Hoxha was in danger of falling into German hands, he and the First Shock Brigade made a kind of Chinese 'long march' and came to the rescue of the supreme command. He commanded the operation for the liberation of Tiranë, and after completing it, he continued fighting to liberate Shkodër and northern Albania. After the liberation of the country in January 1945, when two Albanian divisions had joined Yugoslav units to fight against the German troops in Yugoslav territory, Albanian clan leaders (*bajraktars*) in northern Albania rebelled at Shkodër; Mehmet Shehu responded by simply disarming the insurgents. He set up a court martial and commanded them to hand over their weapons within twenty-four hours.

This was not simply a daring and decisive act of leadership, but was a unique feat in the annals of Albanian guerrilla warfare. The incident was notable because it was the peasants of the North, who had rallied to the *bajraktars* against the new socialist government, that Mehmet Shehu managed to pacify, even though he had no army to back him up. The rebellion was a very serious one in Albanian circumstances. The *bajraktars* were traditionally very important in Albanian society, particularly in waging war. Whenever a *bajraktar* (the headman of a region which could include forty or even sixty villages) called the peasants into battle, they came without fail. The fact that Mehmet Shehu was able to quell such a potentially dangerous rebellion simply by calling on the insurgents to hand over their arms is an indication of the high regard in which he was held by the Albanian clan leaders in the North.

Mehmet Shehu was born on 10 January 1913 in the village of Corush, Mallakastër. He completed the American vocational school in Tiranë in 1932 and continued studies at the military academy in Naples; he had to leave the academy when it was discovered that he taken part in pro-communist activities.[26] He returned home in 1936 and continued his studies in the officers' school in Tiranë. He took part in the Spanish Civil War, and while in Spain became a member of the Communist Party there. He fought in the Twelfth International Brigade, known as the 'Garibaldi' Brigade. Later he became commandant of the fourth battalion. After the International Brigade had fled to France in 1939, Mehmet Shehu was interned in a concentration camp and remained there until 1942. While in the camp, he joined the Italian Communist Party.

Upon his return to Albania in 1942, Mehmet Shehu became a member of the Communist Party committee for the Vlorë district. He formed a partisan unit in Mallakastër. In August 1943 he became commandant of the First Shock Brigade and was awarded the rank of major-general on 28 November 1944. After the liberation he was chief of the general staff of the Albanian army for some time and then attended the Voroshilov Military Academy in the U.S.S.R.[27] Until 1948 he had been kept in the background by the Koçi Xoxe group, which was very powerful in the Central Committee; in February 1948 he was even stripped of his membership of the Central Committee[28] – a victim of the Stalinist purge then going on in Eastern Europe. (Koçi Xoxe, Minister of the Interior and head of the secret police, became the most powerful man in the Party during the period from October 1944 to June 1948 and had ambitions to become the country's leader. After the Cominform meeting in June 1948 he was arrested and executed.) After the fall of Koçi Xoxe, he became deputy prime minister and minister of internal affairs. He was also secretary of the secretariat of the Central Committee. When in 1954 the office of prime minister was separated from that of general secretary of the Party, Enver Hoxha retained his post as First Secretary of the Central Committee, while Mehmet Shehu assumed the office of prime minister.

Enver Hoxha could be described as the theoretician of Albanian policy, and Mehmet Shehu its executant. At the fourth congress of the Albanian Party of Labour in February 1961, during the showdown with the Soviet Union, Mehmet Shehu warned dissidents of the Albanian party that 'those who attempt to disrupt unity will receive a direct blow in the face, and if necessary a bullet in the head'. This served as a warning both to the Soviet guests and to delegates from other 'fraternal parties' that his country would not yield to the increasing Soviet pressure.[29]

(c) HAXHI LLESHI

Haxhi Lleshi, the Chairman of the Presidium and ex-officio Head of State since 1955, was born in Reshen near Dibër in 1913 of a leading family of *Bajraktars* from Dibër, who had taken part in past struggles against the Turks for the independence of Albania. He was a leader of the resistance movement in the Dibër district from the earliest days of the national liberation struggle, and successfully rallied the people of his district to join his partisan battalion and mounted many actions first against the Italians, and later against the Germans and quislings.

He took part in the conference in Pezë in September 1942 and became a member of the Albanian Communist Party in 1943. He was a member of the General Council of the National Liberation Movement, and at the conference in Labinot in July 1943 was made a member of the General Staff of the Albanian National Liberation Army. At the congress in Përmet he was promoted to the rank of colonel, and in 1949 to major-general. In the post-war years he held various governmental and political posts in Albanian, and is a member of the Central Committee of the Albanian Party of Labour. Although formally head of state, he has no real political power, since the Party is supreme.

(iv) *The Large Army of a Small Nation*

The distance from the north to the south of Albania is 340 km.; between the east and west of the country the average distance is 100 km., while the narrowest part is 75 km. – from Peshkopoje to the mouth of the river Mat. Albania is only 76 km. away from Italy across the Strait of Otranto, thus it is in a perfect position geographically to control navigation through the Strait; and this accounts for much of the interest shown by foreign powers in Albania throughout history.

The Albanian strategic concepts and views on the use of armed forces have evolved in step with the overall political orientation of the country. In the post-war years, particularly from 1955, when it became a member of the Warsaw Pact, till 1961, military thinking in Albania was largely subordinated to the interests of a 'coalition' military doctrine. But after it withdrew from the Warsaw Pact (13 September 1968), Albania began to elaborate its own strategy to correspond with its own needs and resources. The essence of this concept is total preparedness of the entire country for a defensive war. In view of the sensitive geographical location of the country, its peculiar international status and its determination to withstand any aggression, from whatever source, the defence concept is, basically, reliance on its own forces.

Until 1925, Albanian had no regular army; in the event of war the entire able-bodied population would be armed. However, when King Zog had consolidated his power, he began to create a standing army.

After the signing by Zog of the pact with Italy in November 1926, that country assumed responsibility for building up the Albanian armed forces and for constructing the military infrastructure in the country. Italian instructors were assigned to each Albanian company, while the British set up the police force. Military service became compulsory for all men between the ages of twenty and fifty, and the total strength of the armed forces was about 10,000 men. The regular army was officially formed on 15 August 1943, two years after partisan detachments and groups had come into existence. In 1944 there were eight divisions in Albania, organized into three corps, with a total of 70,000 men. We have already discussed Albania's military achievements against the Italians and Germans.

The armed forces of Albania are officially known as the People's Army and comprise an army, air force and navy, and units for internal security and territorial defence.

Since the events in Czechoslovakia in 1968, special attention has been given to national defence and the military training of the population, especially the youth. Military training and exercises have been introduced into university and school curricula as an important part of the education process. Since the break with the Soviet Union in 1961, the 'Chinese school' of military thought, which advocates an armed civilian population, has prevailed and Chinese influence on the organization of the standing army is growing.

In 1971, according to some western sources which collect information on strategic problems, Albania had an army of 42,000 men, totalling 2 per cent of the population, which is significantly above the average for the majority of European countries. The armies of Austria, Denmark, Sweden and Finland, which have two to four times more inhabitants than Albania, have armies of approximately the same size as the Albanian army. However, Albania also has border patrols and a police force numbering 35,000 men, so that the total number of men under arms rises to 80,000, or over 3·5 per cent of the population, a percentage considerably above customary peace-time armed forces.

The land-based army has 35,000 men (83 per cent of the total force), grouped into six infantry and one tank brigade. There are 4,000 men in the air force and 3,000 in the navy. Armaments comprise 100 medium-sized tanks, seventy-five fighter planes and forty-five warships, including four submarines and thirty torpedo boats.

Albania allocates enormous resources to the maintenance and the modernization of such a large fighting force, spending up to $100 million per annum (10–11 per cent of the gross national income, which is estimated at about $1 billion. However, the official budget does not list all the actual expenditure on the army, which received assistance in many indirect ways (including Chinese aid), and even earns its own income by engaging in farming, construction and other civil work under the 'self-support' scheme.

The expenditure on internal security forces comes under the budget of the Ministry of Internal Affairs, so that the total amount of money spent on defence has no relation to the country's economic means.

News items appear occasionally in the west about Chinese bases and Chinese divisions stationed in Albania, but these reports are without foundation. There may be military as well as economic advisers, since after the events in Czechoslovakia Albania began modernizing its armaments, adding missiles and other anti-aircraft and naval weapons, but there is no question of any Chinese bases or units. Indeed, the break in relations between Albania and the Soviet Union in 1961 almost certainly came about due to the question of Soviet bases, which would have made Albania lose its autonomous position in conducting domestic and foreign policy in accordance with Albania's own interests.

The strength of Albanian defence and security lies in the resolution of the Albanians to fight against any aggressor: this was proved in the Second World War and would undoubtedly be the case in any future conflict.

(v) *'The First Atheist State in the World'*

The Proletarian Cultural Revolution in China in 1966 must have been a direct inspiration to the Albanian leaders, for they at once launched a 'mini cultural revolution' of their own, called 'measures to revolutionize the Party and life'. The purpose of these measures was to eliminate bodies of religious believers,[30] to emancipate women in society, and to do away with various primitive customs in the Albanian family deriving from religious beliefs and the general primitiveness of Albanian society.

There can be no doubt that in certain phases of Albanian history the church, specifically the Roman Catholic church in the north and the Orthodox church in the south, had a divisive effect on society. Deliberately or unconsciously, the Orthodox church served as a catspaw for the aims of the Greek Orthodox church, while the Roman Catholic church did the same for the Vatican. The altar screen, as well as shielding the mysteries of religion from public view, simultaneously veiled the interests of Greece or Italy.

The Muslim religion also for a while continued to identify with the Ottoman empire and to link the fate of the Albanian people with its interests. However, in view of the fact that ideological bonds with the centre had become tenuous indeed by this time, we should perhaps speak more of tendencies rather than any organized service to the Ottoman empire through religious ties. These tendencies, then, did not become a dominant force for Muslim Albanians, a fact of great importance since Islam is the predominant religion in Albania.

The pluralism of religions and religious communities threw up barriers between the Albanians themselves, and was the cause of friction between tribes and provinces. These religious divisions hampered the Albanians' attempts to unify their efforts to fight foreign domination.

Albanian patriots, regardless of their religion, have always tried to rise above these petty internecine squabbles by stressing national interests above religious and other narrow regional or tribal interests. However, because of the general backwardness of the Albanian people before the First World War and even between the two wars, religious divisions could not be broken down. The government of King Zog, perhaps motivated by the time-honoured wisdom of 'divide and rule', fed the flames of religious conflict rather than trying to overcome the divisions.

After the Second World War, the new government separated church and state. Until 1967 the government tolerated the activities of religious communities, and believers could freely exercise their religious customs. The young generation, brought up in the new way (the Albanian population has a very high percentage of young people) both in schools and at work in factories or farming co-operatives, set less and less store by religion. In its ideological work, the Party tried to make communists and the youth standard-bearers in a war on religion as the 'opiate of the people'.

In 1967 the Party decided to put a damper on the work of the three religions of the country: the Roman Catholics, the Orthodox and the Muslims. The first step taken by the government was to retrain Christian priests and Muslim khojahs and turn them into civil servants. They automatically became state employees or were pensioned off. The second measure was to turn the churches and mosques into museums, halls for physical culture and cultural centres. A total of 2,169 were closed as places of worship. Many of them are preserved as historical cultural monuments. Those which became cultural centres and physical culture halls became centres of youth activities. The administration took no harsh measures against older people who had been brought up in religious faiths, nor were they forbidden to practise their religious rites at home. Care was taken not to deal too harshly with remote villages, where the religious tradition was stronger.

The Party takes great pride in the fact that it has never allowed administrative measures to be taken against religious believers, preferring instead ideological means of persuasion. However, it is believed that in 1973, at the height of the confrontation between the Vatican and the Albanian leaders, one Roman Catholic was executed. The Albanian press branded him as a 'spy, robber and bandit', whereas the Vatican claimed that his only crime had been to baptise an infant.

The Albanian leaders make it a point to show official guests and tourists how well the mosques and churches are maintained and for what purposes they are used. At the same time they stress that theirs is the first atheist state in the world. Visitors both from the west and from Yugoslavia seem to agree that these efforts of the state have had resounding success: there is no trace to be found of any religious life. However, the fact that religious practices can still be found in some places, especially in rural areas, was even mentioned by the official Party organ, *Zeri i popullit*, in articles published during the 1973 drive to do away with political deviations of liberalism and other foreign influences.

In the towns in the traditionally Orthodox south, where many Greeks live, holidays of religious origin are always observed, and people do not go to work at Easter. In the towns of the one-time Roman Catholic north, secret pilgrimages are made to the places where churches once existed, pictures and statues are kept hidden in the homes, women wear crosses on their necklaces and former priests still make the rounds of houses to perform religious rites. Muslims celebrate their holidays in the customary ways, even in some towns.

This subject is a very interesting one, and what is really needed is for field work to be done among the people who had once practised religious customs before any precise judgements could be made on how far atheism has spread and to what extent religion has disappeared among the Albanians. Unfortunately the Albanian authorities have allowed no such studies to be made.

The Albanian leaders cite ideological reasons for their drive to eradicate religion among the Albanians, and the press claimed in 1967 that 'religion was abolished because the people wanted it so'. However, the author feels that the real reason is the leadership's desire to make the nation homogeneous and thus to forestall interference from outside.

It should be noted that the Albanian constitution still guarantees freedom of religion and freedom for believers to perform their religious rites. At the VI Party Congress Enver Hoxha announced that work was being done on adjusting the constitution, which was 'out of line with social practice in Albania'.[31] However, nothing more has been heard about this, nor has anything appeared in the press. Undoubtedly there are problems over how to give legal sanction to the suppression of religion in Albania.

(vi) *Public Health and Social Security*

Very important results have been achieved in the domain of public health and social security. Hospitals, clinics and maternity wards give free medical treatment to the entire population. All medical services are free.

In 1969 there were 158 hospitals and 1,400 doctors. Between 1965 and 1970, the number of people per doctor was reduced from 1,870 to 1,180. The budget for public health in 1969 amounted to 5·3 per cent of the national budget, but in 1971 and 1972 social and cultural expenditure accounted for around 25 per cent: this covers all schools from nursery to secondary levels, universities and other institutions of higher learning, vocational schools, libraries, theatres, hospitals, sanatoria, physical culture, pensions, benefits for mothers with large families, etc. The network of nursery schools and crèches has been well organized. All employed workers enjoy medical care benefits without paying any contributions, and there is a pension system for the aged and destitute. State expenditure is met from the surpluses earned by state enterprises. It is often pointed out in the press that Albania is the only socialist country in Europe which has freed its citizens from all forms of direct taxation. It perhaps needs to be explained that in Albania the distributions of income is not carried out on the principle of work performed or according to 'market rates' of earnings; wages are fixed in advance, and the difference between the highest and lowest wages is minimal. In such circumstances taxation no longer has any meaning.

(vii) *Culture and Education*

Albania is an example of an underdeveloped country which has invested enormous efforts and resources in order to overcome cultural backwardness. After liberation in 1945, over 80 per cent of the population were illiterate; today illiteracy is unknown among the younger generation. According to official figures, at the end of 1972 there were 700,000 schoolchildren and university students, which means that every third citizen was enrolled in some kind of educational institution.[32] Children between the ages of three and six attend nursery schools (*kopshte*); between the ages of seven and fifteen attendance at elementary school is compulsory. Secondary schools in Albania are divided into three categories: twelve-year schools (*shkollat 12-vjeçore*), which give four years of additional education after elementary school; technical and professional schools (*shkollat e mesme tekniko-profesionale*), which combine technical and vocational training with general education, and lower technical schools (*shkollat e ulta profesionale*) for workers in agriculture and industry.

As part of its 'revolutionizing life' programme, it was decided at the eighth plenum of the Central Committee of the Party of Labour in June 1968 to reform the system of schooling, education and training which had followed on the Russian model. University studies were sometimes inordinately long; courses of instruction at the majority of engineering faculties lasted five years or more. For this reason the teaching plans and curricula at all levels of education were revised in 1972.

The new system of education in schools of all levels and at the university is based on a three-pronged approach: *teaching, productive work, phsysical and military exercises*. The participation of pupils and students in productive work is intended for the ideological training and revolutionary motivation of the young generation. The school should be 'in the service of the revolution', since concentration on intellectual work alone gives a one-sided education and leads to a tendency to underrate workers and peasants. According to official Albanian explanations, the previous system of education fostered careerism and revisionism. In secondary schools, the school year now lasts seven and a half months, the rest of the year being spent in productive labour and physical and military exercises. In this way the pupils become acquainted with the 'working class' and the 'production process' at an early stage.

At the tertiary level are the University of Tiranë and colleges and academies in other towns. Students of these institutions of higher education also do production work, military exercises and physical training. The majority of students hold scholarships, which gives them free accommodation in student dormitories, free food, clothing, etc. (they are not in the form of money). Thirty-five per cent of all students are women,[33] a great achievement considering the subordinate place women have traditionally held in the patriarchal Albanian way of life.

Compared with the pre-war era, the country's cultural and artistic life has advanced, and the network of institutions for its cultivation has been increased. Although, in the natural course of events, traditional folklore and folk art are disappearing, the authorities foster them through various artistic and folklore groups, as part of the popular culture and as an expression of the national spirit, which has played an important role in the people's history. There are few peoples who preserved their traditions for so long and in such a pure state as the Albanians, but the aspects of Albanian tradition – especially patriarchalism – which hinder the development of a modern society are gradually being removed. One of the objectives of the Albanian Party of Labour has been to modernize and emancipate the people and to remove those remnants of the past which kept Albanian society from advancing, but in all its plans and programmes, it has aimed to reflect the national character.

Modern life and the national liberation war are the most frequent themes of literature, painting and other forms of artistic expression. Socialist realism is the predominating method, and freedom of artistic expression is restricted within its limits, since otherwise art 'does not serve the interests of the people'. Cultural workers and artists comply with the guidelines of state bodies and the Party of Labour or else risk being accused of 'revisionism' or 'bourgeois liberalism'. At the time of writing, the Albanian press is in the midst of a vehement campaign against 'foreign influences' on the 'national character of literature'. It is further stated that the literature which is again appearing among some poets, artists and musicians and film makers is no accident at a time when in artistic and cultural circles, contacts and co-operation have been established with a public outside the borders of the country.[34] To deal with this subject adquately would require another book, so the task will not be attempted here.

Observers and visitors to Albania from western countries[35] have been struck by the paucity of books on display in book stores.[36] However, the number of cultural centres, cinemas, theatres and libraries is constantly growing. There are many journals and specialized reviews. The state monopoly radio and television services are being promoted and enjoy great popularity. Programmes of Italian, Yugoslav and Greek television can be seen viewed in Albanian homes. This is probably one of the reasons why internal 'ideological problems' have arisen in recent years, primarily in the sphere of culture and arts.

Despite the monotony and stereotypes of Albanian literature and art, there has also been an important breakthrough considering culture in its widest sense. A cultural life has been created – from scratch – in which the broad masses of the people have had an opportunity to participate. Unfortunately, however, the process of democratization of society, including culture and the arts, was brought to a halt by the latest campaign initiated at the Fourth Plenum of the Central Committee in February 1973. Thus the unrelieved uniformity of Albanian literature will continue for some time to come.

NOTES

1 Kushtetuta e Republikës Popullore të Shqipërisë neni 57 de 58. 'Kodifikimi i përgjithëshëm i legjislacionit në fuqi të Republikës popullore të Shqipërisë'. Kodet, Vëllimi I, Botimi i Kryeministrisë, Tiranë, 1961 (in further text, Kushtetuta).
2 Ibid., Article 61.
3 Ibid., Article 63.
4 Ibid., Article 75.
5 Ibid., Article 77.

6 Ibid., Article 79.
7 Ibid., Article 80.
8 Ibid., Article 85.
9 Ibid., Article 86.
10 Ibid., Articles 88, 89, and 90.
11 Ibid., Article 21.
12 See Gilbert Mury, *Le Monde Diplomatique*, No. 214, 4 January 1972.
13 Enver Hoxha, Discussion at the Tenth Plenum of the APL, printed in *Rruga e partisë*, No. 7, 1970.
14 *Zeri i popullit*, 23 October 1973.
15 *Zeri i popullit*, 23 October 1973, p. 2.
16 Before becoming full members of the Communist Party in East European countries (with the exception of Yugoslavia), aspirants must go through a period of preparation as 'candidates', showing their zeal by being very active and studying the theory of Marxism–Leninism.
17 Enver Hoxha, Report to the Sixth Congress of the A.P.L., p. 187.
18 A biography of this outstanding man, who has guided the course of the history of the Albanian people in the last thirty years, has yet to be written. The present profile of Enver Hoxha has been drawn on the basis of his works, which began to be published in Albania in 1968 after his sixtieth birthday, and articles in the Albanian press. Some French and English sources have also been used.
19 Emmanuel Zakhos, *Albanie, Petite Planète*, Paris, 1972, p. 138.
20 Ibid.
21 S. Skendi, op. cit., p. 326.
22 *Dokumenta Kryesore PPSH*, I, 94.
23 Milovan Djilas, op. cit., pp. 110–15.
24 S. Skendi, op. cit., p. 136.
25 Enver Hoxha, speech in Vlorë (Valona) at the sixtieth anniversary celebration of independence and the twenty-eighth anniversary of the liberation. Source: *Rruga e partisë*, No. 12, 1972, p. 9.
26 S. Skendi, op. cit., p. 342.
27 Ibid.
28 Ibid.
29 Paul Lendvai, *L'Europe des Balkans après Stalin. Albanie*, Paris, 1972, pp. 209–49.
30 Muslims accounted for about 70 per cent of the population, Orthodox Christians for 20 per cent and Roman Catholics for 10 per cent.
31 Enver Hoxha, Report to VI Congress of the A.P.L., 1 to 7 November 1971, quoted in *Zeri i popullit*, 2 November 1971.
32 Adbul Kellezi, 'Raport mbi planin dhe buxhëtin e shtetit për vitin 1973' (Report on state plan and budget for 1973), *Probleme ekonomike*, Tiranë, No. 1, 1973, p. 39.
33 M. Snuderl, op. cit., p. 20.
34 Ismail Kadare, 'Mbi ndikimet e huaja dhe karaktërin nacional të letërsisë' (On foreign influence and national character of literature), from *Zeri i popullit*, 8 April 1973.
35 It is not easy to obtain a visa for travel in Albania. Citizens of socialist countries are not allowed in. A small number of Yugoslavs are granted visas, as are Albanians from Yugoslavia who wish to visit relatives. Groups of tourists from Western Europe are allowed to visit Albania. Groups of left-wing youth and student organizations are given visas to take part in voluntary work drives for fifteen days with an additional fifteen days of vacation at the seaside.
36 Diverze, 'Albanian Socialism', *Le Monde*, 6 September 1971.

7

THE FAMILY AND TRIBAL TRADITION

(i) *Albanian Tribal Organization*

Traditionally, the Albanian family has many members – sometimes several dozen – and plays an important social role. Elements of tribal organization can be found even today in remote villages of northern Albania and among the Albanians living in Yugoslavia.[1] The *fis*, considered sometimes as a tribe and sometimes as a clan, consists of a certain number of family households with a common ancestry on the male side. It corresponds to the Latin *gens*. The head of the *fis*, the *vojvoda*, is the oldest male of the parental or grandparental generation, the patriarch. The smaller clan is led by a council of elders (Serbo-Croatian *glavar*, Albanian *plaku*).

There is also a territorial-political organization, the *bajrak*, closely connected with the *fis*. The *bajrak* (Turkish for banner) is a political union of one or more *fis* under a single head, the *bajrabtar*, who convened meetings of the tribe when necessary and represented it. This office is hereditary in certain families. Originally the *bajraktar* had only the modest office of leading the highlanders to the battlefield. It may also be said that each *bajrak*, which has a geographical unity, constitutes an autonomous state governed by customs and other juridical regulations basically common to all the other *bajraks*,[2] When these families were relatively few, they lived in the same village or region. As their numbers grew and they dispersed, they still nourished strong traditions and maintained their family ties with those who had remained in the ancestral village. Even if the genealogy is not correct, it is still carefully perpetuated. A common ancestry is the primary feature of the tribal communities.[3] I could illustrate this with a personal example. In the village where I was born, the clan (families who once lived together) kept up ties with relations whose common ancestors had not lived together for eighty or a hundred years. At least once a year we would pay each other visits, usually in the winter when snow was on the ground and there would be no work in the fields. Visits to relatives were always a special treat.

One important feature of the tribe is that there is no intermarriage. The men of one tribe, particularly when it is a small one, marry only women of other tribes. Thus the ties of kinship were extended to in-laws who were not blood relatives, and in the conditions in which the internally divided Albanian tribes lived during the difficult times of Turkish occupation, these ties of kinship often stood them in good stead.[4] The tribes also had common land, pastures, forests and water. If a member of the tribe needed something that was common property, the entire tribe decided upon his case at a meeting of representatives from all the households. The common property was also collectively defended and linked all the blood-related tribe members into an economic community. In the past, different tribes might come into conflict and even shed blood over pastureland or forests. It was considered a tribal obligation and sacred duty to avenge a relative who had been killed.

What indeed has remained of the old tribal life? It is difficult to answer this question precisely. Today, a large clan or even a good-sized family may be called a tribe. It is safe to say, though, that some features of tribal organization have been preserved, although even these are gradually dis-appearing in the modern Albanian conditions of life and work. Large-scale production in modern industry is replacing the old way of life, in which people grew food and spun cloth for their own needs. Some of those who have studied this aspect of life among the Balkan peoples sug-gest that the rise of the state destroyed tribal life.[5] However, such a view can only be partly correct, since the tribal organization, like any tradi-tional social institution, has left deep marks on the people's psyche and way of life. In northern Albania, particularly, the tribal organizations have been continuous from early times up to this century.[6]

The common chief of the tribe, *bajraktar*, convened tribal meetings whenever necessary and represented it. At his summons, all representa-tives of the tribe and clans would assemble, and would settle internal tribal questions by agreement. Inter-tribal disputes or problems were settled by the chiefs of the tribes concerned, sometimes with the media-tion of a third disinterested tribal community. There was also a tribal court, which passed verdicts according to unwritten customary ordin-ances, embodied in the Canon of Leka Dukagjini; there were rules for every possible situation, right down to the most minute details. The tribal chiefs, who received no remuneration for their duties, were held in high esteem. The tribe demanded loyalty and obedience from each of its members, who, especially in cases involving the honour and reputation of the tribe, were even expected to lay down their lives.

The social and economic importance of the tribe was certainly equalled by the psychological security and intimacy which the members of such a collective enjoyed. The tribe was solidly behind each individual, so long as he complied with the demands and interests of the whole community. The tribe could reprimand any disobedient member, ostracize him or even burn down his house, so that he could no longer live in tribal territory. Serious violations were punished by expulsion from the tribe or even by death. Tribe members thus developed a specific mentality of absolute loyalty to the social collective.[7] The tribes were never a group of close or distant relatives; they were a consolidated society, a community of interests. For all these reasons, the member of a strong tribe felt himself to be strong. The proverbs 'Woe to the brave man in a weak clan' and 'Justice is strong when the clan is strong' are not without foundation.

The tribe, as the organization best suited to the circumstances of the time, was a repository of numerous customs from earlier epochs in Albanian history. One such convention from a patriarchal tribal society which evolved into an ethical or moral institution is *besa* – the word of honour which, when once given, is considered binding. Even the opposite sides in a blood feud can move about freely if they have given each other *besa* (in this instance guaranteeing a truce). Whenever anyone goes back on his *besa*, he loses the confidence and support not only of his tribe members but of all his acquaintances. Such people withdraw into a self-imposed isolation and are the object of general contempt and ostracism.

The material and psychological security that tribal members enjoyed meant that solidarity was very strong. Whenever the house of an individual or household burned down, neighbours and relatives would come to the rescue and with gifts and labour would help to build a bigger and better house than the one which had been destroyed. In the tribe, even another's unhappiness is felt as keenly as one's own. In such communities there is no loneliness and no suicide.

The families and tribes(*fis*) set great store by marriage ties. The men in a household would seek brides from good, reputable families. More attention was given to the stock (lineage and status of the family in society and their observance of the basic social values) than to the bride herself. If a girl was of good stock and from a reputable family, she did not have to be attractive to be assured of a husband, since the children that she would bear were expected to resemble their maternal uncles: Albanians in remote villages in Yugoslavia still today look first at the prospective bride's family and particularly her brothers in making a match.

Special respect for the old was fostered by the tribal organization. The council of elders (*pleqet, pleqnija*) was the supreme court of the tribe, or of several tribes, if their chiefs were discussing intertribal relations. The elders judged according to their consciences, soberly and impartially on the basis of traditional, customary norms. The experience of the elders in a tribe was highly respected, and their advice was usually heeded; whenever they spoke or stated their views, they were listened to with great attention and deference.[8]

As the most important social institution, which possessed elements of independence and self-government, the tribal organization created through the centuries a number of norms of common law which served each successive generation both as theory and for practice. The body of norms governing the life and behaviour of the individual and the tribe as a whole is known as the 'Canon of Lekë Dukagjini'.

The Canon of Lekë is the common law of the Albanians, and comprises conventions from many different periods, some even going back to the very earliest society. However, most of the rules in the Canon took shape during the centuries of tribal organization in northern Albania and later under Turkish rule.[9] The regulations of common law were formulated during the rise and ascendancy of the tribes and tribal autonomy in the north Albanian hills, but they were also a tribute to Leka's leadership in the struggle against the Turks and, of course, to the judgements which he later handed out, and which set precedents. Probably the name 'Canon of Lekë' was first used in the mountains of northern Albania.[10]

This Canon contains statutory, criminal, civil and family laws as well as procedural rules for both criminal and civil courts. Many local differences can be noted in these rules. They became accepted as common law by virtue of long repetition and the precedents set by the councils of elders. There were both legal and moral sanctions for violations of these rules.[11] When the autonomy of Albanians was restricted, particularly in the second half of the nineteenth century, the Canon of Lekë began to acquire an admixture of Muslim religious laws (*sheriat*).

The Canon of Lekë was first published in the Albanian language only in 1933. It was collected and written down by a Franciscan monk, Shtjefën Gjeçovi, from Kosovë, who was well versed in the ethnography, history, folklore, languages and archaeology of Albania, and in Byzantine and Roman culture and civilization. It is due to him that Albanians have such a comprehensive and valuable masterpiece from their past.[12] As we have already seen, the Albanian tribes which had lived for centuries in the mountainous regions enjoyed considerable autonomy and not even at the height of its power could the Ottoman empire subjugate them to its direct control. The autonomous status of the mountain tribes of northern Albania reduced their practical dealings with the Turkish state to little more than the obligation of military service.[13] The Albanian tribes maintained their status and even into the first decades of the twentieth century, each tribe lived in freedom under its chiefs, its only obligation being to serve in the Turkish army, but always under the banner of the tribe.[14]

Turkey tried to stop the disintegration of the empire by centralizing its state administration; the autonomy of the Albanian tribes, which had allowed them to live in their mountains with all their old privileges like a state within a state, had come to an end. Turkey began to replace tribal chiefs with its own officials, and tribal courts with its own judges.

Taxes and recruits were demanded. A conflict with the Albanians was inevitable. The Albanian peasant insurrections were instrumental in awakening the people's consciousness of their national entity, since they were fighting not only on behalf of their tribes but also on behalf of their entire nation.[15]

Our description of the customs and traditions of the Albanians and their social organization in the past would be incomplete without mention of the writings of the Montenegrin *vojvoda* Marko Milanov, entitled *The Life and Customs of the Albanians*. In his foreword he states that 'through thick and thin the Albanian remains steadfast and upright, true to the ancient language and gun that were his birthright. This makes one think that these people have something better and more enduring in themselves than other people, something that has resisted change through all these centuries and all vicissitudes'.[16]

(ii) *The Blood Feud*

According to the official statistics of the People's Republic of Albania, there have been no blood feuds for twenty years. So the blood feud will be discussed here more as a historical phenomenon, than as a present reality; however, it survives to this day in Yugoslavia among the Albanians living in Kosovë, Macedonia and Montenegro.

Many communities at the tribal and familial levels have waged blood feuds, which derived its justification from that most ancient of laws, 'an eye for an eye, a tooth for a tooth', or as the Albanians say *'koka për kokë'* (a head for a head). Since time immemorial vendettas have existed among other peoples inhabiting the Balkan peninsula. The blood feud became particularly widespread after the arrival of the Turks in the Balkans and the renewal of the tribal way of life. The inefficient Turkish state organization could not provide the necessary protection or guarantee sanctions against major crimes;[17] hence the blood feud became an institution of common law according to which members of a community, usually a clan, had not only the right but the duty to avenge the murder of one of their members by killing the murderer or some other member of his family, clan or tribe. As an instrument of familial justice, it has something of the ritual about it. The rules varied from place to place, but they never failed to be strictly observed. Among the Albanians, the victim could not be a woman or a male child who was not old enough to bear arms, and a priest was similarly protected.

In the present age the vendetta seems a shocking anachronism. However, the avenger in a blood feud never thinks that he is doing anything wrong or shameful. He is aware of the gravity of his act, but is convinced that this act is accepted and approved by his milieu. What is. more he is under very strong psychological pressure, because he knows that the milieu will look down upon and spurn him if he does not revenge his murdered kinsman.

When tribal organization was universal, there were no better laws, and personal safety and security were minimal. Not only was it no crime to kill the killer but it was even a necessity. If the murdered relative were not avenged, his killer could murder a second or third time; he might become powerful and constantly commit crimes and cause trouble. For this reason, the fear of revenge was the best guarantee of law and order; it was a warning to all those who would transgress tribal law. The blood feud was less arbitrary than may appear. In many cases a dispute would be judged by the council of elders, which might decree that one clan 'owed blood' to another. The latter then had every right either to kill a member of the first clan, to give a pardon, or even to postpone execution of the sentence for several generations thus keeping the first clan in a state of servitude through fear.

If for any reason the injured side was not able to carry out its revenge, then a substitute would be found to do the job. The person who was hired for a price to do the killing was not in a blood feud with the family concerned; if he were ever discovered, he was not considered guilty, and the blood feud was carried on with the family who had ordered the murder. If it happened that the family had no male members who were of age, the other side waited until they grew up. The act of revenge was a way of showing the social environment and community that justice had been done; the way in which it was done was incidental.[18]

As a consequence of the blood feud and hostilities between various tribes, families began to live in fortified houses built of hard materials and called forts, which were intended to provide refuge for the family, particularly its male members. These forts can be seen to this day among the Albanians in Kosovë, particularly on the plain of Dukagjini.

As yet another ramification of the blood feud as a kind of law and order of tribal society, families brought up their children to be particularly careful and circumspect in what they said. For sensitive mountain people, even a small oath could be taken as an insult and pretext for a fight. Among these hot-tempered, touchy and honour-loving mountaineers, there were often quarrels and even murders over trifles, such as a remark to the effect that someone was of bad family or tribe. An individual would take such an insult as being directed not only at himself but at his entire tribe, and if he did not come to the defence of its honour and dignity the tribe would not come to his defence when necessary. Having grown up in the tribe and with a tribal mentality, the Albanian was very proud and even vain about his tribe, and he would state the tribal name with greater pride if the tribe was large and well known.[19]

Some features of the tribal mentality survive to this day. Members of small communities or of the same village do not intermarry, even though it is allowed by the church or mosque and by civil law. The Albanians traditionally respect and revere their friends, but they prefer them to be from some more distant village, so that they will have less occasion to interfere in their affairs. Then the families would become involved, and after a quarrel there can never be true friendship; someone might even get killed on a slight provocation. We think that there is a connection between the foreign policy of present-day Albania and the old ways of the Albanian people. Relations between states have many similarities with those between tribes or clans. Albania perhaps instinctively avoids having allies that are too close, because they might interfere in its internal affairs.

Among the Albanians in Yugoslavia, the number of crimes committed in vendettas is not only not on the decline but is even rising. Between 1964 and 1970, for instance, the circuit court in Prishtinë tried 320 cases involving blood feuds.[20] There are such feuds in almost every one of the communes of the province of Kosovë, most of them in the remote villages. Thus in the courts of Kosovë, judges have become very familiar with this type of murder or attempted murder. In three communes in Kosovë between 1968 and 1970 there were fifteen murders and about thirty attempted murders, mostly in blood feuds.[21]

The gravity of this phenomenon, however, should not be measured simply by the number of lives lost, but rather by its economic, political, social and psychological consequences, the most grievous of which is certainly the cases of closed families – those which owe blood and live more or less under house arrest, self-imposed of course, often for as long as ten years or more. Such isolation has enormous implications for society – economic (untilled fields), social (restricted movement), political (a suspicion of society and 'the authorities' in general) and psychological (constant fear for one's own life).[22]

The Province of Kosovë, as well as other regions in Yugoslavia settled by Albanians, has undergone far-reaching social and economic transformation: new socialist legislation has been introduced; guaranteeing equal rights to all, regardless of sex, race, religion or social status. However, it is perhaps not surprising that three decades have not been long enough to eradicate the last vestiges of patriarchal relationships and the remnants of common law, including the custom of vendetta.

We mentioned that in Albania the blood feud has disappeared. There are important reasons why Albania and Yugoslavia differ in this respect. In Albania collectivization has abolished private ownership of land, which was one of the main reasons why peasants quarrelled and even killed one another. Today not an inch of land in Albania is privately owned, nor is there any possibility of private initiative. Furthermore, other social causes for feuds, such as religious differences and the buying of brides, have faded into insignificance. Finally, ever since the liberation of the country, perpetrators of blood revenge have been summarily executed, or otherwise severely punished on the spot, and their families are resettled far apart from one another in order to preclude any attempt at prolonging the feud. Hence the blood feud is of extreme rarity in Albania. In Yugoslavia, on the other hand, the steps taken by the authorities to combat it have been less drastic, Efforts are made rather to educate the people and raise their mentality from a primitive level, all of which takes more time.

(iii) *Women in Society*

Until liberation in 1945, an Albanian woman did not enjoy equal civil or political rights; she held an inferior place both in society and in the family life. According to patriarchal views, which were dominant in the town as well as in the countryside, a woman's purpose in life was to bear children and work in the house. The Muslim religious law observed by the majority of Albanians permitted men to have several wives, and many of them did, especially the wealthy beys and feudal lords. Thus religion and patriarchalism and the low level of economic development made the position of the Albanian woman in society exceptionally difficult.

The establishment of the new socialist government in Albania marked the beginning of women's equality in the legal and political and social sense, and all forms of exploitation and oppression of women, in whatever spheres of life, were abolished. The Muslim law was replaced by new socialist law, originally inspired by the Soviet model. It was forbidden for women to wear the veil, which they had done until liberation. Particularly important measures were taken in the sphere of education. Immediately after the war over 240,685 women were attending courses to learn to read and write.[23] The younger generation of women has been brought up with normal schooling and further education. In 1970 there were 268,896 girls enrolled in schools. The number of women students at the university was 2,928, or 36 per cent of the total enrolment.

Once it was a rarity to see a woman working in an office or shop; but thirty years after liberation this situation has completely changed. In 1972, 178,671 women were employed in the state sector, or 40 per cent of the total number of employed in the country; just ten years before in 1960, women had accounted for only 26 per cent of the total work force.[24] Clearly women have acquired a new status in society and the production process, and their emancipation has come a long way. In 1966, as part of its 'ideological and cultural revolution', the Albanian Party of Labour devoted special attention to the role of the Albanian woman in society and the family. The traditional Albanian family with its conservative, patriarchal way of life and attitudes towards women was

a stumbling block for the Party in its implementation of a number of
actions and measures to transform social relationships.

The Party of Labour and its leaders decided that very little had been
done to change the role of women in the family and society, and that
steps should be taken to this end and to 'strengthen socialist democracy
in the family'. All Party members who still acted like 'despots' towards
their wives in the family and who qualified as 'heads of household'
according to the old patriarchal laws, written and unwritten, were
brought under sharp attack. At a meeting in Tepelene in 1969, the third
senior man in the Albanian leadership, Hysni Kapo, called all those
party members who still viewed their wives as inferior 'Anatolians'.[25]
At the elections in September 1970 for the Albanian People's Assembly,
seventy-two women were elected, out of a total of 740 deputies.[26]
Tens of thousands of women are activists in socio-political and sports
organizations and in local administration. Formerly 'male' jobs and pro-
fessions are being filled by women – in the oilfields; on the estates of
farmers' co-operatives; in factories, offices and administration; as doctors and university professors, and even in military exercises for national
defence.

The industrialization, which is still in progress, and the collectivization of agriculture have also brought about radical changes in the structure of Albanian society. In 1964 the number of families working outside agriculture was 26·6 per cent of the total population, while in 1955
it had been 16 per cent.[27] The process of industrialization has attracted
many families from the countryside to the towns: the urban population
grew from 15·9 per cent in 1945 to 33·3 per cent in 1967. Although rural-
urban migration is administratively regulated, the rural population
is progressively dwindling. In 1955 there were 155,200 families with
the status of peasant families, whereas by 1960 this number had dropped
to 150,197 familes, i.e. to 58·6 per cent of the total population.[28] However, in the country's present level of development it is difficult to provide the jobs in the cities and the housing, schools, utilities and other
services necessary to cope with a large influx of peasants from the countryside. For this reason migration is strictly controlled.

According to some sociological research, the pattern of marriage has
acquired many strikingly new features among young people in Mirëdité
(a backward region in northern Albania). Before the Second World
War, marriages were arranged by the parents, and the bride and groom-
to-be were not consulted. Now, of the fifty-four married couples sur-
veyed in the small town of Rreshën in northern Albania, twenty-six
had chosen their own partners, fifteen had married on the initiative of
their parents, but with their own consent and thirteen couples had been
married according to the old customs – without giving their consent.
At the height of the campaign after 1966 to transform the family in the

backward rural environment, over 3,718 engagements which had been made in the old way were broken.[29]

The replies of the boys and girls asked about the role and influence of their parents in matchmaking are interesting. To the question, 'Who should decide on the marriage?' 39 per cent answered that they should decide themselves, while 61 per cent answered that they should decide together with their parents. Thus the majority of young people thought they should consult their parents over the choice of a partner.[30]

The Albanian family, where traditional moral values are very strong, tends to be stable. In 1969, 15,322 marriages were performed, or 7·4 for every 1,000 inhabitants.[31] In that same year the divorce rate was 0·8, one of the lowest in Europe.[32] The reasons for seeking a divorce were largely the breakdown of relations or adultery.[33] In addition to the fact that the right of divorce is guaranteed by family law, people's courts, particularly in recent years, hold public discussions before they allow a marriage to be dissolved. It is noted that men and women file for divorce in almost equal numbers.

The campaign to 'strengthen socialist democracy in the family', which was carried out as part of the 'ideological and cultural revolution', takes a large share of the credit for the improvement in women's place in society and the family.

NOTES

1 Dr. Mirko Barjaktarović, 'Plemensko uredjenje kod Albanaca', from *Istorija Albanaca*, Beograd, 1969, p. 104.
2 Stavro Skendi, op. cit., p. 14.
3 Ibid.
4 Ibid.
5 See Milan Suffley, *Srbi i Arbanasi*, Beograd, 1925.
6 Barjaktarević, op. cit., p. 108.
7 Ibid., p. 110.
8 Ibid., p. 115.
9 Dr. Surja Pupovci, *Gradjanskopravni odnosi u Zakoniku Leke Dukagjinija*, Prishtinë, 1968, p. 282.
10 Ibid.
11 Ibid.
12 See *Kanuni i Lekë Dukagjinit*, collected and collated by Shtjefën Gjeçovi, Prishtinë, 1972.
13 Dimitrije Tucovic, *Srbija i Arbanija*, Beograd–Zagreb, 1954, p. 54.
14 Ibid., p. 56.
15 Ibid., p. 57.
16 Marko Milanov, *Život i običaji Arbanasa*, Titograd, 1967, p. 10. Also of interest are the books of Edith Durham. This Englishwoman studied the laws, character, customs, history and culture of the Albanians during those troubled times when the Albanian people were entering history and were most in need of true friends who would help them realize their historical aspirations to form a nation-state. See Edith Durham, *The Burden of the Balkans*, London,

1905; *High Albania*, London, 1914; *The Struggle for Scutari*, London, 1914; *Twenty Years of Balkan Tangle*, London, 1920.

17 The vendetta and banditry have flourished in Sicily, Sardinia and Corsica, which are far removed from the metropolitan seats of power, for the same reason.

18 Ibid.

19 Ibid., p. 118.

20 'Nedelne informativne novine', NIN.

21 *Politika* daily newspaper, Belgrade, 3 March 1973.

22 M. Karan, op. cit., p. 7.

23 Vita Kapo, 'Për emancipimin e plotë të gruas' (For a full emancipation of women), *Rruga e partisë*, No. 11, 1969, p. 38.

24 *Zeri i popullit*, 25 May 1973, p. 2.

25 Hysni Kapo, 'Mardhanjët në shoqri dhe familje – fushë e gjerë e luftës klasore' (Social and family relations – a wide scope for class struggle), *Rruga e partisë*, No. 1, 1970, p. 69.

26 Godišnjak Instituta za medjunarodnu politiku i provredu 1970, p. 257.

27 Alfred Uçi, 'Familja, martesa dhe çkunorizimi në Shqipëri' (Family, marriage and divorce in Albania), *Rruga e partisë*, No. 4, 1969, p. 76.

28 Ibid.

29 Ibid., p. 78.

30 Ibid., p. 79.

31 *Vjetari Statisikor i RPSH 1969 dhe 1970*, p. 27. The figures are provisional.

32 Ibid., p. 33.

33 Family Law of Albania, Article 57.

8

SOCIAL AND
ECONOMIC DEVELOPMENT

(i) *The First Period of Economic Development 1945–8*

The building of a socialist society in Albania was begun under very
inauspicious circumstances. The problems looming largest were the
very low level of productive forces and a society still in the bondage of
its feudal past, when workers and poor peasants were not only exploited
by the domestic bourgeoisie and semi-feudal landlords (who in turn
were dependent on the foreign concessionaires in Albania), but also had
to cope with the basic problems of poverty and hunger.

Economically, in comparison with other European countries, Albania
was on the lowest rung of the ladder. Between the two wars capitalist
industrialization was in its infancy; in 1938 the proportion of non-
agricultural activities in the economy taken together was estimated at
between 8 and 9·8 per cent of the national income.[1] In the countryside
subsistence farming was the rule.

During the Second World War the economy was completely
devastated,[2] so the whole spectrum of economics had to be dealt with
by the Communist Party of Albania on assuming power. It had not
only to renew the war-torn economy but to ensure a rate of development
befitting a socialist society – two complementary needs.

The post-war economic development of Albania can be divided into
three periods, each with its phases which correspond to the five-year
plans of economic development.

The first period covers the years 1945–8. The new democratic
government which had been formed while the national liberation war
was still raging, passed the first measures of social and economic reform
in 1944, 1945 and 1946.[3] The first important measure was agrarian
reform, after which all economic organizations (factories, transport
enterprises, banks, etc.) were nationalized. Planning was introduced, and
the work of laying down the foundations of a socialist economic system
was begun.[4]

Since Albania was predominantly an agricultural country, the
agrarian reform was of momentous importance for the peasantry. Prior
to the socialist revolution, 52·43 per cent of all land in Albania was owned

by beys and semi-feudal landlords; small farmers accounted for 28·07 per cent of the land, and the state owned 18·71 per cent. The agrarian reform changed this situation radically. The once large estates of the semi-feudal lords were cut down to 16·38 per cent of the total land in Albania; small farmers increased their holdings to 43·17 per cent and landless proletariat in the countryside were given 34·63 per cent of the land area. As it had always been the Albanian peasant's fondest dream to own land, this reform was immensely popular.

During this period, economic development was achieved through co-operation with Yugoslavia. Annual economic plans passed in 1947 and 1948 were aimed at activating domestic resources. Emphasis was placed on developing the extractive industry and modernizing its equipment, on building up manufacturing and reconstructing plants, and in agriculture on producing crops used in industry and pharmaceuticals. Since construction of new communications was of primary importance, work began immediately on the first railway lines (Durrës-Elbasan and Durrës-Tiranë).[5]

Under an agreement on economic co-operation between Albania and Yugoslavia, signed on 1 July 1946, a mixed Albanian–Yugoslav society was set up[6] and the principles of economic co-operation between the two countries were laid down.[7] In addition to the agreement on economic co-operation and the formation of mixed societies, an inter-governmental treaty on co-ordinating economic plans and on a customs and monetary union was signed on 27 November 1946.[8] The principle underlying the treaty was that a mutually fair economic co-operation and mutual solidarity should be established.[9] However, the co-operation with Yugoslavia aroused suspicion and resentment among some Albanian leaders. In 1948, after Yugoslavia's expulsion from the socialist camp, all treaties and agreements between the two countries were annulled.

(ii) *The Second Period of Economic Development 1949–61*

The second period of economic development covers the years between 1949 and 1961; it comprises the two-year plan of 1949–51, the first five-year plan of 1951–5, and the second five-year plan of 1956–60. At the very beginning of this period, Albania formed firm ties with the countries of the socialist camp belonging to the Council for Mutual Economic Assistance (Comecon) and pursued a corresponding policy of economic development.[10] The two-year plan marked a change in the concept of economic policy to emphasis on industry, neglecting agriculture and completely ignoring the people's standard of living. This emphasis was also predominant in the first and second five-year plans. To be sure, after 1953 the plan was revised, following the reversal of policy in the U.S.S.R. and other East European countries; the construction of some industrial plans was postponed, and greater attention was now paid to agriculture and to improving living standards. However, heavy industry continued to enjoy priority treatment, and agricultural production showed little growth (see Table 15); this stagnation can also be accounted for by the collectivization carried out in the very short space of three years – 1958–61.

Despite certain weaknesses in the first and second five-year plans, the Albanian economy achieved considerable results in this period, to which the loans granted by the Soviet Union and other Eastern–European socialist countries contributed.[11] The country's G.N.P. increased by more than six times.[12] This is undoubtedly no small achievement, in view of the backwardness of the Albanian economy immediately after the war. However, Albania was not satisfied either with the amount of credit granted by the Soviet Union and other East European socialist countries (the slow growth rate and its oscillations were blamed on inadequate loans), or with the political relationships within Comecon. For this reason, Albania was among the first of the Eastern European countries integrated within Comecon to begin criticizing the discrimination shown by the Soviet Union against other socialist countries in Comecon – this was in 1957. Although the credits and assistance from the Soviet Union and other East European socialist countries were vital for the growth of the Albanian economy, the Albanian leaders were convinced that this assistance was less than could have been made available.[13]

As is well known, after the XX Congress of the C.P.S.U. at the end of the 1950s the philosophy of Comecon was that the Soviet Union, as the leading socialist country, should undergo accelerated economic development in order to catch up with the United States (this being one of the prerequisites for successfully opposing the 'imperialist bloc'). This policy in certain ways subordinated the economies of the small and medium-sized countries in Comecon to the Soviet economy. During his visit to Albania in 1959, Khrushchev recommended to its leaders that their country should be turned into a specialized producer of tropical fruit and industrial crops. On this occasion, Khrushchev said that Albania 'had no need to produce wheat, since it used as much wheat as the mice eat up in the Ukraine', going on to say that the Soviet Union would supply Albania with grain and would endeavour to turn Albania into a 'flower garden'. All of this greatly incensed the Albanians, and it became clear to both Enver Hoxha and Khrushchev that relations between their two countries were heading for a breakdown and that it was only a matter of time before it occurred.[14]

(iii) *The Third Period of Economic Development 1961–70*

The third period includes the third, fourth and fifth five-year plans, and begins with the conflict in 1961 with the Soviet Union and other East European socialist countries, and the Soviet economic blockade.[15] At this time, changes were made in the model of development of the Albanian economy. The concept of intensive economic development with a parallel growth of industry and agriculture was adopted, with self-sufficiency as the password. Foreign credits (only from China) were to play only a supplementary role. The autarky which had previously been the main feature of the Albanian economy was to be gradually abandoned, and economic criteria were to be given greater scope. For this reason, new trends became evident in the Albanian economy in the course of the fourth and fifth five-year plans. The dynamics of economic development took on realistic proportions, and domestic economic resources began to be used more intensively. There is no doubt that this orientation contains numerous positive elements and that there have already been satisfactory results.

The break in relations with the Soviet Union and the economic blockade caused a great setback to the growth of the Albanian economy. The Soviet Union cut off its aid and loans and cancelled the economic agreements. Supplies of industrial equipment were stopped, so that construction of many projects which had already started had to be postponed.[16] This was the reason for the low growth rate (6·7 per cent) during the third five-year plan (1961–5). To add to Albania's problems, in 1961 and 1962 the country was plagued by drought and floods. The rate of capital accumulation under the third five-year plan was 25·7 per cent, which shows the trend towards further industrialization.

After the break in relations with the Soviet Union, the People's Republic of China granted loans for Albania's third five-year plan (1961–5) amounting to 100 million roubles.[17] These credits were used to build twenty-five factories.[18] Thus Albania succeeded – thanks primarily to its own efforts but also to Chinese assistance, which the Albanian leaders are anxious to stress was motivated not by a selfish interests but by a spirit of internationalism – in overcoming these difficulties within a remarkably short time.

According to unofficial figures, China approved credits to Albania amounting to between $360 and 400 million between 1953 and 1970. Credits of $130 million are thought to have been given for the plan running from 1971 to 1975.[19] This assistance has been based on the eight well-known principles which the Chinese leadership made public in 1964.[20] These figures should be taken with some reservation, since no official figures on the amounts of Chinese credits exist either in Albania or in China. It is clear that they only refer to the construction of new industrial plant and exclude loans for equipping the Albanian army.

In addition to the Chinese loans for construction of large industrial projects (e.g. the hydro-electric plant at Vau i Dejës on the Drin, the textile mills in Berat, a glass factory and a sulphuric acid factory) the rate of capital accumulation increased at a rate of 15·7 per cent per annum, and had risen by 1969 to a level of 81·1 per cent higher than in 1965. What is more, in this period (according to Albanian sources) the volume of consumer goods rose by 55 per cent, and the national income (1966–9) rose at an annual rate of 9·3 per cent.

The high rate of capital accumulation made possible a high growth rate in production, but there was no corresponding rise in the standard of living.[21] Besides the reasons already mentioned, large outlays were made in this period for national defence. In 1970 alone $84 million were earmarked for defence, an increase of 9·2 per cent over the preceding year.[22]

The fourth five-year development plan (1965–70) called for a growth in industrial output of 8·7 per cent a year, and an 11 per cent growth of agricultural production.[23] In short, one of the goals of the fourth five-year plan was to alleviate the disproportions within industry and between industry and agriculture. In other words, in addition to further industrialization, one of the prime goals of the fourth plan was to achieve a relatively faster growth in agriculture than in industry. Actually, this plan envisaged a certain change in the status accorded to agriculture; most of the increase in agricultural output (i.e. 82 per cent) was to be achieved by increasing crop yields, while the remainder would be reached by breaking up virgin land.

However, during the fourth five-year plan an average annual growth rate of industrial output of 11 per cent was achieved, and the growth of production of producer goods was 15 per cent (the plan envisaged a growth of 10·8 per cent per annum).[24] The growth rate of agricultural production averaged 5·8 per cent, that is agricultural output in 1969 was 29 per cent greater than in 1965. It would seem then that the plan was not fulfilled in this sphere, probably because its targets were over-ambitious. Many of the tasks set by this plan in the sphere of agriculture will have to be carried out under the fifth five-year plan. Today Albania is producing about 215,000 tons of wheat and 220,000 tons of maize.[25] However, grain production is still not enough to obviate grain imports, despite the fact that in recent years wheat yields have been averaging 15 metric centners per hectare, and maize yields at 19 metric centners.[26] These yields considerably exceed those of previous years, when wheat harvests averaged 9·8 mc per ha., and maize 13·9 mc. During this plan period, some 100,000 ha. of virgin land were broken. This campaign was carried out under the slogan 'Agriculture is the concern of the entire nation'.

(iv) *The Fifth Five-Year Development Plan 1971–5*

As it had done in the past, the VI Congress of the Albanian Party of Labour in 1971 adopted directives on the fifth five-year development plan (1971–5). The tasks laid down by these directives could be summarized as follows:

(*a*) By the end of these five years, the economic level achieved by Albania should make it primarily an industrial country rather than an agricultural one. This would be achieved primarily by giving industrial development top priority. In this way, the economic strength of the country would be enhanced, but parallel with industrial development, further intensification and expansion of agricultural production are planned.

(*b*) Overall economic development, management and organization of labour should be based on scientific principles. The prerequisites for achieving this target of the plan already exist since Albania has well-trained professional and technical personnel who are able to apply scientific and technological innovations and thereby to spur the process of integration of the Albanian economy into the international division of labour.

(*c*) The country should rely on its own resources. It may be true that self-sufficiency is largely a political rallying cry in the country, but efforts are being made to supplement it in the economic as well as the political sphere.

In 1975 production in the social sector should be from 54 to 58 per cent higher than in 1970. Of this amount 70 per cent will be achieved by increasing labour productivity. A growth in industrial output of 10·3 per cent a year is also planned (see Table 2). Production of some leading commodities will increase: oil production to 2,700,000 tons, lignite to 1,250,000 tons, chrome ore to 900,000 tons, copper ore to 600,000 tons, nickel to 650,000 tons, artificial fertilizers to 330,000 tons, electric power to 2 billion kilowatt hours, and there are goals of 64 million metres of cloth and 5 million pairs of shoes.[27]

Under the plan, investment will continue to be concentrated on capital formation (known as 'Group A'), while the manufacture of consumer goods ('Group B') is scheduled to grow much more slowly. The Albanians will have to forgo a higher standard of living for some time to come in the interest of further industrialization of the country. These aims of the new five-year plan can be seen clearly from the structure of overall investment in the five-year period 1971–5.[28] The credits given Albania by China will greatly facilitate realization of the plan.

This plan also envisages the construction of the metal processing, chemical and machine tool industries. In the past the machine tool and equipment industry was neglected. According to the plan, an industrial base will be built which will subsequently make possible the production of heavy machinery. In this way the foreign trade balance can be improved.

One of the large industrial plants to be built is a metallurgical combine in Elbasan, the largest in the country, of which the first phase is due for completion by 1975. Several hydro-electric plants and steam plants (the largest at Fier) will be built; several new mines will be opened and existing ones expanded. The production of cobalt and sulphuric acid will begin, as will oil refining and production of oil derivatives, various steel products, and so on. Light industry and the food processing industry will grow at a moderate pace, with the emphasis on improving the range and quality of products and rationalization of production.

The directives of the plan also call for expansion and modernization of agriculture. A 10·8 per cent annual growth rate is planned in agricultural production and the production target for 1975 is 65 to 69 per cent more than the 1970 level. Grain harvests should increase by between 70 and 74 per cent compared with 1970, and a 60 to 64 per cent growth in animal husbandry is envisaged.[29] There will be greater mechanization on the farm and use of artificial fertilizers, but this is a far cry from guaranteeing that productivity and yields will rise to the desired level. Formidable problems are still faced by agriculture.

Improvements in crop farming were previously given priority over investment in livestock breeding which was neglected and remained at a low level, although it had been a traditional Albanian pursuit. This is the first plan to provide measures designed to upgrade animal breeds and animal husbandry techniques. A shift to intensive breeding and fattening methods requires time and capital; hence farming in general is still largely extensive, even though efforts are being made to intensify it, and the method of remuneration provides little incentive for greater labour productivity.

It was apparently in recognition of this fact that Enver Hoxha announced at the VI Party Congress the innovation in agriculture that the co-operative farms in the plains would be handed over to the work collectives, which would be responsible for production, growth and earnings. Actually these farms have the most modern equipment and had previously been under state control. The state would give assistance in the form of grants-in-aid. This experiment may prove to be a watershed in the further development of agricultural production, although the system of income distribution remains the same.

The plan also devotes great attention to the problems of work organization and management of the economy on scientific principles – about which much more has been said and written than done in recent years. The Congress acknowledged this fact and stressed scientific

management as an important component in future economic development, adding that these efforts were founded on healthy Marxist
principles and opposed to 'revisionist practices'. In the Albanian view,
the practice of 'worker self-management and economic reform' has led
'revisionist' countries into capitalism by virtue of the fact that they
change socialist economies into capitalist economies.

Given the base achieved by the Albanian economy both materially
and in terms of professional and skilled personnel, there is a high
probability that the basic targets of the plan in the sphere of industrial
production will be realized.

(v) *Industry, Mining, Transport*

In all the post-war economic development plans, industry has been
given the top priority, and impressive results have been achieved in
industrial growth. By 1950, industrial output had already more than
quadrupled compared with the pre-war level and continued to grow at
a rate of 22·8 per cent between 1951 and 1955, at 17 per cent between
1955 and 1960, at 6·8 per cent between 1961 and 1965, and at 12·7 per
cent between 1966 and 1970.[30] The fifth five-year plan (1970–5) set the
annual growth rate of industrial output at 10·3 per cent.[31]

Albania has substantial raw material resources, which were hardly
tapped before the war. In 1938 oil production was only 117,000 tons,
and the bitumen produced in 1939 was 10,000 tons.[32] Now, however,
oil extraction and refining have become a leading industry, and the oil
provides three-quarters of the country's power needs. Oilfields extend
between the rivers Semani and Vijosë in the south-western part of the
country (Patos, Mariksa and Qyteti Stalin). The current development
plan up to 1975 for oil and oil derivatives is very ambitious.

There is very little coal, but lignite is mined in Memaliaj, in the Vijosë
river valley, near Korçë, Mborje and Drenova, in Kraba e Vogël between
Tiranë and Elbasan, and in some other parts of the country. Electricity
generating is another important industry which is undergoing accelerated development. In 1965, 340 million Kwh. were generated (70 per
cent hydro-electric power); in 1973 the figure was 1,552 million Kwh.,
and the goal for 1975 is 2,000 million Kwh. By 1971, all villages and
settlements were completely electrified.

In mining, one of the principal ores is chrome. Over six chrome mines
are being exploited, the largest being the Bulqizë mine, north-east of
Tiranë. In 1965 320,000 tons were mined, and in 1973 628,320 tons; an
output of 900,000 tons is planned for 1975. The largest copper mine is
at Rubik, which also has a copper smelting plant (2,600 tons of copper in
1965 and 6,730 tons in 1973),while other important mines are located at
Kukës and Kurbesh. There is a copper wire factory in Shkodër. Iron ore

and nickel are worked in three mines in the Mokra mountain west of Lake Ohrid, and in 1973 380,982 tons were produced. A large iron works is under construction in Elbasan, of which the first phase will be completed in 1975. There are also large salt works on the coast.

Albania has only rudimentary heavy industry and extractive industries. However, the groundwork is being laid for these industries in the five-year plan now in progress, and rapid development is expected in the near future. The most important factories are the copper smelting plant in Rubik, two oil refineries, a cokery, an engine factory in Tiranë and metal-working plants, producing agricultural machinery, automobile parts, kitchenware, tools, etc., in Durrës, Kavajë, Qyteti Stalin and Gjirokastër. Electric motors are being manufactured in Tiranë, and there is a shipyard for the construction of fishing-boats in Durrës. In recent years the chemical industry has begun to develop, but is still in its infancy. A modern factory producing sulphuric acid and superphosphates has been built in Laç near Shkodër, and there is a factory of nitrogen fertilizers in Fier. Plastics are manufactured in Tiranë and Durrës. Other important factories include the porcelain factory in Fier, glass factories in Korçë and Tiranë, cement works in Shkodër, Tiranë, Elbasan, Fush-Krujë and Vlorë, and a caustic-soda factory also in Vlorë. Silenice is the main source of bitumen. In addition to these factories, there are several light industries such as the sugar mills in Maliq, textile mills in Tiranë and in some other towns, tobacco factories in Shkodër, Durrës and Gjirokastër, a tannery in Korçë and several footwear factories. Most industries are located close to their prime source of raw materials. Tiranë has become the leading industrial centre, followed by Durrës, Elbasan, Vlorë and Shkodër.[33]

One of the largest stumbling-blocks impeding the development of the Albanian economy has been the poor state of communications. Priority has therefore been given to road building. In 1969 the quantity of motor vehicles in use was as follows: passenger cars 2,700 and trucks and buses 7,700. The total road mileage amounted to 1,926 miles (3,100 km.).[34] Main highways run from Shkodër in the north all the way to Vlorë in the south, and also link the east and west, from Durrës to Korçë and Gjirokastër. Four-fifths of all commodities are transported by road. Railway transport only became of any significance after the Second World War; in 1937 only 12 km. of railway track existed in the country. Two hundred km. of railways have now been built and when the northern and southern systems are connected, there will be a total of 260 km. In 1973 the Prujas–Elbasan line was completed, having been built by volunteer groups numbering over 400,000 young people, with the assistance of pensioners, office workers, intellectuals and war veterans. In Albania every citizen must spend one month taking part in work drives; even diplomats roll up their sleeves and give a hand in the work brigades when they are home on leave. A new railway line was built in 1974 by volunteer youth groups and citizens doing their compulsory one-month stint.

These railways only run within the country and have no links with other European systems. Consideration is being given to linking the Albanian system with Yugoslavia: it would connect with Prizren in Kosovë, either via Shkodër and Titograd or eastwards via Ohrid. Such a link would greatly stimulate the Albanian economy.[35] While the Albanian railway system is not very modern, it is adequate for the country's needs and its very existence is a boost of public morale.

(vi) *Agriculture*

Nearly half (42 per cent) of the land surface of Albania is used for agricultural purposes. Crop farming accounts for a little over 17·5 per cent of the land under cultivation.

Land reclamation, virgin lands projects and the ploughing of meadows and pastureland have doubled the land under cultivation since 1945. In 1964, 15 per cent of the land was owned by the state, 44·7 per cent by co-operatives, and 21·9 per cent consisted of farmsteads belonging to farm workers. The private sector owned 8·4 per cent of the arable land. By 1967 the Albanian countryside had been completely collectivized, and today it is only possible to speak of co-operatives or state farms in Albania and not of private property, since farmsteads allowed to workers are minimal. Rural households usually have up to 2,000 square metres and some livestock. Peasants can earn more from the sale of meat from their livestock than from the small crops they can raise – mainly vegetables, never grain.

In the first and second periods, there was virtually no investment in agricultural development. After 1960, however, greater efforts were made to accelerate its growth. Outstanding results have been achieved in mechanization of crop farming, in irrigation and in extending areas under cultivation, the draining of swamps, use of artificial fertilizers and increased crop yields. Pre-war Albania had been plagued by its many swamps, but the new government has drained all of them. M. Šnuderl, a professor at the University of Ljubljana, who had spent two years in Albania during the First World War, visited the country again in 1971, and his description of his impressions conveys the changes that have occurred.

I was left speechless when we flew over Shkodër and Lezhë and I saw the land-scape below us. In 1917 there had been marshes stretching endlessly from the coast all the way to the hills in the north-east. These swamps were breeding grounds for malarial mosquitoes. Bites from these mosquitoes, which were impossible to fend off, were often fatal. The areas most afflicted with malaria were the districts of Lezhë, Shengjin, Durrës and farther south towards Fier, Lushnje and Elbasan. Of the 90,000 Austrian soldiers who held the front along the Vijosë river before Vlorë in 1917 and 1918, 80 per cent suffered attacks or died from tropical malaria between April and November and had to be replaced by new troops. Almost every day the white hospital ship flying the Red Cross insignia docked in Durrës and took aboard soldiers who had gone down with malaria. Many died during the voyage. In Durrës, where I spent most of my time in Albania, from sundown onwards we had to wear netting over our faces and gloves to protect ourselves from the thick swarms of mosquitoes in the air and on the city streets. Windows, doors and beds were all protected with thick mosquito netting. But all to no avail, as the small insects found a way through. The natives of the marshy parts were debilitated and unhealthy, yellow in the face, and children over three years of age had swollen bellies, like pregnant women. The inhabitants of other regions, particularly the mountain areas, were strong and healthy.

Looking down from the plane, I was mainly surprised by the extensive and carefully tended fields where there had once been endless marshes. At the cost of great sacrifice and labour over ten years, new Albania drained all the marshes. They dug canals and pumped out the water, desalinated it and made the land fit for crop growing. Now there are no more mosquitoes in the towns. Malaria has disappeared and is a thing of the past. In Durrës (in the south) there is a lovely beach several kilometres long, and in the place where there were once marshes there are now hotels and bungalows for the tourists[34] along the tree-lined avenue. I was there, and they told me that it was the same wherever there had once been infertile and disease-bearing marshland. What such an enormous and thorough land reclamation has meant for the health of the population is obvious![37]

In 1938 over 92 per cent of all land cultivation was done by draft animals. The picture has completely changed today: in 1965, 84 per cent was done by tractor, and 90 per cent of the ploughing, 60 per cent of the harvesting, and 40 per cent of cultivation was mechanized. In 1970 there were 10,000 tractors, as compared with 4,540 tractors of 1,500 cc. in 1960.

Farming is organized by co-operatives and state farms. The co-operative farms comprise between 900 and 4,500 ha., while the state farms are larger (2,300–13,000 ha.) and organized more rationally. Each co-operative or state farm has its tractor station, which belongs to the state. In recent years there has been a consolidation of co-operatives to pool resources and agricultural machinery. Albania has also gone a long way in irrigating farmland. Well over half of all land under cultivation is now being irrigated, a fact which gives great promise for the future intensification of agricultural production.[38]

According to the guidelines of the present plan running to 1975, increases in agricultural production should primarily be achieved by modernization and greater productivity. However, as we have already seen, the targets set by the plan are very ambitious.

(vii) Foreign Trade

The volume and structure of foreign trade are good indicators of the level of a country's economy. However, in these terms Albania is a developing country in which industrialization is still under way. Imports show a steady rise, particularly of capital equipment and producer goods. Export trends are variable, but the balance of payments has been in deficit almost every year; for this reason Albania depends on loans from its leading trade partner, China.

The composition of reports has shown drastic changes since the war: in 1950 for example, 62·7 per cent of Albanian exports were unprocessed commodities, while only 27·3 per cent were manufactures; in 1970 manufactured articles accounted for 58·7 per cent of exports, and unfinished commodities for only 41·3 per cent.[39]

Chrome (of which Albania is among the major exporters), ferro-nickel, nickel, silicate, bitumen, copper, copper wire and cables account for 55 per cent of the total of exports. More than 25 per cent of exports comprise commodities of light industry, primarily textiles, and the food processing industry, while the remainder is made up of tobacco, cigarettes, tinned foods, livestock products, fruit and spring vegetables. In 1970 there were 200 articles on the export commodity list. The official slogan now in Albanian foreign trade is 'Without exports, there are no imports'.

As a developing country, Albania imports most of its machinery, industrial equipment, spare parts, derv, metals, industrial consumer goods and, in general, what cannot be produced within the country. In 1970, 37 per cent of imports were of machinery, equipment and spare parts, 24 per cent of fuels and metals, 10 per cent chemical products, 11 per cent food products and 10 per cent industrial consumer goods. In terms of tonnage, exports are three times greater than imports, but the value of imports is much greater.

Albania's annual foreign trade amounts to between $230 and $300 million, about half of which is with China. The Comecon countries (except for the Soviet Union, with which it has no trade relations) come after China as Albania's major trade partners. Trade relations are also maintained with many industrially advanced West European countries, but trade with these countries amounts to only 10 per cent of overall trade. In 1970 Albania maintained trade relations with over fifty countries in Europe, Asia and Latin America. With the majority of these countries, Albania has foreign trade agreements, although trade with some countries is carried out on the basis of contracts between Albanian foreign trade enterprises and firms abroad.

In 1971 Albania and Yugoslavia signed their first long-term agreement on trade for the period 1971–5. (Before 1968, trade with Yugoslavia was negligible and any other kinds of relations non-existent.) A trade volume of $114 million in both directions was fixed. Similar trade agreements have been concluded with Italy, Albania's most important West European partner, and with Greece, after a thirty-year lapse of any kind of economic or political ties. In 1972 the export of electric power was begun to Yugoslavia and Greece.

Foreign trade has been planned to correct the pattern of domestic production, and in view of the orientation of the economy and its strategy of development, will have increasing importance. Albanian foreign trade is carried out within the strict limits of the quotas set by the plan. Foreign trade enterprises are organized according to industries, and every contract is approved by the foreign trade ministry.

That great earner of foreign exchange, tourism, is in its infancy. There are exceptionally favourable conditions for its development – the unspoiled beauty of its coastline, lakes, rivers and mountains, a mild climate, and archaeological monuments.

More is now being done for tourism than before. Many places have been made accessible by road for the first time, and modern hotels have been built. However, the huge allocations for industrialization have stunted investment into the necessary infrastructure for motorized tourism. Tourism will no doubt grow more rapidly now that relations have been normalized between Albania and its neighbours, Yugoslavia and Greece. An added attraction is the favourable tourist currency exchange rate.

(viii) Urbanization and Regional Development

Albania has made it a policy to promote agriculture and local industry in all parts of the country. Mining and agriculture largely determine the distribution of economic activity, but the case of Albania, as well as of other countries, shows that natural resources do not necessarily mean that the settlements where they are located will be centres of population and thus important poles of development.

In view of the previous extreme backwardness of the country, the initial stages of industrialization have been highly successful. Industry today employs some 110,000, which has increased from 86,650 only since 1965. This sector (which carries the main burden of changing the traditional structure of the country) was largely concentrated in a few towns on the Adriatic coast in the central part of the country.[40] Of the twenty-six districts in Albania, the five districts of Berat, Durrës, Elbasan, Tiranë and Vlorë account for 38·3 per cent of the total population, and 54·6 per cent of the industrial output. About 20 per cent of total industrial production is produced by 8·6 per cent of the population living in Tiranë[41] which, of all Albanian towns, has undergone the most dynamic growth. In addition to being the capital, it is the hub of manufacturing, commerce and services. In 1923 its population was only

11,000; on the eve of the Second World War it was 40,000, and by 1970
it had risen to 180,000.

These concentrations have not been sufficiently offset in other parts of
the country by a corresponding growth rate in agriculture. On the
contrary, these five districts also have the most favourable conditions for
agriculture and achieve the highest growth rates in this sector.[42] The
political and geographical isolation of Albania in various phases of its
development has certainly been partly responsible for a pattern in which
a restricted number of sub-regions began to develop an embryonic
industrial economy within the traditional economy. The special feature
of Albania is that the distribution of industry is being carried out in social
conditions quite different from those that existed under capitalism. If the
same tendencies are manifested, then concentration of industry and
population in centres would appear to be an inevitable by-product of
development, which cannot be avoided even in a socialist system, and is
even more pronounced where the level of development is low.[43]

Economically, Albania can be divided into five regions. The northern
region, which includes Shkodër, is the most diversified, it abounds in
minerals, forests and livestock, and has an abundance of hydro-electric
power, with a large hydro-electric plant being built there (the Mao
Tse-tung plan at Vau i Dejes). However, this region has no railway
links. The most advanced part of the country is the central region around
Tiranë, which includes the lowlands between the Mati and Shkumbin
rivers. Tiranë is linked by rail with Durrës, the principal port, and also
with other important centres. There Albanian manufacturing industry
is concentrated. The third region is also economically important and
is the largest in size. This is the Elbasan–Berat region, stretching between
the rivers Shkumbin and Vijosë. In addition to Mediterranean cultures
and cotton, this area provides the country's entire oil production and
contains all the refineries. Elbasan is advanced industrially, and as part
of the present five-year plan the largest metallurgical combine in the
country is being built there. The first phase of this project will be completed by 1975. The fourth region is the south-west centre, Vlorë, which
has slightly over 50,000 inhabitants. Vlorë is also a manufacturing centre.
However, industry is not as well developed as it could be, although
bitumen and lignite are relatively abundant there. Such sub-tropical
cultures as olives and sisal are also principal products. The fifth region is
the south-east part of the country, with its centre at Korçë. This area
stretches southwards from Lake Ohrid and Prespa along the Greek
border. Agriculture is the main activity in the valleys, where wheat,
maize and sugar-beet are the leading crops; livestock breeding is also
important. There are several manufacturing industries here as well.[44]
There has been a notable growth in the national income in post-war
Albania. The average annual growth rate of the national income was

8·6 per cent between 1951 and 1965, and 8·8 per cent between 1966 and 1970;[45] *per capita* national income has grown less fast.[46]

The growth index of the G.N.P. (at constant prices) was 185 in 1968, based on 1960, and the very high average annual growth rate in this period was 10·1 per cent.[47] Thanks to this accelerated growth of the economy, the *per capita* national income was $500 in 1968,[48] and its present-day level is estimated at $600. In 1970 the share of industry in the national income (at 1971 prices) was 42·4 per cent, and of agriculture 34·5 per cent. These figures indicate that Albania has created all the prerequisites of even faster economic growth in the 1971–5 period.

However, surplus manpower in agriculture is still considerable, due to the high rate of population increase. In 1970, 66·4 per cent of the population lived in the countryside: this percentage could not be reduced, despite intensive industrialization, and the process of intensifying the economy will simply exacerbate this problem in the foreseeable future. Not only is manpower underemployed in agriculture, but the same problem occurs in industry, if international criteria are applied. Hence productivity in Albania, as in the economies of other socialist countries, is still relatively low. For this reason, the 1971–5 plan calls for most of the increase in the G.N.P. to be achieved by a 70 per cent increase in labour productivity.[49]

Urbanization has been accompanied by significant improvements in living and working conditions. Before the war, over 85 per cent of the population was rural and lived in backward and unhygienic conditions, with a high illiteracy rate. Since the revolution this ratio has been completely altered.[50] Between 1950 and 1970 the number of permanently employed workers quadrupled, and in the same period 190,000 flats were built; the rent for housing is low (2–3 per cent of the nominal pay of a worker). Against an average life expectancy in 1938 of 38·8 years, that in 1960 was 64·9 years, and in 1970 68 years. Malaria and other infectious diseases which once ravaged Albania are now completely eradicated. There is one doctor for every 1,182 inhabitants. The standard of living is decent rather than high, but compared with life for the masses under the old regime it is miraculously high.[51] Even though industry received priority over consumer goods, much has been done since 1955 to make the life of the average Albanian much more comfortable.[52] The Albanian leadership set itself the goal, particularly in the most recent phase of Albanian development, of revolutionizing and transforming the masses not only in terms of their material standard of living but in a spiritual and cultural sense. They have achieved a large measure of success in this respect. The radical changes in the way of life of the Albanian people have genuinely emancipated them.

(ix) *Conclusions*

Could such results have been achieved in a system based on the profit motive in which there was no strong collective discipline—in other words in a capitalist society? A small country like Albania can achieve notable results in the economic, cultural and social spheres, but under another system it would be very dependent. Considering the conditions in which development was begun, and the level of the country at that time, the results that have been achieved are quite remarkable, and socialism as a system gives the optimal opportunities for development. It is no accident that many 'third world' countries have opted for socialist forms of development.[53]

Professionally trained manpower is an essential asset for any country, and a prerequisite for keeping abreast of modern development. After the war there was a great need for such highly skilled personnel as agronomists, engineers, technicians and doctors, and great emphasis was therefore placed on education. Professionals at first received their training in other socialist countries, but later they could be accommodated in Albania: the Albanian university was founded in 1957. By 1970 Albania had 15,100 highly skilled workers – 2,071 doctors and dentists, 37,700 workers with secondary technical training and over 12,000 full-time university students. At the end of 1972 there were almost 600,000 children and students enrolled in schools.[54]

After the revolution, as in other socialist countries, enormous efforts had to be made to overcome the backwardness which was the legacy of the past, while seeking the best ways to build the material base of society and to transform the economy. However, in the post-revolutionary enthusiasm, these efforts gave rise to a number of inconsistencies and deformations which were heightened by outside factors, particularly relations among the countries of the socialist camp.

The strategy of economic development in Albania has been completely subordinated to the political aim of achieving complete political and economic independence. Post-war development was based on the rapid growth of heavy industry at the expense of light industry. Similarly, production of machine tools and the means of production grew 71·4 times in post-war development, while production of consumer goods has grown by only 55·1 times since 1948.[55] Although priority was placed on industry, disproportions arose between individual industries and between industry and agriculture. Since most available resources were being ploughed into capital investment, the standard of living tended to lag behind the country's overall advance. The model of economic development and investment policy was for the most part based on Stalin's thesis that a faster growth rate of industry as a whole and of the means of production in particular are the key to industrialization.[56]

After 1961 this model was combined with an accelerated development and intensification of agricultural production, no doubt under the influence of Chinese development concepts.

One of the main weaknesses facing the Albanian economy at its present level of development is a widening of the gap between various sectors of the economy and even within different branches of industry. It is difficult to see how they can be overcome rapidly within the concept of autarkic economic development which has reigned supreme for so long even though in recent years, particularly since the fourth five-year plan, this concept has begun to lose favour, giving way to the idea of a developed, modern economy able to provide both for internal demand and for participation in the international division of labour.

Greater recognition than before is being given today to the operation of *economic* as opposed to administrative rules. Incentives are being introduced in income distribution in order to stimulate the interest of workers in achieving a better, more economical and more rational production. Wages are paid on the basis of piece work and by the hour; special stress is placed on the latter. The trend now is towards reducing the differences between the highest and the lowest incomes by administrative fiat; however, it remains to be seen whether such a course will provide enough incentive to initiative and individual creativity or whether some other way will have to be found.

More is heard these days about the need for consolidation within the economy and the advantages this would entail for enterprises and producers. Co-production and specialization are becoming more common, and large technical and economic systems are being set up.

The new processes set in motion by economic growth will certainly give results. However, they will undoubtedly work in tandem with the still dominant bureaucracy, both in directing and in carrying out economic affairs, as well as in other spheres of national life. There is growing awareness that the bureaucracy has become a stumbling-block to further economic and social development, and measures are being taken to restirct its power and influence.

In the future we can expect Albania to follow the strategy of an open economy. As a European and Mediterranean country, it will trade more with West European countries, but for political reasons will probably not undertake co-production or raise credits to stimulate economic growth with any country other than China. At one time in the backward agrarian category, Albania after 1975 will have become an industrial-agricultural country with a medium-developed economy.

The Albanian economy is centrally organized and run entirely according to the official plan. Management is the preserve of the central administration. In 1966 measures were passed against excessive bureaucratic control and red tape, and worker control was introduced in the enterprises as a check upon the managerial class. The Central Committee of the Albanian Party of Labour discussed these problems at its tenth plenum, held in June 1970. The Politburo report stated that 'there are still glaring instances of too much centralism and bureaucratic tutelage' and that 'forms of organization and management should be adopted which would increase the number of people consulted when decisions are made in enterprises, national committees and ministries'.[57] Enver Hoxha spoke at the plenum about the problems of managing the economy and about the situation of Albanian society in general. He called for a change towards greater democracy and human freedom, and towards freedom to criticize both the political leadership and managerial personnel in the economy, in party life and in all spheres of social life. Some of the ideas contained in this speech, one of his most important in several years, are being put into effect, especially in the economy. However, so far as cultural life and literature are concerned, three years after this speech (when a new quickening appeared in intellectual life) there are demands for an end to 'bourgeois-revisionist' influences in the country, which has 'become mired down in liberalism and revisionism'.[58] It would seem that successive thaws and freezes (particularly in culture and ideology) are a phenomenon common to all socialist countries.

The present organization for running the economy is becoming less functional, and is in fact a brake on further socio-economic progress. There is a great need for structural changes in the economy and in the organization of productive forces and a growing awareness that something must be done to change the existing situation. Efforts are now being made to put the management of the economy on a scientific basis, to relieve the ministries of some managerial functions, and to give greater initiative and autonomy to enterprises and co-operatives. The need to apply scientific and technological innovations has also been recognized, and in recent years consultations have been held and articles written on how to use technological breakthroughs in the economy. A change is surely imminent, since the existing bureaucracy, which is still a dominant force in society, is incapable of carrying out innovation and technological advance. The effect of all this on Albanian society, and the speed with which these new processes will develop remain to be seen.

After the war industrial and economic development began in co-operation with Yugoslavia and later with aid from the Soviet Union, but after 1961 'self-sufficiency' became not just a slogan but a reality in Albanian political and economic development.[59] Certainly journalists who have visited Albania in recent years have returned with reports that the entire country has become one enormous building site, where the people are all working to fulfil the plan targets, often adding that Albanian achievements should be measured not by European criteria but by the difference between Albania 'then' and 'now'.[60]

After taking power, the Albanian communists, like many others in Eastern Europe, believed that socialism was equivalent to Lenin's well-known formula 'industrialization plus electrification'. Experience proved otherwise, and they realized that constant efforts were necessary to transform nature in the way suggested by Karl Marx. For this reason, the targets set by almost all the economic plans so far have been unrealistic and over-ambitious. Their achievement has depended largely on outside factors, i.e. on political relations among the socialist countries. As was pointed out at the VI Congress, Albania has pulled itself up by its boot-straps out of its state of economic backwardness. By now there is probably enough skilled manpower to carry forward the new processes in all spheres and to achieve the goals set by the latest five-year plan. Despite various weaknesses in Albanian society, the social development of Albania has not only preserved the values of the Albanian revolution but has imbued Albanian society with new socialist values. The material base of society has been created at a dynamic rate, and new relationships in society have been established, based on the principles of a socialist society.

This tempo will no doubt be sustained by the marked 'trend towards revolutionizing life', a large-scale mobilization of the masses in the interest of 'higher aims', i.e. the interests of the party and state, which look after the people and their welfare. There have, for example, been large-scale work drives, involving tens of thousands of people, which have been organized to complete projects, such as irrigation systems or cultivation of virgin lands, of importance for a given region and to 'revolutionize the masses'. These work drives have been carried out under the slogan, 'Think, Work and Live for the Revolution'.[61] It is claimed that the socialist spirit of competition in these drives has been responsible for greater labour productivity and better business results by enterprises and districts, and has served to strengthen the conviction that collective interests have priority over personal ones.

NOTES

1 Dr. Augustin Lah, *Naše sosedne države* (Our Neighbour States), Ljubljana, 1969, p. 43.
2 Enver Hoxha, *Works*, Tiranë, 1969, III, p. 443.
3 S. Skendi, op. cit., p. 229.
4 A. Lah, op. cit., p. 43.
5 V. Dedijer, 'Jugoslovensko-albanski odnosi 1939–1948' ('Yugoslav–Albanian Relations 1939–1948'), *Borba*, 1949, p. 183.
6 The first societies were modelled after Yugoslav–Soviet mixed societies.
7 V. Dedijer, op. cit., p. 175.
8 *Keesing's Contemporary Archives*, Vol. VI, 1946–8, A. 8337.

9 It should be mentioned here that this co-operation was intended according to some sources as a kind of groundwork for a future unification of Yugoslavia and Albania into a joint federation. *See* M. Djilas, op. cit., pp. 110–15.

10 William E. Griffith, *Albania and the Sino-Soviet Rift*, Cambridge, Massachusets, p. 21. *See also* Skendi, op. cit., p. 221.

11 Foreign investment credits averaged 46–63 per cent of total annual capital investment.

12 According to Albanian economists, the economic base for socialism had been built by 1960.

13 Dr. Radovan Vukadinović, *Odnosi medju evropskim socijalističkim državama* (Relations between European Socialist Countries), Zagreb, 1970, p. 75.

14 W. E. Griffith, op. cit., p. 34.

15 *Europe Year Book: A World Survey*, Volume I, 1969, pp. 507–9.

16 Ibid.

17 A long-term economic agreement was concluded between Peking and Tiranë as early as 1954. Under this agreement, China sent Albania 20,000 tons of wheat, 2,000 tons of rice, 2,000 tons of sugar, 100,000 metres of silk, etc., as a gift (W. E. Griffith, op. cit., p. 34).

18 Selmanaj O. Selman, 'Uslovi i koncepcije privrednog razvoja NR Albanije' (Conditions and Concepts of the Economic Development of the People's Republic of Albania), master's dissertation, Economics Faculty of the University of Belgrade, January 1973, p. 74.

19 Cited in *Current Scene*, September 1972.

20 The eight principles on which China's assistance to Third World countries is based are as follows: (1) equality and mutual benefit; (2) respect for the sovereignty of the country receiving help; (3) credits are granted at very low interest rates or are interest-free, and repayment can be made over a very long period; (4) assistance is given in order to support the economic independence of the recipient country; (5) no assistance is given for building facilities requiring little investment and providing rapid returns; (6) the best possible equipment is given at world prices, under the condition that faulty equipment be exchanged for new; (7) technical training of personnel in the recipient country; (8) Chinese experts in developing countries live under the same conditions as the people in those countries, with no right to any special privileges. (*Source: Peking Review*, 197 No. 17, p. 15.)

21 At the Sixth Congress of the Albanian Party of Labour, the President of the Ministerial Council made a comparison of social trends and growth in production between 1970 and 1960 (*Source: Rruga e partisë*, No. 1, 1971).

22 *Source:* the Journal *Military Acts*, No. 1, Belgrade, 1971, p. 142.

23 The plan called for an increase of 70 per cent in agricultural production in 1970 relative to 1965.

24 Prime Minister Mehmet Shehu presented figures on the results of the fourth five-year plan at the VI Congress of the Party of Labour, 1 to 7 November 1971 in Tiranë.

25 *Source: Statistical Yearbook U.N. 1969*, figures for 1968.

26 Wheat yields in the plains areas are above the average at between 25 and 30 mc per hectare.

27 Since no figures are available for 1970, we are giving the figures for 1964 supplied by official Albanian statistics: 763,723 tons of oil, 476,129 tons of oil derivatives, 291, 626 tons of brown coal, 306,822 tons of chrome ore, 144,673 tons of copper ore, 350,741 tons of nickel ore and 288,399 million Kwh. of electric power.

28 *Source:* Report on the directives of the 1971–5 plan at the VI Congress of the Party of Labour, *Rruga e partisë*, No. 12, 1971.

29 Ibid.

30 These figures have been taken from the reports delivered at the third, fourth and fifth congresses of the A.P.L. by the prime minister, Mehmet Shehu.

31 Méhmet Shehu, Report at the VI Congress of the A.P.L., printed in *Rruga e partisë*, No. 12, 1971.

32 A. Lah, op. cit., p. 47.

33 A. Lah, op. cit., p. 48.

34 The New Encyclopaedia Britannica Micropaedia, Vol. I, p. 191, 1974.

35 *Tariff Transport News* of the Yugoslav Railways for 1972.

36 Domestic tourism is well developed, in contrast to the reception of foregin tourists.

37 Makso Šnuderl, 'Sa puta po Albaniji. Kod radnih i prijatnih ljudi' (Travels in Albania. An Industrious and Pleasant People) *Delo*, Ljubljana, 12 June 1971, p. 20.

38 Figures from the Albanian yearbooks and reports by the president of the Planning Commission, Abdul Kellezi, to the National Assembly.

39 *Source: The People's Republic of Albania and Thirty Years of the Albanian Party of Labour*, Tiranë, 1971, p. 141.

40 Kosta Mihajlović, *Regionalni razvoj socijalistickih zemalja* (Regional Development of the Socialist Countries), Beograd, 1972.

41 Ibid., p. 49.

42 Figures taken from the Albanian statistical yearbook 1967-8 (quoted in K. Mihajlović, op. cit.). See Table 12.

43 K. Mihajlović, op. cit., p. 50.

44 A. Lah, op. cit., p. 50.

45 *Source: Economic Survey of Europe in 1970*, Geneva, 1971.

46 This is explained by the high rate of population increase (3.2 up to 1960, and 2.8 since).

47 *Source: Monthly Bulletin of Statistics*, U.N., November 1970.

48 *Source: The People's Republic of Albania*, op. cit., p. 16.

49 Mehmet Shehu, VI Congress of the Albanian Party of Labour.

50 Enver Hoxha, Report at the 25th anniversary celebration of the independence of Albania on 27 November 1969, as quoted in *Rruga e partisë*, No. 12, 1969, p. 9.

51 M. Duverger, 'Albanian Socialism', article in *Le Monde*, 6 September 1971.

52 *Source:* Documents on the fourth and fifth five-year plans 1966-70 and 1971-5 as presented at the V and VI Congresses of the Party of Labour.

53 Duverger, op. cit.

54 *Source: Probleme ekonomike* (Economic Problems), Tiranë, No. 1, 1973, p. 39.

55 Selmanaj, op. cit., p. 195.

56 Stalin's theses on industrialization were religiously followed by all socialist countries for a long time, and in some they are still being applied to this day.

57 *Rruga e partisë*, No. 7, 1970.

58 *Rruga e partisë*, editorial entitled 'A Resolute Struggle against Foreign Influences in the Sphere of Culture and Education', No. 4, 1973.

59 See materials from the V and VI Congresses of the Albanian Party of Labour.

60 E.g. Maria Adele Teodori, 'Report from the Loneliest State in Europe', article in *L'Espresso* as reprinted in Naši razgledi, Ljubljana, 9 July 1971.

61 The 'Elbasan example' and drives in the districts of Dibër and Librazhd are often cited. In Librazhd more than 10,000 people took part in the drive in a single day to open a 17 km.-long irrigation canal. In the Elbasan district the annual plan for breaking new ground was fulfilled in eleven days.

9

ALBANIA'S PLACE IN THE WORLD

(i) *Retrospect: Relations with Western Countries*

The position of Albania in the international community has undergone very important changes in the last three decades. The country emerged from the Second World War as a member of the victorious anti-Hitlerite coalition, yet was denied the status of victor by the western allies because a new socialist government had been established after the national liberation war. Hence, after the victory of the socialist revolution, the prime concern of the new government, the sole legitimate representative of Albanian identity and sovereignty, was the question of international recognition for the country's socialist revolution.[1]

The democratic Albanian government had proclaimed the principles of its foreign policy as early as November 1944, when it arrived in Tiranë. Co-operation with the allies and neighbouring countries, Yugoslavia and Greece, formed an important part of this policy.[2] On 4 January 1945 the government sent an official note to the allies – the Soviet Union, the United States and Great Britain – requesting recognition.[3] From the standpoint of international law, this presented no problem, since the new government was the only government to emerge from the people's struggle during the Second World War; there was no other government, either within the country or abroad. The Soviet Union unconditionally recognized it on 10 November 1945. Yugoslavia, the principal ally of the new government, since it had also had a revolution and shared the same goals, recognized it as early as 28 April 1945. Yugoslavia was followed by Hungary, Bulgaria and Poland. However, the British and American governments informed the Albanian side on 10 November 1945 through their representatives in Tiranë that their recognition would be conditional on the holding of free elections devoid of intimidation or anti-democratic practices. The elections should be held at an early date, all anti-fascist parties should be enabled to put up candidates, and foreign journalists should be allowed to report on them freely. It was also made clear that recognition of the provisional government 'should not be construed as prejudicing consideration at a later date of other questions of an international character involving Albania'.[4] French recognition was notified on 26 December 1945.

Elections for the constituent assembly were held on 2 December 1945, and over 96·18 per cent of the voters cast their ballots for Democratic Front candidates.[5] The election results were a good indication of the popular feeling toward the new democratic government, which had come into being during the socialist revolution; however, the western allies continued to exert pressure. Recognition was next made conditional on the government's agreement to assume the obligations contained in treaties made before 7 April 1939 between the government of King Zog and the United States and Great Britain.[6] The Albanian government categorically rejected all these conditions, which were contrary to the decisions of the Congress of Përmet and the Second Session of the Anti-Fascist Council of National Liberation in Berat. Albanian sovereignty was at stake; however, the Albanian government agreed to review the treaties, provided diplomatic relations were first established.

Enver Hoxha tried to influence the United States government to change its attitude through the good offices of Fan Noli, the well-known Albanian writer and former politician, who was then living in the U.S.A.,[7] but all came to nought. The governments of the United States and Great Britain undoubtedly believed that the Albanian democratic government would finally have to submit, but they had miscalculated. They considered Albania, as a small country, to be the weak link in the chain of socialist countries which emerged from the Second World War. For this reason they supported Greek territorial claims to southern Albanian, called by the Greeks 'Northern Epirus' with the towns of Gjirokastër and Korçë, and long opposed Albania's admission to the United Nations. These actions were not in the spirit of statements made by the British and United States foreign ministers in December 1942.[8]

At first Albania was denied the right to participate in the Paris peace conference; then the ministerial conference decided to allow it to take part in the work of committees and the plenary session so that Albania's views on the signing of a peace treaty with Italy could be heard. The Albanian delegation was led by Enver Hoxha, who vigorously defended his country's interests. He said, among other things: 'Statements about protecting the interests of small nations have often been heard at this conference, but when it is my nation, then things are different. . . .' To make the irony even greater, the Paris peace conference considered the Greek demand for discussion of the Albanian–Greek border, in which designs on Albanian territory were expressed. Eleven states supported the Greek demand, seven opposed it, and two abstained. Afterwards, Enver Hoxha told newsmen that 'no conference has the right to question the Albanian borders, which do not contain even an inch of foreign soil',[9] and 'history will be the true judge of the injustice done to Albania at the peace conference in Paris'.[10] Albania's interests were defended at the peace conference by the Soviet Union, Yugoslavia and other socialist countries. The Greek territorial aspirations, which had no solid foundation,[11] were supported by the western allies. As a result of this split, the Greek demand was finally rejected.

After the Paris peace conference western pressure on Albania steadily escalated. The British, American and French military missions in Albania, which had had diplomatic status, were withdrawn; Britain recalled its first diplomatic emissary to Albania as he was on his way to take up his post.[12] As bloc divisions deepened, relations between the west and Albania grew increasingly strained. In the west Albania was considered a dependent country, a Soviet or Yugoslav satellite. In 1946 British warships carried out several provocations in Albania's territorial waters, until on 22 October 1946 the destroyers *Saumarez* and *Volage* hit a minefield within those territorial waters in the Strait of Corfu, and sank, with the loss of forty-four officers and sailors. The British government sent a protest note to the Albanian government and submitted a complaint to the United Nations Security Council.[13] The Albanian representative in the Secutiry Council said that Albania had not laid the mines, did not possess the equipment to do so, and did not know who had laid them. After a debate, the Security Council turned the case over to the International Court of Justice at the Hague. The Court, presided over by Dr. Guerrera of El Salvador, reviewed the Albanian-British dispute on 26 February 1948. The Albanian delegation was led by Khreman Ylli, head of the Albanian mission in Paris, and the British delegation by W. E. Beckett, legal adviser to the Foreign Office.[14] By a decision handed down on 9 April 1949, awareness of the existence of the minefields could not be ascribed to Albania simply on the basis of the fact that the mines were discovered in Albanian territorial waters.[15] However, even though an active part in laying the mines was not established, the court sentenced Albania to pay damages to Great Britain because the Albanian state had not carried out its duty to safe-guard its territorial waters from the laying of mines and did not announce that mines had been laid. Every state bears a vicarious respon-sibility for infringements of international law that take place in its territory, and the extent of this type of responsibility is still controversial in international law. However, in the Albanian-British dispute, the Hague Court merely charged Albania with negligence and failure to attend to the regular duties of a territorial state.

Until 1947 Great Britain was the major power with the most visible presence in this area, and its pressure was exerted most forcefully on Albania and Yugoslavia; later the United States began to take a hand. President Truman's message to Congress on 12 March 1947, concerning so-called financial and social assistance to Greece and Turkey, actually contained a new political and economic programme, known as the 'Truman Doctrine'. Through this programme the United States displaced the British in Greece and elsewhere in the Mediterranean and the Middle East and took over their obligations there.[16]

During the cold war confrontation, the western countries stepped up their pressure on Albania. In the spring of 1950 the United States and Great Britain sent Albanian emigrants into the country in the hopes of changing its social system; H. A. R. Philby informed the Soviet authorities of this action. The Albanian armed forces quickly put an end to this incursion.[17] However, in 1955 the United States and Great Britain did not stand in the way of Albania's admission to United Nations. They abstained from voting, but did not use their right of veto. The polarization which had arisen in the mid-1950s within the socialist camp caused a lessening in American and English provocations against Albania. Nevertheless, diplomatic and other relations have still not been established between Albania and these countries.

The attitude of the United States and Britain was largely responsible for Albania's foreign policy in the first decades after the war, just as the eastern countries influenced its orientation in the 1960s.

(ii) *Relations with Neighbouring Countries*

The Albanian leadership attributed great importance to relations with neighbouring countries, particularly Yugoslavia and Greece. On the arrival of the democratic government of Albania in Tiranë on 28 November 1944, Enver Hoxha, while addressing the citizens of the capital, talked about the co-operation between Albania and Yugoslavia during the national liberation war: for the first time in recent history, the Albanian and Yugoslav people had worked closely together and, led by the communist parties of their countries, had opened a new page in the history of the Balkans.

After the revolution had been put down in Greece by foreign intervention, the bourgeois parties and monarchy voiced their demands for the annexation of southern Albania. As well as confrontation between Albania and Greece on a political and diplomatic level, there were even armed clashes. The detachments of General Zervas provoked border incidents and massacred members of the Albanian national minority in the Cameria region of Greece; of these over 20,000 fled into Albania.[18]

In this address in Tiranë, Enver Hoxha also said,

. . . The Greek premier Papandreou has expressed aspirations to annex the towns of Gjirokastër and Korçë and their hinterlands. Such aspirations impede good relations between our countries. Our borders are inviolable, since they contain only land which our grandfathers have left us. No one dares touch our borders, because we shall defend them.[19]

He also spoke of the rights and freedoms which the new democratic government would guarantee to the Greek national minority in Albania:

The national liberation movement of Albania . . . will guarantee the same democratic and national rights and freedom to the Greek national minority for which the best sons of the Greek national minority fought heroically in units of the national liberation army.[20]

However, the Greek government continued its border provocations and, with the support of the western allies at the peace conference in Paris, tried – unsuccessfully, as we have seen – to engineer the annexation of southern Albania. When Great Britain and the United States announced their intention of establishing diplomatic relations with the new Albanian government on 10 November 1945, there was a protest demonstration of over 150,000 people in Athens.[21] During the Greek civil war, Albania, Yugoslavia and Bulgaria supported the Marxist partisans. The 'Greek question' was put before the Security Council, which on 16 December 1946 passed a resolution setting up a commission of inquiry to establish whether or not assistance was being given to the rebels in Greece by Albania, Yugoslavia and Bulgaria. As was to be expected, many Greek communists had fled to those countries on account of the civil war. The communist groups fighting in Greece sought, and obtained, help from their communist neighbours. Albania Yugoslavia and Bulgaria held that the proper subject for investigation was rather the *cause* of the situation in Greece and that there was no need to set up such a commission,[22] which served as a launching-pad for much recrimination against Albania, Yugoslavia and Bulgaria in the early years of the cold war. In the end, as the result of the division of spheres of influence at Yalta, British troops were sent in and quelled the revolution.

At the third session of the United Nations General Assembly in November 1948, these three states were called upon to cease giving assistance to the Greek insurgents.[23] Relations between Albania and Greece were strained, and sometimes border incidents still occurred. The Albanian side made several overtures to Greece for a normalization of relations, but the Greek government showed no interest.

From the standpoint of international law, the abnormal relations between Albania and Greece lasted thirty years. Ever since 1940 when Italy, having occupied Albania, invaded Greece from Albanian territory, Albania and Greece had formally been at war with each other. However, the subsequent détente in Europe and changes in Greece made this situation an anachronism. In 1971 relations between the two countries were normalized, with the establishment of diplomatic relations and the exchange of ambassadors. Thus a European dispute which had lasted for more than three decades was finally settled.

The mutual solidarity and co-operation established between Albania and Yugoslavia during the war continued in the years immediately after liberation – the period of post-revolutionary euphoria. Yugoslavia defended the interests of its small neighbour in international bodies and at the Paris peace conference. All authentic and autonomous revolutions try, more or less openly, to impose their experience on others, and few resist the temptation to raise much that was the product of specific circumstances to the level of a universal law and model.[24] Such attempts have been made by the majority of socialist countries and were present in the relations between Albania and Yugoslavia.

One of the key questions in the years immediately after the war was that of a Balkan federation – of Yugoslavia, Bulgaria and Albania. The idea of a Balkan federation had not originated in the Balkans, nor had it been held by Yugoslav or other Balkan communists during the Second World War, even though they later embraced it with enthusiasm. An idea of this kind had been implanted in the Balkans by tsarist Russia when the spirit of nationalism was awaking in Southern-eastern Europe, particularly among the South Slavs, who sought to free themselves from the two empires which extended into the Balkans – Austria-Hungary and the Ottoman Empire. Tsarist Russia wished to penetrate into the Balkans and take the place of these empires, which had become anachronisms in the modern age. It reasoned that the South Slavs could only achieve their aspirations if they united in a joint struggle; Russia wished to be their 'protector' and thus eventually gain access to the Mediterranean.

These ideas were later taken up and modified by the Balkan socialists and communists. After the First World War, when the Albanian people felt disappointed at being divided, ideas of a Balkan federation began to obsess some Albanian intellectuals, and were still alive after the Second World War – fed by the existence of the Albanian national minority in Yugoslavia. The Albanian leadership began to take sides on the issue. The majority, led by Enver Hoxha, took a more realistic view since they were aware of the realities of the situation and of the long-standing desire of the Albanian people to be independent and autonomous and to have their own state. Some three decades later, we can see that such a federation would probably have been short-lived. Outside factors would have played their part in the break-up, the different levels of development of the Balkan countries and the historical differences between them would not have been conducive to harmony, and such a rapprochement, not to speak of unification, among the Balkan states would hardly have served the interests of some of the great powers, which could have stepped in to arbitrate relations within the federation. Feelings ran high in Albania, both among the leaders and among the citizens, since it was apparent what very different conceptions of federation were expressed by Yugoslavia, Albania and Bulgaria.

Despite conflicting ideas on the formation of a federation, political and economic co-operation was on the increase in the early post-war years. On 10 June 1946 Albania signed a treaty of friendship and mutual assistance with Yugoslavia and in December 1947 with Bulgaria. Such treaties were concluded in South-east and Eastern Europe between the socialist countries as part of a special system of regional security; Albania calculated that through ties with the socialist countries its international status could be secured.[25]

In September 1947 at a consultation of representatives of communist and workers' parties from eight countries (including France and Italy) held in Poland, the Information Bureau (Cominform) was set up to serve as a forum for exchanges of experience among the communist parties and 'in the case of need for co-ordination of their activities on the basis of mutual agreement'.[26] It is noteworthy that Albania was not invited to this meeting.

In June 1947 Enver Hoxha paid his first official visit to Yugoslavia, and a month later spent ten days in the Soviet Union at the head of a government delegation and met Stalin. The content of his talks with Stalin has never been divulged either in Albania or in the Soviet Union.

(iii) *In the Socialist Camp*

Albania consolidated its international status by forming ties with the socialist countries, but the difficulties and convulsions within and between these countries were felt acutely in Albania. Albania invariably based its policy on national interests, subordinating them to 'universal' and 'internationalistic' interests only when it was clear that her national interests would not be jeopardized.

In the conflict which arose between Yugoslavia and the Soviet Union in 1948, the Albanian Party of Labour endorsed the letter of the Central Committee of the C.P.S.U. on the situation in the Communist Party of Yugoslavia and the Cominform resolution[27] that followed, breaking off party and diplomatic relations with Yugoslavia, and annulling all treaties. In view of the intimacy which the two countries had enjoyed earlier, this move was traumatic for the Albanian Party of Labour and its leadership.

The Communist Party of Yugoslavia and Marshal Tito were opposed to Stalin's and the Soviet Union's quest for hegemony over the other parties and the new socialist countries. This was not just the refusal of a small country to take orders from a large one; it was a demand for equality in relations between socialist countries and the right of every state to seek and to follow its own road to socialism. The question of equality and autonomous socialist development continues to be upper-most in relations between socialist countries and communist parties even today and will no doubt continue to be so. Yugoslavia, which was then and still is prepared to give a resounding 'No' to any attempts to impose hegemony, managed to withstand the pressures exerted upon it, and immediately after the conflict in 1948 was able to reject the concept of bureaucratic socialism and blaze the trail of democratic self-managing socialist development.

In the circumstances, Albania decided to protect its security and strengthen itself internationally by taking the side of the Soviet Union, whose support in international affairs and grants of loans and assistance could enable Albania to achieve its goals of socialist revolution. This was during the time of the cold war, the formation of power blocs and acts of aggression in international affairs. Such a situation paved the way for the countries of Eastern Europe, including Albania, to become the first places in the world where the concept and practice of Stalinism, previously codified only within the Soviet Union and institutions of the international workers' movement, appeared in an international setting.[28] In these years, Albania's entire foreign policy and international activity was focused on the socialist camp.

In January 1949 in Moscow, six socialist countries founded the Council for Mutual Economic Assistance ('Comecon'). Although it joined Comecon later,[29] Albania was not present at this meeting. There is no official explanation of why Albania was absent from the Comecon and other communist bloc meetings at this time, but the Societ Union was probably not interested in inviting Albania, since it did not border with the U.S.S.R. and was the most backward of all the countries in the communist bloc.

After Stalin's death, Soviet policy, particularly foreign policy, became more flexible and this resulted in an easing of international tensions. The new Soviet leadership began to seek ways of revamping relations with other socialist countries so as to achieve greater equality and unanimity. At this time the term 'socialist camp', which was in general use during the Stalinist years, was abandoned in favour of 'the community of socialist states'.[30] However, in response to the strengthening of the western alliance and the admission of West Germany to N.A.T.O. in 1954, the prime ministers, foreign ministers and defence ministers of the Soviet Union, Poland, Czechoslovakia, Hungary, Rumania, Bulgaria, Albania and East Germany signed a treaty of friendship, co-operation and mutual assistance known as the Warsaw Pact on 14 May 1955. In the mid-1950s, Comecon and the Warsaw Pact were assigned the task of strengthening their political, economic and military

ties *vis-à-vis* the west, even though there were already twenty-year
treaties of friendship, co-operation and mutual aid in existence between
all the East European socialist countries, which served as the cornerstone
of the Soviet system holding Eastern Europe together.[31]

Changes in the communist movement set in motion by Khruschev
at the XX Congress of the C.P.S.U. were opposed by Albania, a fact
which led to new polarization within the Albanian Party of Labour. At
the municipal party meeting in Tiranë in 1956, demands were made in
the spirit of the XX Congress of the C.P.S.U. as the result of which
Liri Gege and Dali Ndreu were expelled from the party and liquidated.
Pressure was even brought to bear on the Albanians by the new Soviet
leadership to rehabilitate Koçi Xoxe, who had been liquidated after the
1948 Cominform resolution. This pressure was designed to install a
clique at the head of the Albanian party and government that would
serve the interests of the Soviet Union; however, Enver Hoxha deftly
nipped these plans in the bud. Events in Hungary and Poland made
Albania take a serious look at its place in the international workers'
movement. The Albanian leadership was strongly opposed to the
process of de-Stalinization, which would sap its ability to fight effectively
against outside pressure.[32] Enver Hoxha managed to stop at the Albanian
borders the winds of change that were blowing in various East European
countries in the mid-1950s.

The subsequent crisis in the international communist movement and
the sharp Soviet–Chinese polarization caused the Albanian Party of
Labour to move closer to the People's Republic of China. At the
Bucharest meeting of East European communist parties (excluding
Yugoslavia) in June 1960, the representative of the Albanian Party of
Labour refused to endorse Khrushchev's condemnation of the Chinese
Communist Party, and at the Moscow consultation of communist
parties in 1961, the A.P.L. took views identical with those of the
Chinese.

At the XXII C.P.S.U. Congress, Khrushchev publicly denounced the
Albanian leadership. These accusations were actually intended for the
Chinese Communist Party, at a time when the conflict between the
C.P.S.U. and the Chinese Communist Party was still an internal affair
and had not become public. Chou En-lai, who headed the Chinese
delegation to the Congress, responded by criticizing Khrushchev and his
way of 'condemning another fraternal party at the Congress'; he then
walked out. The conflict between these two great countries in the
communist world had come into the open and took its toll in the relations
between other communist parties.[33]

After the XXII C.P.S.U. Congress, there was a rapid deterioration in
Soviet–Albanian party and governmental relations. The Soviet Union
cut off all the credits it had granted Albania, withdrew its advisers,

broke off trade, suspended the scholarships of Albanian students, annulled agreements on cultural, scientific and technical co-operation and brought a halt to military co-operation. Soon afterwards there was a break in diplomatic relations. Albania's relations with other East European socialist countries also began to show the strain.

The break with the Soviet Union caused considerable hardship for Albania. The third five-year plan was not completely carried out, and industrial growth only attained a modest 6·7 per cent between 1961 and 1965. The V Congress of the Albanian Party of Labour, held in 1966, called these years the most difficult period in the country's economic life since the war. Contrary to expectations, however, the conflict with the U.S.S.R. caused no major upsets either within the party or in social and political life. Albania severed ties with the Soviet Union and the 'fraternal community' in a more or less painless fashion. (The break with Yugoslavia in 1948 was far more traumatic, as we have seen, and had far greater repercussions in the Albanian Party of Labour.)

After the break, Albania *de facto* withdrew from the Warsaw Pact and Comecon. In September 1968, after the intervention in Czechoslovakia, the Albanian National Assembly *de jure* sanctioned the decision to withdraw from the Warsaw Pact.

(iv) *Isolationism and Co-operation with China*

In the mid-1960s, after the break with the Soviet Union and other East European socialist countries, Albania entered a period of isolationism, and contacts with the outside world were reduced to a minimum. The nature of its relations with neighbouring countries forced Albania to shift the focus of its foreign policy away from the Balkans. Except for economic co-operation and diplomatic relations with Italy, France and Austria, co-operation with other Western European countries was out of the question. In the words of the Albanian leadership, this was the time of the most severe 'capitalist-revisionist blockade and encircle- ment'; Khrushchev was branded as the biggest 'renegade' against Marxism–Leninism. It was a time of sharp Sino–Soviet polemics and confrontation; Albanian foreign policy and propaganda were very active in support of China, which was Albania's only window on the world.

The international activity of the Party of Labour was spent in the struggle against 'contemporary revisionism'. The line of the Party was, and largely still is today, that the 'victory of revisionism' and 'restoration of capitalism' are established facts in the Soviet Union and other East European socialist countries. According to the Albanian view, this victory of revisionism was caused by both internal and external factors. According to the Albanians the main reason for this is the new bour-

geoisie, which has arisen, especially in the government and party, under
the influence of bourgeois ideology and as a result of high wages,
various perquisites of office and aloofness from the masses; and there
has been a progressive degeneration of the party as the result of bureau-
cratization and formalism in the context of present-day retrogressive
processes in the Soviet Union and other East European countries.
Revisionism, according to the Albanian press, is marked by timidity and
capitulation to imperialism.

The Albanian-Chinese reports on the meetings between Mehmet
Shehu and Chou En-lai in Peking and Tiranë in 1966 contain the
fundamental assessments of the Communist Party of China and the
Albanian Party of Labour concerning events in the socialist world and
the international communist movement. The emphasis of all these
reports is on the need for a complete break, and the drawing of a 'line
of demarcation' between contemporary revisionism and true Marxism-
Leninism.[34]

After the break in relations with the Soviet Union, the Albanian
Party of Labour ceased co-operating with East and West European
communist parties. It now works only with the Communist Party of
China and workers' and communist parties in South-east Asia, as well
as 'Marxist–Leninist' parties or groups in Europe, Latin America and
elsewhere. Twenty-eight foreign delegations attended the V Congress
of the Albanian Party of Labour in 1966 and twenty-six attended the
VI Congress in 1971 – which, however, was not attended by the Chinese
Communist Party which decided after its IX Congress and the
Cultural Revolution, not to send delegations to the congresses of
fraternal parties.

(v) *Some Basic Ideas on Revolution and Contemporary Trends*

At recent Congresses of the Party of Labour – notably the V and VI –
the international situation was assessed as being auspicious for the
revolutionary cause. The centres of contemporary revolutionary trends
are in Asia, Africa and Latin America. Changes in the modern world
have not changed the nature of the world's contradictions or the
aggressive nature of imperialism. One of the overriding features of the
present international situation is the alliance and co-operation between
the Soviet Union and the United States. The Albanian line is that this
alliance is the 'greatest counter-revolutionary force' obstructing the
struggle of peoples for freedom and socialism. These two powers are
pictured as co-ordinating their activity in all areas – military, economic
and political – in order to further their hegemonistic aims and intentions.
This alliance is thought to be directed against the People's Republic of
China, which is the vanguard of revolutionary processes in the modern

world; all this was stated at the VI Congress of the A.P.L. However, the deep contradictions which exist between the Soviet Union and the United States are acknowledged.

Albania was not happy to see President Nixon's trip to China to hold talks with Albania's principal ally in February 1972. Nixon's trip to Moscow in May the same year was strongly criticized in the Albanian press, as was the trip by Leonid Brezhnev to the United States in June 1973. An Albanian article stated that 'Nixon, anti-communist America and all international reactionary circles need not fear "Soviet communism", since it is no longer Leninist but rather a surrogate which agrees with them in all spheres and in all directions.'[35] The article goes on to call for an uprising by the Soviet people and the Red Army, 'which should not permit a degenerate clique to sell out the country to American imperialism'.

The leaders of Albania are convinced that the Soviet Union and the United States have formed an alliance on the basis of joining interests and a division of zones of influence to ensure domination of the world. The Soviet leaders are thus painted as being prepared to sacrifice other communist and independence movements. The socialist countries which hold revolutionary tenets and the world proletariat are said to form the nucleus of a growing front against imperialism and revisionism, based on an alliance with oppressed peoples.

In a report to the VI Congress of the A.P.L. in 1971, Enver Hoxha set forth the ideas and concepts of revolution:

. . . The great People's Republic of China and Albania, countries which consistently adhere to Marxism-Leninism and building socialism, are an important factor in the revolutionary movement, an example of encouragement and inspiration in spreading the revolutionary and independence struggles of nations. Their success in the socialist revolution, their economic, political and ideological consolidation, their resolutely uncompromising and successful struggle on two fronts against imperialism led by America and modern revisionism led by the Soviet Union, their clear revolutionary policy and support for the national liberation struggle, all encourage nations and revolutionaries and strengthen their faith in their victory and the victory of socialism, to which the future belongs.[36]

The Party Congress hailed the growing number of Marxist-Leninist parties which are in the vanguard of the world revolutionary and national liberation struggle. The youth and student movement was singled out as the revolutionary force of our time, with particular importance in the class struggle against capitalist exploitation and the policy of imperialism. The youth in the capitalist world are dissatisfied both with their position in society and with the present system, which bars all their prospects for the future. They are seeking the true way which will lead to unity with the working class – with the revolution.[37]

A central theme in Albanian ideology is that the driving force of world history and the history of each country is the class struggle, which will raise up the proletariat to become the dominant class in all societies. The Albanian concept of revolution in various countries and of revolution on a global scale is virtually identical with that of the Chinese. However, the two countries are putting their theories into practice in quite different ways, especially since emerging from their previous isolation.

As for other important world trends, enlargement of the E.E.C. has been criticized in the Albanian press as a concentration of capital and the operation of a financial oligarchy in Western Europe, while initiatives to convene the conference on European security – which began in Helsinki on 3 July 1973 – have been portrayed as a farce staged by the blocs and superpowers to hoodwink European nations; the Soviet Union in particular wants to establish security in Europe in order to leave its hands free to conduct its dispute with China. For these reasons, the Albanian government refused the invitation by the Finnish government to send a representative to the conference of ambassadors in Helsinki. A long explanation was sent to the Finnish government as to why Albania would not take part in the European security conference. It stated that the Albanian government 'feels that the intra-European conference, because of the circumstances in which it is being held, and especially because of the manipulation of the two superpowers, actually cannot help achieve European security, nor can it truly ensure the protection of European countries and peoples from the threat of war and aggression. . . . This conference will do no more than increase insecurity in Europe.' The note went on to say that the initiators of the conference were those very powers 'which are maintaining aggressive blocs – N.A.T.O. and the Warsaw Pact' – and that the plan on European security and co-operation is a smokescreen for the plans of the two superpowers to perpetuate the *status quo* and their spheres of influence.[38] These Albanian views on European trends were not inspired by China.

As we have already said, there are no diplomatic, trade or any other relations between Albania and the Soviet Union. Since Khrushchev's fall in 1964, the new Soviet leadership have on many occasions expressed the desire to normalize relations, but of course cautiously and with explanations of past mistakes accounting for the break; Leonid Brezhnev even spoke of this at the XXIV Party Congress.[39] However, the Albanian leadership has rejected these overtures as 'pure demagoguery' and 'attempts at self-justification', since 'they owe so much to Albania politically, economically and ideologically'.[40] Thus Enver Hoxha told the A.P.L.'s VI Congress that normalization would occur when 'the Soviet people and true Bolsheviks take a hand to achieve revolutionary Marxist-Leninist justice in this case'.[41]

Albania's relations with the East European countries belonging to the Warsaw Pact, with the exception of Rumania, have a rather low profile, and trade is carried on within very restricted limits. On the eve of the military intervention in Czechoslovakia in 1968, Bulgaria expelled Albanian diplomats, and two days later Albania responded in kind. After 1970 diplomatic representation was resumed, and is maintained at the level of *chargés d'affaires*. At the VI A.P.L. Congress the blame was placed squarely on the East European countries, since 'the leaderships in these countries are completely subordinated to Moscow and, blindly carrying out its foreign policy, are pursuing an unfriendly policy *vis-à-vis* Albania', with harmful consequences.[42] Enver Hoxha said that, even though their plans had failed, they were continuing to pursue an anti-Albanian policy.

(vi) *Albania opens up to the World*

Momentous changes have taken place since the late 1960s in international affairs, and the position of Albania in the world has changed in many respects. The most striking difference is the lively activity of Albanian diplomacy, notably in establishing relations with some West European, Scandinavian, Mediterranean and neighbouring countries. Albania maintains relations with more than fifty countries, but does not have diplomatic missions in all of them. Albania is also making its voice heard more often in the United Nations. The General Assembly on 25 October 1971 adopted the historic 'Albanian resolution' on the admission of the People's Republic of China to the United Nations and the Security Council and on the expulsion of the Chiang Kai-shek regime.[43]

All this is a far cry from the days when Albania's role in foreign affairs went no further than maintaining ties with its principal ally, China. Of course, China remains Albania's principal ally in foreign affairs and gives assistance towards its industrialization and economic growth. However, Albania's relations with China are based on different principles from those underlying its earlier ties with the Soviet Union and East European socialist countries, when it was militarily, politically and economically integrated in the Warsaw Pact and Comecon. Especially since the seven-day war in the Middle East in 1967 and the events in Czechoslovakia in 1968, Albania has taken a greater interest in trends in the Balkans and the Mediterranean. The presence of the superpowers in the Mediterranean, their military build-up and their mutual negotiations are carefully watched in Albania. Enver Hoxha was following the example of some other governments of Mediterranean countries when he told the VI Party Congress: 'It is the responsibility of all nations and progressive forces in the Mediterranean area to demand and fight for the removal of foreign navies from the Mediterranean and to withstand any hegemonistic policy in this part of the world. The Mediterranean belongs only to the Mediterranean nations and states. . . .'[44]

Special attention is now given to fostering relations with neighbouring countries. As we have seen, those with Yugoslavia and Greece were normalized in 1971. Albania has responded to some initiatives for co-operation on a multilateral basis in this region – with reservations, because of its bad experiences in the past. As was stated at the VI Congress,

. . . Friendship and negotiation between the Balkan countries should have their foundation in the people. We have no intention of proposing, nor would we agree to, the formation of various blocs and alliances. The People's Republic of Albania desires and will endeavour to strengthen friendship with the Balkan peoples on the basis of the principle of peaceful coexistence. The form of government each nation has is its own affair. We do not interfere in the internal affairs of others, and others should not interfere in ours. This is not to exclude mutual criticism or polemics.[45]

Towards selected countries in the west a more flexible attitude is very cautiously being made apparent. Relations were first established with small and neutral states and with the Scandinavian countries; still, it is Italy, France and Austria which have the most extensive relations with Albania. The United States and Britain have indicated their interest in establishing diplomatic and other ties with Albanian. In May 1973 Kenneth Rush, Assistant U.S. Secretary of State, in an address to cadets at the Annapolis Naval Academy, stated that

the United States is willing to respond to any overture by Albania to restore diplomatic relations between Washington and Tiranë. This hint brought no response from Albania. Similarly, at the beginning of 1973, news agencies reported the first contacts in Rome between Albanian and British diplomatic representatives, who discussed aspects of economic co-operation. After this meeting, the Foreign Office announced that there had been no change regarding the establishment of diplomatic relations and that Britain would be happy if a way could be found to eliminate existing difficulties.[46]

The principal reason why, despite the fact that both countries recognize each other, Albania and Britain have not had diplomatic relations since the end of the war is the unresolved incident of the two British destroyers which were sunk in the Corfu Strait. Albania refused to recognize the competence of the International Court of Justice, which ruled that it should pay damages, and would not take responsibility for the incident; for its part, Britain impounded Albanian gold deposited in London banks.

Even in Albania's relations with China certain changes are taking place; co-operation is continuing wherever points in common do not jeopardize the pragmatist policy of each country, while in those areas where their interests differ, each state acts according to its own lights.

To conclude, Albania bases its co-operation and political relations with other countries on the principles of peaceful co-existence and the United Nations Charter, with respect for the sovereignty and integrity of other states and nations and non-interference in their affairs. Its ties with some West European countries, especially medium-sized and small advanced countries, have an economic as well as political significance, because of its need as a developing country undergoing industrialization to import the most up-to-date know-how and technology. Above all, Albania's foreign policy and activity in world affairs are based on the Albanians' concern to preserve their autonomy and integrity and the sovereignty of their state at all costs. After 1961 Albania was able to extricate itself from political and economic membership of a bloc. Thus its foreign policy can be said to be successful and to gain for the Albanian people something of the best of both worlds.

NOTES

1 See: Decisions of the Congress in Permët, May 1944, and of the Second Session of the Anti-Fascist Council of National Liberation of Albania, in Berat, October 1944. According to Enver Hoxha, op. cit., Vol. 2, pp. 206–24 and 373–83. Also see the chapter concerning the special features of the Albanian socialist revolution in this text.

2 Hoxha, op. cit., Vol. 2, pp. 421–31.

3 Hoxha, op. cit., Vol. 3, pp. 1–5.

4 *Keesing's Contemporary Archives*, January 1–15, 1946, A.7634.

5 Ibid. Only the Democratic Front was represented in the elections. However, although no other party was standing, not all the candidates on the Democratic Front list were members of the Communist Party.

6 Hoxha, op. cit., Vol. 3, pp. 189–90.

7 Ibid., pp. 329–32. Fan Noli had formed a democratic bourgeois government in Albania in 1924, which was overthrown six months later by Zogu with foreign help. Fan Noli left the country for the United States and took up residence in Boston, Mass. He was active there in organizing the cultural activities of the local Albanian colony. Besides being an Orthodox bishop, he was an outstanding man of letters. He gave Albanian literature a translation of Shakespeare such as few small nations can boast of. His translation of poems by Edgar Allen Poe, particularly 'The Raven', read as if originally written in Albanian. Fan Noli was one of the greatest of Albanian writers and is still popular today. He died in Boston in 1965.

8 Official war documents later made public at the British Public Records Office and research by the Albanian historian Arben Puto show that despite Britain's material assistance to the resistance movement in Albania, British diplomacy throughout the war displayed cynical and hypocritical attitudes to Albania. The Foreign Office always upheld Greek claims to Southern Albania and even the pretensions to Albanian territory of the Yugoslav

government in exile. According to Puto, in the first years of the war some British historians were asked to plan a federal monarchy or confederation between Greek and Yugoslavia in which Albania would be an insignificant member. This creation would supposedly serve as a *cordon sanitaire* against socialism in the Balkans. See Arben Puto, 'In the Annals of British Diplomacy', *Nendori* (monthly publication for literature and socio-political questions), Tiranë, No. 12, 1972, and Nos. 1, 2 and 3, 1973.

9 Hoxha, op. cit., Vol. 3, p. 448.

10 Ibid., p. 447.

11 Between 40,000 and 60,000 Greeks live in Albania, but in Çameria there used to be many Albanians – until they were resettled throughout Greece in order to be assimilated.

12 Arben Puto, op. cit., No. 12, p. 56.

13 *Keesing's Contemporary Archives*, C.8313.

14 Ibid., April 3–10, 1948.

15 Dr. Smilja Avramov, *Medjunarodnu javno pravo*, Beograd, 1963, p. 86.

16 Group of authors, *Yugoslavija u medjunarodnom radničkom pokretu*, Beograd, 1973, p. 85.

17 Nicholas C. Pano, *The People's Republic of Albania*, Baltimore, 1968, p. 94.

18 Hoxha, op. cit., Vol. 3, pp. 357–60.

19 Ibid., Vol. 2, p. 428.

20 Ibid., Vol. 2, p. 429.

21 *Keesing's Contemporary Archives*, January 1–15, A.7634.

22 Ibid., July 12–19, 1947, A.8719.

23 Branko Petranović, Čedomir Strbac, Dr. Stanislav Stojanović, *Jugoslavija u medjunarodnom radničkom pokretu*, Beograd, 1973, p. 85.

24 Branko Pribičević, *Autonomo u teoriji i praksi socijalizma* (Autonomy in the Theory and Practice of Socialism), Beograd, 1972, p. 9.

25 Group of authors, op. cit., p. 97.

26 Ibid., p. 98.

27 On 28 June 1948 at Bucharest. The Yugoslav Communist Party and its leadership headed by Marshal Tito were excommunicated from the socialist camp, the decision being endorsed by all the other communist parties in the world except that of Poland.

28 Draginja Arsić, *Društveno-ekonomski kóreni staljinizma* (Socio-Economic Roots of Stalinism), Beograd, 1972, p. 183.

29 Dr. Radovan Vukadinović, *Odnosi medju evropskim socijalistíčkim zemljama* (Relations among the European Socialist Countries—a discussion of Comecon and the Warsaw Pact), Zagreb, 1970, p. 42.

30 Ibid., p. 194.

31 Ibid., p. 201.

32 Griffith, op. cit., pp. 24–7.

33 Ibid., pp. 89–99.

34 *Keesing's Contemporary Archives*, A.21610.

35 'The General Secretary of the C.P.S.U. talks with the Leader of American Imperialism', *Zeri i popullit*, 21 June 1973, p. 4.

36 Enver Hoxha, *Report to the VI Congress of the Albanian Party of Labour*, Tiranë, 1971, p. 12.

37 Ibid., p. 10.

38 'Tanjug', 3 July 1973.

39 *Keesing's Contemporary Archives*, A.24655.

40 Enver Hoxha, *Report to the VI Congress*, Zeri i popullit, 2 November 1971, p. 4.

41 Ibid., p. 4.

42 Ibid.
43 Albania had been calling for the admission to the U.N. of the People's Republic of China for twelve years.
44 Enver Hoxha, Report to the VI Congress, *Zeri i popullit*, Tiranë, 2 November 1971.
45 Ibid., p. 4.
46 Tanjug news item datelined 23 January 1973, London.

PART THREE

IO

THE ALBANIANS IN YUGOSLAVIA

(i) *Historical Background*

Within the Ottoman Empire, the Albanians lived in four *vilayets* (provinces), those of Shkodër, Kosovë, Manastir and Janina. In some of these *vilayets* the Albanian population lived alongside the Christians, Serbs, Macedonians and Greeks. During the decades between the Berlin Congress and the Balkan wars, in all the *vilayets* where they lived, particularly in Kosovë, the Albanians organized a number of armed risings in order to win political autonomy within the Turkish state and later to create their national state. In the European part of the Ottoman Empire, the Young Turks' revolution broke out in 1908, and would have had little success without Albanians, who figured prominently in the revolution as officers in the army and government officials and who furthermore formed an élite corps in the army. The Young Turks promised the Albanians social, national and political reforms, but the Albanians soon found out that they had been deceived and so in 1909 and 1911 they again rose up, in the north as well as in the south of Albania. Because of the political and economic circumstances at the time, these uprisings could not acquire a national character, and the Turkish army, despite its weaknesses, was strong enough to suppress the rebellions. Yet the Turkish government which was becoming ever more vulnerable, mainly owing to the unceasing uprisings of the peoples still under its rule, was forced to negotiate with the rebels. In the summer of 1912 the Kosovë Albanians again rose up under the leadership of Isa Boletin and Hasan Prishtinë; they succeeded in liberating Skopje, seat of the *vilayet*. The sultan was forced to grant Albanian self-government in the *vilayets* of Shkodër, Kosovë, Manastir and Janina which disturbed the Christian population as well as the neighbouring countries. For decades the latter had been dreaming of extending territorially over Macedonia and Albania, and the Albanian revolts precipitated the wars between the Balkan states and Turkey.

In the years before Turkey was expelled from the Balkans, Bulgaria, Serbia and Greece already had their national bourgeoisies, and capital of foreign origin and its interests at times coincided, and at times conflicted with those of the domestic bourgeoisies. The leaders of national rebirth, particularly in Serbia and Bulgaria, had been trying ever since the middle of the nineteenth century to convince public opinion that it was essential to expand territorially in the Balkans at the expense of the decaying Ottoman empire, and by 1910 those states had strong, modernized standing armies to back up such a policy. The domestic bourgeoisie in Serbia and Bulgaria justified the need for expression in Macedonia and the Albanian regions not only in terms of expanding their markets, which would be the logic of capital penetration, but also in terms of historical myths of the period before the Ottoman conquests. Some of the remnants from that past are found to this day in the Balkan nations, in relations between the Bulgarians, Serbs, Greeks, Albanians, Macedonians and Montenegrins. The spirit of nationalism in the Balkan peninsula, which was kindled at the Berlin Congress, burst into flames when the Balkan peninsula was divided into spheres of interest.

Following Turkey's expulsion from the Balkans after the first Balkan war, Macedonia was carved up by Serbia, Bulgaria and Greece. Secret agreements existed among those countries and Montenegro on the division of Albania, but they did not succeed because of the proclamation of Albanian independence by patriots at the Congress in Vlorë on 28 November 1912 and its subsequent recognition by the Ambassadors' Conference of the great powers in London in December 1912. Meanwhile, the armies of the neighbouring countries had penetrated deep into Albania, and their governments, abiding by the secret agreements, refused to withdraw them and opposed the formation of an Albanian state. The Albanians reacted with armed resistance, whereupon the invading armies introduced terror and violence in the Albanian regions. The deep-rooted mistrust which still taints Albania's relations with neighbours originated then.

When the other Balkan states refused to withdraw their troops from Albania, the big powers, particularly Austria-Hungary, were compelled to intervene. The Ambassadors' Conference in London, on 22 March 1913, drew up Albania's frontiers with Serbia and Montenegro, deciding that Shkodër and its surrounding territory should be allotted to Albania, whereas a major part of the Dukajgin Plain (Metohija), Kosovë and Macedonia should devolve to Serbia and Montenegro.[1] Even though Serbia kept regions which had been mostly inhabited by Albanians, it was not satisfied because its ambition to have access to the Adriatic was frustrated; it then arrogated to itself the right to determine a 'strategic border', which stretched nearly all the way to Mat in central Albania.[2] Similarly, Montenegro refused to withdraw its troops from Shkodër. The Albanian government organized armed reisistance in September 1913 to recover the areas which the Ambassadors' Conference had allotted to Albania. The organizers of the uprising included Kosovë patriots who refused to accept the Ambassadors' Conference's decision on Albanian borders.[3] The Albanian rebels in Djbër and the Plain of Dukagjin succeeded in expelling the Serbian troops, but the Serbian army was mobilized and succeeded in quelling the Albanian rising. Thus the Serbian troops again marched towards the Adriatic, and their violence and crimes were denounced by the young Serbian socialists, notably Dimitrije Tucovič in his book *Serbia and Albania:*

The bourgeois press clamoured for a merciless extermination, and the army executed the orders. The Albanian villages, from which the people had made a timely flight, were burnt down. There were at the same time barbaric cremateria in which hundreds of women and children were burnt alive. . . . Once again it has been seen that a popular rebellion by the most primitive tribes is always more humane than the practices of a standing army which a modern state uses to quell rebellions. . . .

The Albanian uprising in Kosovë and the Serbian incursion into Albania nearly brought about an Austrian invasion. The Vienna government asked the Serbian government to withdraw its troops from Albania and Germany gave Vienna a free hand to have it out with Serbia. The Russian government counselled Serbia to give in, whereupon the Serbian troops withdrew from Albania.[4]

During the second Balkan war and the 1914–18 war, there were attempts by Turkey, Bulgaria and Austria-Hungary to draw Albania to the side of the central powers, thus creating a Turkish-Bulgarian-Albanian alliance, and to make war on Serbia and Greece. The first Albanian government under the leadership of Ismail Qemal Vlora opposed these attempts and preserved its neutrality. Nevertheless, it permitted the representatives of the Young Turks to bring arms to Albania secretly and to form fighting units along the borders with Serbia. It was not long before this action was disclosed. On 22 January 1914, to put an end to squabbles and anarchy, the Albanian government resigned and transferred all powers to the international control commission[6] which was set up by decision of the London Conference of Ambassadors. There were two other commissions formed to draw the Albanian borders. These international commissions became a battlefield in miniature between the Central Powers and the Allies; when the First World War began they ceased functioning, but Albania remained a bone of contention up till the Versailles Peace Conference.

(ii) *In Bourgeois Yugoslavia*

Albanians in Kosovë and other regions which had been incorporated into Serbia and Montenegro, and particularly the leaders of the national liberation wars in the years before the creation of an Albanian state, who had formed a 'Committee for the Liberation of Kosovë' in Constantinople, urged the Albanian government to declare war and

seize the areas inhabited by Albanians. During the First World War,
Kosovë and the other areas inhabited by the Albanians were intermittent-
ly 'conquered' by one army and 'liberated' by another. The Serbian
army again acted with brutality in those areas: any trouble among the
Albanian masses was suppressed with bloodshed 'to teach them a lesson'.
Many Albanian families fled to Albania – and some even to Turkey.

The desire to join the motherland, as well as the crimes of the Serbian
and Montenegrin armies and later of the police and civil authorities, gave
rise to a very strong irredentist movement among the Albanians in
Yugoslavia. It was strong between the two wars because of the distinct
national, economic and cultural status accorded to them. Many Albanians
in Serbia, and later in Yugoslavia, organized groups popularly known as
kochaks and *komitajis*, which took to the forests and waged guerrilla warfare against the authorities by force of arms. Prominent among these was
Azem Bejta, whose group of fighters gave trouble to the police and the
Yugoslav army until 1924. This movement, essentially one of liberation,
lasted till the late 1920s, but was suppressed by the Serbian authorities
who rounded up many extended families of up to fifty members and
detained them all together on pain of death until the 'outlaws' surren-
dered. This proved highly effective; in fact there was no other means of
suppression, as these were very small and highly mobile units which enjoyed popular support, and used to flee into the mountains after skirm-
ishes with the police or the army.

In bourgeois Yugoslavia political conditions were extremely difficult
in the regions inhabited by the Albanian minority, which did not have
even elementary national and democratic rights. According to the 1921
population census there were 439,658 Albanians in Yugoslavia, and by
the time of the 1931 census, the number had risen to 500,000. However,
the succeeding governments of the kingdom of Serbs, Croats and Slovenes, and later of Yugoslavia, consistently followed a policy designed to
'correct the national composition of the old Serbian areas'; this policy
they conducted in various ways. Although constituting a compact territory, Kosovë, and Metohija were divided up and attached to the three
different *banovinas* of Morava, Zeta and Vardar. Economic pressure was
exerted through an unjust agrarian reform and taxation policy. Settlers
from Montenegro, Hercegovina, Lika and other places were brought to
live in the region of Kosovë, 228,080 ha. of land being sequestrated in the
agrarian units of Pejë (Peć), Ferizaj (Uroševac) Mitrovica and Prizren.
By 1940, 17,679 families had been settled and the government had
built 15,943 houses for them.[7] There were even cases where fertile
land and houses were taken away from Albanian peasants and given to
the settlers. Djordje Krstić, the chief agrarian commissioner with headquarters in Skopje, who was responsible for the colonization of Kosovë,
said in his book *The Colonization of Southern Serbia*, published in 1928,

that in the Lab district north of Prishtinë the colonization had thoroughly changed 'the ethnic composition of the entire region', in which in 1913 'there had been not a single Serbian inhabitant'.

On the eve of the Second World War, the Yugoslav and Turkish governments concluded a convention on the conditions governing the resettlement of the Yugoslav Albanians in Turkey. The Albanians opposed those measures, but the shadows of the approaching war were the main reason why the Yugoslav government could not carry them out.

In the areas inhabited by the Albanian national minority between the two wars, economic and social conditions were hard. Despite the large raw material and mineral resources abounding in Kosovë, the Yugoslav bourgeoisie showed little interest in investing its own or international capital in that area. Only the Trepça lead and zinc mine near Mitrovica, in which British capital showed some interest, and several smaller mines were opened up.

Agriculture was primitive. Of the total economically active population, more than 87 per cent were engaged in farming. Because of the prevailing economic conditions, the population, and the peasantry in particular, were impoverished. Because of poor living conditions, one in every two new-born children died soon after birth, and the population's life expectancy was thirty-eight years. Epidemics were rife. In Kosovë just before the war, there were only a few doctors and about 350 hospital beds. There were 294 four-year primary schools, four high schools, and 36,000 pupils. Teaching was done only in the Serbian language. The rate of illiteracy among the Albanians was 90 per cent. In these regions there were more police posts than schools and public health and welfare institutions.

Thus the status of the Albanians in Yugoslavia between the wars was characterized by difficult living and working conditions; in addition their national, cultural, economic and social rights were repressed. No expression of the Albanian national consciousness and the Albanian revolutionary movement, which essentially had a national and social character, was allowed. Of course, the denationalization policy of bourgeois Yugoslavia failed to suppress the Albanian national consciousness, which came into its own in the Albanian participation in the socialist revolution.

(iii) *The Revolutionary Movement and National Liberation Struggle in Kosovë*

The only force in Yugoslavia between the two wars which opposed this denationalization policy was the Communist Party. It is not accidental that in Kosovë and Macedonia the revolutionary movement was at its peak at the time of the 1921 elections for the constitutional assembly. A period of retreat and defeat followed, in which the movement all but disappeared. Only in the 1930s did the revolutionary movement in Kosovë revive and begin to grow again.[8] This was particularly the case after 1937 when Josip Broz Tito came to head the Party. On the eve of the war the communist party organizations, which had had a sectarian attitude towards Albanians, started to admit them to party membership. At the time of the German occupation of Yugoslavia in April 1941, it was the communists in Kosovë who called the people to arms and later organized armed resistance against the invader and domestic traitors. After the dismemberment of Yugoslavia, the major part of Kosovë and the Plain of Dukagjin, as well as five districts of western Macedonia, were annexed to Albania by Italy.[9] The three Kosovë districts, those of Mitrovica, Lab and Vuçitrnë, were allotted to the military government of Serbia because of the Trepça mines, and were ruled directly by the German command. A few other districts, including those of Gnjilane, Kaëanik and Shtrpce, were given to Bulgaria.[10]

The Italians tried to present themselves as the 'liberators' of Albanians in Kosovë and elsewhere, claiming that they had returned them to their homeland, and brought their historic aspirations to realization. They established Albanian schools, administration, press and radio; they endeavoured to supply the market with consumer articles, on the basis of which domestic merchants and quislings who had placed themselves at the service of the Italian invaders quickly enriched themselves. They bought scarce goods on favourable terms and sold them to the poor peasants at prices two to three times higher. Between 1939 and 1945, according to Italian figures, goods worth 600 to 650 million Albanian francs, or 4 billion lire, were imported into Albania.[11] The Albanians in the 'liberated regions' – in fact occupied by the Italians, like the whole of Albania – saw this situation as a liberation in comparison with their position in bourgeois Yugoslavia. It was for this resaon that most of the quislings and supporters of the Italian regime were Albanians from Kosovë or from northern Albania.

In these conditions communal hatred between the Serbs and Montenegrins on the one hand and the Albanians on the other became virulent, especially in the case of those Serbs and Montenegrins who had been settled in Metohija on land which during colonization had often been unlawfully expropriated from the Albanian peasants. However, during the war years there were many examples of the Albanians opposing those among their ranks who tried to disturb the *status quo*. It was in this context that the communist party leadership from Kosovë and Metohija, from the earliest days of the occupation, made preparations for an armed uprising. Many revolutionaries of Albanian nationality who had been communists and anti-fascists returned from Albania, whither they had gone under Italian auspices. Together with the communists of Montenegrin and Serbian nationality, they organized armed resistance as early as 1941. In 1942 and 1943 the resistance movement in Kosovë and western Macedonia acquired larger dimensions, and armed actions against the Italian, and later the German, fascists were carried out by several partisan detachments and brigades composed of Serbs, Montenegrins and Albanians. Some of the detachments, such as those of Zejnel Ajdini, Emin Duraku and Bajram Curri, were composed exclusively of Albanian fighters who, among other things, had the task of drawing the Albanian masses into the anti-fascist struggle.

One of the principal organizers of the uprising and resistance movement in Kosovë was Fadil Hoxha,[12] who was born on 15 March 1916 in Gjakovë, near the Yugoslav-Albanian border. In 1932 he escaped to Albania to continue his education, because at that time in Yugoslavia the Albanians, as a disenfranchised national minority, could not go beyond primary school education.

Dissatisfied with the position of the Albanian nationality in Yugoslavia and with the conditions of the Albanian people in Albania itself, he joined the revolutionary workers' and communist movement, like many other young Albanians, while still at high school at Shkodër in 1935 and 1936.

Because of his revolutionary activity, he was forced to leave the Shkodër high school, so he continued his education in the teachers' training college at Elbasan, where he soon became the leader of the Shkodër communist group. After the Italian invasion of Albania, together with other revolutionary comrades and Albanian patriots, he organized a battalion of volunteers for the purpose of resisting the Italian invaders in Durrës. He worked for a while in Tiranë in the party headquarters and formed party cells in northern Albania. On instructions from the Shkodër communist group, he established contacts with the Yugoslav Communist Party's regional committee for Kosovë and Metohija. After the occupation of Yugoslavia in April 1941, he went to Kosovë and with the other communists dedicated himself to organizing armed resistance. He soon proved himself an outstanding leader and organizer, and in 1943 he became commander of the National Liberation Army and partisan detachments in the region of Kosovë and Metohija. After the war he performed various political duties in Kosovë. He enjoys great prestige and popularity in Yugoslavia, especially among the Albanians. Since 1969 he has been a member of the Executive Bureau of the Presidency of the League of Communists of Yugoslavia, and belongs to Tito's party caucus. He has been nominated a member of the Presidency of the S.F.R.Y. in Kosovë, the body which in the post-Tito period will serve as collective president of the republic.

Politically and organizationally, the leadership of the resistance movement in Kosovë was linked with the leadership of the Yugoslav resistance movement, with the Central Committee of the Communist Party of Yugoslavia and with the general headquarters of the National Liberation Army and partisan detachments of Yugoslavia. Otherwise, political and military decisions were taken independently, according to prevailing circumstances. The partisan detachments and brigades from Kosovë and Metohija during the war carried out operations in the neighbouring regions – in the border areas of Albania, Macedonia and Southern Serbia.

Under an agreement reached between the Germans and the Italians in Vienna in April 1941, occupational zones in the Balkans were established. Most of the areas of Yugoslavia inhabited by Albanians went to the Italians, who annexed these areas to the Tiranë quisling government with the catchword of creating a 'greater Albania'. The leadership of the Albanian resistance movement and the Central Committee of the Communist Party of Albania did not accept or recognize the establishment of zones of occupation; nor did the leadership of the resistance movements of Yugoslavia and Kosovë and Metohija.[13] In this the Communist Party of Albania differed completely from that of Bulgaria which demanded that the Macedonian Communist Party should be joined to it, since Macedonia and some parts of Serbia, as well as a part of Kosovë, had been incorporated into Bulgaria; the Comintern had to settle this dispute between the Yugoslav and Bulgarian Communist Parties.

However, the leadership of the Albanian resistance movement was interested in the fate of the Albanians in Kosovë and Metohija and in other areas in post-war Yugoslavia – an attitude which was motivated by a desire for co-operation with the neighbouring nations, and influenced by their people's past experience with the great powers. It was in this sense that Enver Hoxha spoke at the Second Conference of the National Liberation Committee in Labinot near Elbasan (held on 4–9 September 1943) about the catchword of an 'ethnic Albania', which was bandied about by the Balli Kombëtar organization. In that part of his report where he referred to the problem of the Albanians outside Albania, he said:

The National Liberation Committee had a clear line and policy for Kosovë and Çameria and endorses this policy, because it is the most correct one. Our national liberation struggle is the poeople's common struggle with the Allies against the Axis powers. A sound and active alliance is worth more than any charters [reference to the agreement of Mukje between the National Liberation Front and Babli Kombëtar]. Our aim is to continue the joint struggle [meaning the resistance movements in Albania, Yugoslavia and Greece] and to forget the past, because we are fighting against our common enemy; at the conclusion of the struggle we who have fought shoulder to shoulder with the greatest understanding will settle any misunderstandings.

The Albanian people, who have suffered for so long, do not wish to oppress and divide other peoples. . . . The national liberation movement has the task of making the Kosovë people conscious of their aspirations, and they will succeed in liberating themselves only through a struggle against fascist invaders or the eventual Yugoslav occupier, Draza Mihajlovic.[14] We must see that the people of Kosovë decide for themselves which side to join [Albania or Yugoslavia] . . . and to oppose the Yugoslav régime which would attempt to oppress them.[15]

Similarly, at the end of November 1943, the Central Committee of the Yugoslav Communist Party sent a letter to its Albanian counterpart referring to Kosovë and Metohija:

To raise today the question of unification would mean giving a helping hand to various reactionaries, including the enemy himself . . . and it is hardly necessary to emphasize that between us and a democratic and anti-imperialist Albania this cannot possibly be an issue. . . . The new Yugoslavia which is in the making will be a land of free nations, and consequently there shall be no room for national oppression of the Albanian minorities either. . . .[16]

After the II Session of the Anti-Fascist Council of National Liberation of Yugoslavia, the first conference of the National Liberation Committee for Kosovë and Metohija was held at Malesi të Gjakovës, in the liberated territory in Albania, from 31 December 1943 to 1 January 1944, attended by forty-nine delegates. The conference worked in the spirit of the II Session of the Anti-Fascist Council of National Liberation of Yugoslavia which had preceded it, and approved its decisions. The formation by Tito of a government of Yugoslavia was viewed as a happy event for all the Yugoslav peoples, particularly the Albanian people in fear of a return to the inhuman treatment of Yugoslavia born at Versailles. To quote Mehmet Hoxha: 'We know that Kosovë and Metohija are inhabited mostly by the Albanians who want to unite with Albania. However, to bring about the realization of the people's idea, there is no way other than to continue the armed struggle against the fascist invader and his lackeys, joining with the other nations of Yugoslavia and with the National Liberation Army of Albania.[17]

The meeting adopted the following resolution: 'Kosovë and Metohija form a region in which Albanian inhabitants preponderate; they, as always, still wish to be united with Albania. Consequently, our duty is to point to the true way which the Albanian people should take in order to achieve their aspirations. The only way for the Albanians of Kosovë and Metohija to unite with Albania is through a common struggle with the other nations of Yugoslavia against the invaders and their forces, because it is the only way to win freedom, when all the nations, including the Albanians will be able to choose their own destiny, with the right to self-determination – including secession. The guarantee is the National Liberation Army of Albania, with which it is closely linked. A further guarantee is our great allies, the U.S.S.R., Great Britain and the United States (the Atlantic Charter and the Moscow and Teheran Conferences).'[18]

The material from the first session of the National Liberation Committee of Kosovë and Metohija was sent to the Central Committee of the Yugoslav Communist Party; the Anti-Fascist Council and the National Committee of Yugoslavia were asked to give their opinions on the resolution and the other material adopted at the first session. The Central Committee, in a letter of 28 March 1944 to the leaders of the resistance movement of Kosovë and Metohija signed by Milovan Djilas, made an assessment of the first regional conference. It endorsed the orientation of the National Liberation Committee of Kosovë and Metohija, but indirectly criticized the part of the resolution referring to the aspiration of the Albanians from Kosovë and Metohija to join Albania.[19] Similarly, a letter was sent to the Yugoslav Communist Party's regional committee for Kosovë and Metohija dated 2 October 1943, by Svetozar Vukmanović-Tempo a delegate from the general headquarters of the Yugoslav National Liberation Army and the Central Committee of the Communist Party of Macedonia and Kosovë and Metohija. He had stayed among the partisans in Kosovë and wrote:

Regarding the question of the future borders between Yugoslavia and Albania, it will be resolved by brotherly agreement and co-operation between the National Liberation Army of Yugoslavia and the Council of National Liberation of Albania on the basis of the right of self-determination of nations. How the borders will be drawn will depend on the evolution of the political situation in Yugoslavia and Albania. At present we must not make any definite statements on this issue.[20]

After a letter from the Yugoslav Party's Central Committee dated 28 March 1944, the leadership of the resistance movement in Kosovë and Metohija undertook to amend that part of the resolution of the first conference of its National Liberation Committee where the problem of the union of these parts with Albania was referred to.[21]

However, it was undoubtedly the desire of the Albanian masses which made the resistance movement in Kosovë and Metohija pass that part of the resolution. They feared a return to the pre-war situation, either in Yugoslavia or in Albania, as the result of international pressure or intervention. Allied pressure on the small nations had already begun, and plans were afoot for a division of the Balkans into spheres of interest. The Balkan peoples, particularly the Albanians, had too often been the object of bargaining and haggling among the great powers in the past. However, the Yugoslavs and the Albanians have in the intervening years become for the first time masters of their own destinies. Since the socialist revolution had won a victory in Albania as well as in Yugoslavia, there was no reason why the areas inhabited by the Albanians in Yugoslavia should become a bone of contention between the new Albania and the new Yugoslavia. Marshal Tito made this point repeatedly in speeches and articles throughout the war; Yugoslavia should not come out of this weakened and disintegrated; it was becoming a federal and democratic state in which all the peoples and nationalities would have guaranteed national, political, economic and cultural rights. Thus the sensitive question of the areas inhabited by the Albanians in Yugoslavia was resolved peacefully between the resistance movements of Yugoslavia and Albania.

After the liberation of Kosovë and Metohija, the entire military and administrative government in the province went to the leadership and organs which emerged from the national liberation struggle. Military government was established in the province, with the tasks of liquidating certain areas of counter-revolution, associated with the Balli Kombëtar organization. This situation was quickly brought under control by the National Liberation Front of Kosovë and Metohija in which the National Committee of the Albanians in the province operating within the democratic front under the leadership of Fadil Hoxha took a strong part.

Soon after the pacification of Kosovë the military government was replaced by a civilian government. In the middle of April 1945, Marshal Tito received a delegation of the National Committee of Albanians from Kosovë and Metohija, to whom he promised the same rights as the other peoples of Yugoslavia, saying that they would be an important element in the building of a new Yugoslavia. The injustices committed by the bourgeois regime would be put right particularly the unjust agrarian reform measures. This meeting had a great impact on the Albanians in Kosovë.[22]

In the summer of 1945 delegates were elected for the second meeting of the National Liberation Committee of Kosovë and Metohija which was held from 8 to 10 July 1945 at Prizren. A resolution was passed on the uniting of Kosovë and Metohija with the Federal Republic of Serbia within a democratic federal Yugoslavia, with the status of an autonomous province. It amended a part of the resolution from the first session, as discussed above. The Albanians of Kosovë together with the other nationalities exercising the right to self-determination gave their support to socialist Yugoslavia.[23]

(iv) *In Socialist Yugoslavia*

What is the position and what are the special preoccupations of the Albanian nationality in Yugoslavia in the 1970s? Are they in favour of Tito's Yugoslavia or are they the Achilles heel of the federation?

Considering the level of economic and political development before the socialist revolution, the Albanians have made astonishing progress during the first three decades of socialism in Yugoslavia. The Albanians' cultural life has developed enormously, and a new intelligentsia has emerged. The number of employed has risen and the percentage of highly trained and skilled personnel and workers has risen substantially. An impetus has been given to the building of new factories, whole branches of industry with modern plants, a communications network, schools, hospitals, and agricultural-industrial complexes, which have become an important base for modern agricultural production and the transformation of the countryside. According to the 1971 census in Kosovë province farmers comprised 51·5 per cent of the population, compared with 64·1 per cent 1961.[24] The *per capita* national income averages about $300, and was planned to reach $450 in 1975. From its fund for the development of the backward republics and the Province of Kosovë the federation undertook to allocate the larger share for the economic and social development of Kosovë. Kosovë has large natural resources, including lignite, lead, zinc and magnesium, bauxite, chrome and other ores, and existing capacities will be expanded and new industrial plants erected. It is no accident that because of natural and other resources experts are calling Kosovë the Yugoslav Ruhr.

Despite its dramatic economic development, Kosovë still lags behind in relation to the rest of Yugoslavia. In 1947 the G.N.P. of the province of Kosovë was 50 per cent of the average level for Yugoslavia as a whole, whereas in 1970 it had fallen back to 33 per cent. Until 1960, investment in Kosovë had been almost nil. Thus the *per capita* level of investment in 1950–70, if Yugoslavia is taken as index 100, was 131 for Montenegro, 104 for Macedonia and 79 for Bosnia and Herçegovina, three republics with the status of underdeveloped areas, and 61 for Kosovë. Since 1971 the development of Kosovë has been given priority.

The Albanian village and urbanization provide a very interesting illustration. On the one hand, there is evidence of a fast rate of urbanization since 1960, whereas on the other hand the total rural population is on the increase. Thus in Kosovë in 1947, 80 per cent of the population was agricultural, whereas by 1971 this figure had dropped to 51·5 per cent, which is favourable enough. However, if in 1953 the index of the agricultural population for Yugoslavia is taken to be 100, it was 118 in Kosovë, and by 1970 it had risen to 139, as a result of the population explosion in the province.

When the 1971 population census was taken, there were 1,309,523 Albanians in Yugoslavia, 916,168 in the Province of Kosovë, 179,871 in Macedonia, 35,671 in Montenegro and 65,507 in Serbia proper, mainly in the communities of Bujanovac, Preševo and Medvedja.[25] While the Albanian nationality accounts for 6·4 per cent of the total population of

Yugoslavia, it constitutes, in the areas which it inhabits, the majority of the population. Thus in Kosovë Albanians account for 73·6 per cent of the total population, whereas in most communities in western Macedonia they constitute 70 to 80 per cent. Of all the Albanians in the Balkans, 42 per cent live in Yugoslavia. In Kosovë the proportion of Albanians in the total provincial population increased by 6·7 per cent, more than was forecast, between the censuses of 1961 and 1971. This is due to the population migrations, which have always been important in these parts, as well as to a high rate of expansion. It is interesting to note that the Albanians are among the 'youngest' peoples, not only in Europe but in the world. Among the Albanians in Kosovë, 42·5 per cent of the total population belongs to the age group up to and including 14, and 50·2 per cent belongs to the age group 15 to 59. The average Albanian family has 3·6 children, the Serbian 2·1 and the Slovenian family 2·5 children. A household in Yugoslavia during 1971 had an average of 3·8 members, while in Kosovë it had 6·6 members.

Many families in Kosovë still live in family communities of between fifty and ninety members, although industrialization and labour migrations to other parts of Yugoslavia and West European countries have helped to break up the villages and large family communities. In such communities the house rules are laid down by the head of the community, and all the members are bound to carry out the tasks assigned by him. In many cases the community head has his assistants, each charged with a specific duty. These communities are becoming adapted to the modern conditions of life, work and production, as well as of the market. Children in such communities are being sent to schools, right up to university level, and there is a special item in the community budget for education. When a decision is required that affects the entire family regarding work, production, family relationships, and so on, it is taken by a council composed of all the male members and presided over by the head of the community. The parlour in which adult men discuss matters and spend their evenings takes on the appearance of a parliament in miniature. As in all parliaments, there are influential and less influential members. In such family communities, food is prepared and bread baked collectively. Meals are served out of a single vessel on low round tables, where men eat separately from women and children. This patriarchal way of life has been preserved in the Albanian villages in Yugoslavia.

We have already noted the high rate of population increase among the Yugoslav Albanians. Between 1961 and 1971 the Yugoslav population as a whole grew at an annual average of 1·14 per cent. Above the average were Macedonians (1·39 per cent), Montenegrins (1·69 per cent), Muslims (2·24 per cent) and Albanians in Kosovë and western Macedonia (3·05 per cent). In 1972 the rate of natural increase per thousand inhabitants in Yugoslavia was 9·6; in Kosovë it was 29·6. The public health services in Kosovë and other areas where Albanians live achieved important results in decreasing the mortality rate, which was 17·0 in Kosovë in 1950, and had fallen to 8·6 by 1970. A similar trend has occurred in the rate of infant mortality of Kosovë, which has fallen in the last ten years from 142 deaths per 1,000 live births to 90. Epidemics and contagious diseases used to be rife in these areas, but have now almost been eradicated. Most Kosovë villages have been electrified, and by 1975 the process of electrification is expected to be complete.

Especially important results have been achieved in education. Immediately after the liberation, nearly 90 per cent of the population were illiterate, but in 1971 the Province of Kosovë had 825 primary schools (eight years) with a total of 239,393 pupils, 175,249 of whom were of Albanian nationality, and eighty-two secondary schools of all types, with an enrolment of 38,761 of whom 23,150 were Albanians. At the University in Prishtinë, which was founded in 1969, there are over 15,000 registered students, of whom more than half are Albanians. There is thus a great thirst for education in this underdeveloped area of Yugoslavia, and the literary and artistic achievements of the Albanians in Yugoslavia, where creative life is free and not directed as in the other socialist countries, are far greater than in Albania itself. Yet, despite these achievements, 30 per cent of the Albanian population in Yugoslavia are still illiterate – mostly old people, it is true, but also including a considerable percentage among the younger generations.

(v) *Some Acts of Discrimination before 1966*

Immediately after the socialist revolution, the post-revolutionary impetus was in evidence in the areas inhabited by the Albanians. But after 1949 there was discrimination against Albanian participation in political life, in the government, the economy, and so on. The Albanians were accorded the status of second-class citizens, especially by the secret police, which played a part in exacerbating relations between Yugoslavia and Albania. In 1956, when relations between Yugoslavia and Albania had improved, the secret police in Kosovë brought violent pressure to bear on the Albanians to collect firearms – from the many families who possessed them. It was then that Albanian families in Kosovë started migrating to Turkey (as long as they declared themselves to be Turks, they could enter Turkey without any trouble). It is estimated that some 15,000 families took up residence in Turkey. Leaders of political and other associations in Kosovë, western Macedonia and elsewhere were mainly Serbs, Macedonians and Montenegrins, with only an insignificant proportion of Albanians. The Serbian and Macedonian languages had the status of 'national languages', used in the administration, courts of law and schools, but Albanian did not have this status.

The role of the Autonomous Province of Kosovë and Metohija, which was set up in 1945, was reduced to that of an administrative unit. This situation, which caused a revival of irredentism, had to be changed.

A turning-point in the status and role of the Albanians in Yugoslavia was reached in 1966 with the fall of the head of the secret police, Aleksandar Ranković, a leading proponent of centralism and unitarism, who had aspirations to seize power in Yugoslavia after Tito. The leadership of the League of Communists of Yugoslavia, Serbia and Kosovë denounced the acts of the secret police and declared that discrimination against the Albanians was contrary to League policy. Members of the state security who had committed criminal acts in Kosovë were tried, and many were removed from their posts.

The Yugoslav party showed its strength in thus openly acknowledging its weaknesses before the rank and file.

(vi) *Full Equality within the Yugoslav Federation*

The constitutional amendments of 1969, 1971 and 1973 basically changed the status and role of the socialist republics and autonomous provinces in the Yugoslav federation. Thorough changes were made, particularly in regard to the (similar) positions of the autonomous provinces of Kosovë and Vojvodina. The name of the autonomous province of Kosovë and Metohija was changed to the Socialist Autonomous Province of Kosovë and in place of its previous statute, a 'constitutional law' of Kosovë was promulgated. The delegation of Kosovë in the Federal Assembly and other federal bodies, although numerically smaller than the republican delegations, is equal to the republican delegations: the rights and duties of an autonomous province in the Yugloslav federal system are equal in the areas of economics, culture, education and welfare and foreign policy to those of the republics. It is true that the province of Kosovë forms part of the Republic of Serbia, within which only certain questions are dealt with jointly, with the consent and agreement of the autonomous provinces. It is true that the Albanians do not like to emphasize the fact that they have been incorporated within the Republic of Serbia, because they prefer to owe their full allegiance to Kosovë, but it is a reality which they have accepted. Ever since Turkish times, the Albanians have traditionally been wanting autonomy and self-organization.

During the public discussions in 1967 and 1968 concerning the change in the Yugoslav constitution and the position of the republics and provinces within the federation, there were demands in some quarters in Kosovë, and particularly among a part of the Albanian intelligentsia, to make of the Autonomous Province of Kosovë the seventh Yugoslav republic. These demands were rejected by the leaders of the Albanian minority as unrealistic. This attitude needs to be explained. First, this would be acceptable neither to the other nationalities in Kosovë – specifically the Serbs and Montenegrins – nor in the Republic of Serbia; nor would the other republics and peoples of Yugoslavia endorse this change without the agreement of the Serbs. The Serbian nation survived the Turkish occupation by nurturing the folk-memory of its medieval history, which was centred on Kosovë. Kosovë has a similar importance in the struggles of the Albanians for national emancipation and their efforts to form a national state. For this reason, the area has always been a bone of contention between the Albanians and Serbs, and it is therefore extremely difficult to strike a true balance. History has left deep scars on both nations, and conditions following the Second World War helped to keep them fresh and make relations in some periods very tense.

The community leaders in Kosovë, particularly those of the Albanian community, fully understood the implications of demands for the formation of a republic of Kosovë, and therefore rejected it. Under the constitutional law of Kosovë, the Albanians were then guaranteed the right to use their national symbols, in particular the Albanian national flag.

On 27 November 1968 demonstrations of an openly separatist and nationalistic character took place in Prishtinë and some other places in Kosovë in which several hundred students and high school pupils demanded a republic of Kosovë. The demonstrators carried Albanian flags and hailed Enver Hoxha; they also broke shop windows, especially those bearing Serbian inscriptions. The provincial leadership of Kosovë denounced the demonstrations as 'nationalistic, reactionary and anti-constitutional, designed to disorient the Albanian population'. Demonstrations also took place on 23 December 1968 at Tetovo in north-western Macedonia, which is mostly inhabited by Albanians. In these demonstrations too several thousand young people took part, and called for an Albanian republic in Yugoslavia, to incorporate western Macedonia. The organizers of both demonstrations were tried and imprisoned.

The idea of an Albanian republic in Yugoslavia was also rejected by the Central Committee of the League of Communists of Yugoslavia at its session presided over by President Tito on 4 February 1969. The demand for an Albanian republic was seen as a 'demand for changing state frontiers', which would 'not only threaten the security of Yugoslavia and its territorial integrity, but would also imply the danger of international complications in the Balkans'. It was then that President Tito, who had always favoured equality among the nationalities of Yugoslavia, decided to meet all the demands of the Albanian nationality in Kosovë for a broad autonomy which would give them the same rights and duties as the republics. Thus the Autonomous Province of Kosovë has remained part of the Republic of Serbia, in satisfaction of the Serbian leaders' demands. Attempts by the secret police and its chief, Aleksandar Ranković, to be 'guardians of Kosovë' were a failure.

The Albanians in Yugoslavia do not regard themselves as second-class citizens. Nationalism and separatism do exist among them but less than ever before. Their attitude towards Yugoslavia has altered considerably due to their national, political and cultural emancipation and through the general economic progress of Kosovë and the other areas which they inhabit in the federation.

Foreign observers who regard the Albanians as one of the weak points in the Yugoslav federation base this assessment on the pre-occupations of the Albanians before the socialist revolution, when bourgeois Yugoslavia was a prison for them. It was natural then that the demand for secession should be strong. However in the multi-national federal Yugoslavia of today, in which they enjoy equal rights and cultural, political and economic emancipation, they feel at home and are committed to maintain the security and integrity of their homeland. The Albanians as well as the other Yugoslav peoples are aware who would profit from a possible conflict in this part of the Balkans. There is similar awareness in the People's Republic of Albania and in this aspect the situation has not altered since 1945. The Albanian nationality in Yugoslavia is interested in an equal co-operation in every area between Albania and Yugoslavia, and in the free circulation of people, ideas and goods. Until 1966 no such co-operation was possible, but since 1970 when inter-governmental relations became normalized, the possibility has existed and has not yet been fully exploited. After a break of nearly twenty years and the chequered history of these relations, improvements must be gradual, because any sudden improvement would bring difficulties to both countries. Consequently the cautious policies pursued by both governments can be approved of as realistic.

NOTES

1 *Histori e popullit shqiptar*, Prishtinë, 1969, p. 372.
2 Ibid., p. 388.
3 Ibid.
4 Dr. Vladimir Dedijer, *Istorija Jugoslavije*, Beograd, 1972, p. 344.
5 *Histori*, op. cit., II, 397.
6 Ibid., p. 400.
7 Yugoslav archives, Fond Agrarne reforme (Fund of the Agrarian reform), p. 48. See Dr. Ali Hadri, *National Liberation Movement in Kosovë* (Albanian language), Prishtinë, 1971, concerning the Albanian language, p. 22.
8 Most of the movement's adherents at that time were the children of settlers, especially Montenegrins.
9 V. Dedijer, op. cit., p. 461.

10 Dr. Ali Hadri, op. cit., pp. 95–105.
11 Stavro Skendi, op. cit., p. 228.
12 No relation to Enver Hoxha. Hoxha is a common Albanian name.
13 Enver Hoxha, *Works*, I, 508–11. See *Histori*, op. cit. II, 674, and Dr. Ali Hadri, op. cit., p. 95.
14 Mihajlović was a representative of the royal government in exile, who collaborated with the Germans in fighting Tito's partisans.
15 Enver Hoxha, *Works*, I, pp. 357–8.
16 Quoted from Vladimir Dedijer, *Yugoslovensko–Albanski odnosi 1939–1948* (Yugoslav–Albanian Relations 1939–1948), Beograd, 1949, p. 134.
17 From a speech by Mehmet Hoxha, President of the National Liberation Committee of Kosovë and Metohija (now [1974] retired and living in Belgrade). Cited according to Dr. Stanoje Aksić, 'Prva Konferencija (zasedanje) Narodnooslobodilačkog odbora za Kosovǝ i Methoiju' ('First Conference [Session] of the National Liberation Committee for Kosovë and Metohija'), in the journal, *Anali pravnog fakultata u Beogradu* (Annals of the Belgrade Law School) Nos. 3–4, May–August 1969, p. 422.
18 Ibid.
19 Ibid., p. 427. The letter is preserved in the Regional Historical Institute in Prishtinë, document No. 246.
20 Quoted from Dr. Stanoje Aksić, op. cit., p. 428. The original letter is preserved in the Regional Historical Institute in Prishtinë, document No. 177.
21 Pavle Jovicević, the article 'Prvo zasedanje Narodnooslobodilačkog odbora' (The First Session of the National Liberation Committee), in the book *Kosovo i Metohija 1943–1944*, Prishtinë, 1963.
22 *Rilindja*, a periodical in the Albanian language published in Prishtinë, 15 April 1945.
23 The National Committee of the Autonomous Province of Kosovë and Metohija 1943–53. Documentation from the session in the Serbo-Croatian language, Prishtinë, 1955, p. 44.
24 Provincial Bureau of Statistics of the Socialist Autonomous Province of Kosovë. Statistics published in Prishtinë, May 1972, p. 15.
25 Federal Institute for Statistics, *Statistical Calendar of Yugoslavia*, Beograd, 1973, p. 32.

I I

CONCLUSION

Albania has devoted the past three decades, with extraordinary single-mindedness and despite great obstacles, to building a socialist society. In the process it has undergone far-reaching transformations. After the victory of the revolution, the main concern of the new government was to create a material base and transform the economy, overcoming the backwardness it had inherited. The process of industrialization has been remarkably successful and the country has gained in economic strength. In the second decade of economic development (1960–8), Albania qualified as a country undergoing accelerated economic development, with a growth rate in the G.N.P. of 10·1 per cent. With the building of new factories, railway lines, asphalted roads, blocks of flats, etc., a modern infrastructure was laid down, and employment and adequate living standards have been provided for the people.

With the creation of this material base of society, the way in which the economy has been managed hitherto is becoming obsolete and could soon become a brake on further socio-economic progress. Structural changes in the economy and organization of productive forces seem to be imperative. There is an awareness of this in the country and ways are being sought to reduce the role of the bureaucratic apparatus. It can be surmised that the technical and professional cadres that have been formed will be able to initiate new processes and give fresh stimulus in all spheres of social life as well as in achieving the goals of the new five-year plan. The Albanian economy will then be able to make the change from being an agrarian-industrial economy to being an industrial-agrarian one. The forces of history make it likely that Albania will remain a relatively closed and centrally directed state and society. In such a small country strong central control is easy to maintain.

As a result of Albania's social and economic institutions entering a new and higher phase of development in recent years, the country's position in the international community has changed. Its national policy, bred of a traumatic past, of relying on its own forces both in domstic affairs and in international relations, was overshadowed at a time when Albania's geo-political and strategic considerations made it natural that it should be a member of the socialist camp, adopting a hostile stance towards the western powers. However in the early 1960s, when developments in regional and inter-bloc relations made it clear to the Albanians that the national interests of small and medium-sized countries would not be served by bloc adherence, this policy reasserted itself.

The Balkan peninsula, once termed a 'powder keg', has often served as a political barometer for the general atmosphere in Europe, and the Albanian question has traditionally been the fuse. The political and strategic importance of the Balkans is still important today, because of the many different foreign interests that converge there – mortgages from the past – and because of the different orientations of the Balkan countries. But now more than ever before these countries have real opportunities and means for overcoming the existing differences and for promoting mutual co-operation based on the principles of respect for sovereignty and territorial integrity, regardless of the political orientation and socio-political system of the various states. In an era of *détente* in Europe, the beneficial influence of which is also being felt in the Balkans, the normalization of relations with series of countries – neighbours and Mediterranean countries – was crowned by the establishment of diplomatic relations with Greece. The impact of this was felt throughout the world, since it marked the end of a European anomaly which had lasted for more than three decades.

This diplomatic and political success was not achieved overnight. Overtures has been made previously to normalize relations, but they bore no fruit. But it was at a time when both countries were preoccupied with their own problems and interests, as well as with Balkan and Mediterranean realities, that it was seen that their standing mutual antagonisms could be overcome after all. There is no doubt that the normalization of relations between Albania and its neighbours, Yugoslavia and Greece, will promote Albania's policy of independence and autonomy both internally and in its foreign relations.

Albania has consistently turned a cold shoulder toward Soviet advances for a normalization of relations but has maintained relations at various low levels with other Warsaw Pact countries. This situation will remain unchanged for some time to come. Albania's opening towards the west will be gradual, although the attitude of the West towards Albania is more flexible than it used to be. Albania's attitude towards one superpower largely determines its behaviour towards the other. In all probability China will continue to be Albania's principal ally in the world at large as a counterweight to Soviet influence in the Balkans, but here too there have been changes. For many years Albania was China's only window on Europe, while China was Albania's only link with the world. Economic assistance and credits are another reason for friendship with China, even though the fundamental policy of the Albanian government has been to develop the economic resources of the country without outside help.

Albania has carved a special niche for itself in international relations and in its internal development, proudly exercising its right not to have to belong to any political or economic bloc. It may open itself up to the world by slow steps; it will never give away an ounce of its independence.

APPENDIX : TABLES

APPENDIX

Table 1
SURVEY OF POPULATION GROWTH

	1938	1950	1960	1965	1970	1971
Total inhabitants	1,040,400	1,218,900	1,626,300	1,865,300	2,135,600	2,188,000
Base index	100·0	117·3	156·3	179·3	205·3	210·3

Source: Vjetari statistikor RPSH 1969 dhe 1970, Tiranë 1971, p. 24 (cited below as *Vjetari statistikor*).

Table 2
URBAN AND RURAL POPULATION

Year	Total population	Urban	Rural	Percentage Urban	Percentage Rural
1938	1,040,400	160,000	880,400	15·4	84·6
1950	1,218,900	249,800	969,100	20·5	79·5
1960	1,626,300	502,500	1,123,800	30·9	69·1
1965	1,865,300	620,000	1,245,300	33·2	66·8
1970	2,135,600	719,000	1,416,600	33·6	66·4
1971	2,188,000	740,000	1,448,000	33·8	66·2

Source: Vjetari statistikor.

Table 3
COMPOSITION OF LABOUR FORCE BY OCCUPATION

	1950	1960	1970
Total labour force	100·0	100·0	100·0
Blue-collar workers	11·2	29·1	32·9
White-collar workers	10·1	11·3	11·3
Farmworkers, total	74·3	58·7	55·7
In cooperatives	1·6	41·6	55·4
Private farms	72·7	17·1	0·3
Artisans and shopkeepers	4·4	0·9	0·1

Source: Republika popullore e Shqipërisë, Tiranë 1971.

Table 4

BIRTH RATE AND MORTALITY RATE
(percentage)

	1938	1950	1960	1969	1971
Live births	34·7	38·5	43·3	35·3	33·5
Infant mortality	17·8	14·0	10·4	7·5	8·1
Population increment	16·9	24·5	32·9	27·8	25·2

Source: Vjetari statistikor.

Table 5

BLUE- AND WHITE-COLLAR WORKERS

Year	Total of blue- and white-collar workers	Blue-collar workers		
		Total	%	% increase over 1950
1950	82,642	54,969	66·5	100·0
1960	202,248	153,843	76·1	279·8
1965	268,419	203,740	75·9	370·6
1970	392,282	307,052	78·3	558·5

Source: Vjetari statistikor.

Table 6

ABLE-BODIED AND WORK UNFIT POPULATION

Year	Total population	Able-bodied	Approx. employed in total population (%) (3:2)	Work-unfit population(a)			Share of work-unfit in total population (%)
				Under 16	Over 59 or 54	Total under 16 and over 59 or 54	
1950	1,218,900	589,200	48·4	497,700	129,900	627,600	51·5
1955	1,391,500	672,000	48·3	572,400	140,200	712,600	51·1
1960	1,626,300	774,900	47·6	694,500	153,600	848,100	52·2
1965	1,889,800	878,500	46·6	837,400	173,900	1,011,300	53·4
1967	1,991,100	923,200	46·7	879,200	179,700	1,058,900	53·3
1969(b)	2,046,800	1,000,600	48·8	862,700	183,500	1,046,200	51·2
1970(c)	2,122,000	1,044,500	49·2	897,500	183,000	1,074,500	50·8

(a) According to official statements, the able-bodied population comprises males between 16 and 59 years of age and women between 16 and 54 years of age.

(b) Estimate, 31 December 1968. *Source*: Hans-Joachim Pernack, 'Probleme der wirtschaftlichen Entwicklung Albaniens', *Südosteuropa-Studien*, München 1972, Table 2, p. 161; for 1969, *Vjetari statistikor*.

(c) *Estimate data source*: *Vjetari statistikor*.

Table 7

EMPLOYED PERSONS WITH HIGH SCHOOL AND
UNIVERSITY DEGREES

	1938	*1950*	*1960*	*1965*	*1970*	*1971*
Total	2,380	3,650	15,845	31,700	52,900	59,013
University-level degrees	380	620	4,245	9,200	15,200	16,905
High school degrees	2,000	3,030	11,600	22,500	37,700	42,108

Source: Vjetari statistikor.

Table 8

GROWTH OF INDUSTRIAL OUTPUT
(at 1971 prices)

	1955	*1960*	*1965*	*1970*	*1971*
Total industrial output	100	220	300	560	557
Producer goods	100	230	320	670	755
Consumer goods	100	210	290	460	505

Source: Republika popullore e Shqipërisë, op. cit.

Table 9

COMPOSITION OF INDUSTRIAL OUTPUT
(at 1971 prices)

	1955	*1960*	*1965*	*1970*	*1971*
Total industrial output	100·0	100·0	100·0	100·0	100·0
Producer goods	47·0	49·1	49·7	56·6	57·1
Consumer goods	53·0	50·9	50·3	43·4	42·9

Source: Republika popullore e Shqipërisë, op. cit.

Table 10

MECHANIZATION OF AGRICULTURE

	1938	*1950*	*1960*	*1965*	*1970*
Tractors	28	285	2,712	4,331	6,015
Combine harvesters	—	—	349	554	890
Threshers	75	280	322	814	1,286
Cultivators	—	65	728	718	969

Source: Vjetari statistikor.

Table 11

OUTPUT OF LEADING INDUSTRIAL PRODUCTS

Product	*1938*	*1950*	*1960*	*1964*	*1971*[a]	*1975 (planned)*
Crude oil	108	132	728	764	1,657	2,700
Oil derivatives	—	56	369	476	1,334	
Petrol	—	5	54	52	88	
Coal	4	41	291	292	675	1,250
Chrome ore	7	53	289	307	502	900
Copper ore	—	14	81	145	—	600
Iron nickel ore	—	—	255	351	400	650
Cotton	—	—	6,857	8,630	—	
Electric power (kwh.)	9,311	—	—	288,399	1,103,600	2,000,000

(Coal, Chrome ore, Copper ore, Iron nickel ore, Cotton bracketed: × 1000 tons)

Source: Hans-Joachim Pernack, 'Probleme der wirtschaftlichen Entwicklung Albaniens', op. cit., Table 14. Figures for 1970 and 1975 according to the development plan ending 1975.

(*a*) *Source: Vjetari statistikor.*

Table 12

COMPOSITION OF INVESTMENTS BY FIVE-YEAR PLANS

(at 1971 prices, %)

Five-year plans	Total real investment	Industry	Agriculture	Transport	Education and public health	Housing construction	Other
1st 1951–5	100·0	52·0	12·0	13·0	6·0	8·0	9·0
2nd 1956–60	100·0	44·0	18·0	13·0	5·0	8·0	12·0
3rd 1961–5	100·0	49·0	15·0	11·0	4·0	8·0	13·0
4th 1966–70	100·0	47·0	16·0	11·0	5·0	7·0	14·0
5th 1971–5	100·0	66·0	12·0	6·0	4·0	5·0	7·0

Source: Republika popullore e Shqipërisë, op. cit.

Table 13

COMPOSITION OF NATIONAL INCOME BY
ECONOMIC ACTIVITIES
(at 1971 prices %)

Year	Total national income	Industry	Agriculture	Construction	Transport and retail trade
1938	100·0	3·8	93·1	0·8	2·3
1950	100·0	11·0	76·3	4·6	8·1
1960	100·0	32·7	44·4	10·9	12·0
1965	100·0	35·0	43·0	10·1	11·1
1970	100·0	42·4	34·5	10·2	12·9

Source: Republika popullore e Shqipërisë, op. cit.

Table 14

POPULATION AND GROSS INDUSTRIAL PRODUCT OF ALBANIA BY PROVINCES 1965 AND 1971

| Province | Area (sq. km.) | | Population | | | | Gross Industrial Product | | | |
| | | | Total | | Per sq. km. | | (millions of leks) | | (per capita in 100 leks) | |
	1965	1971	1965	1971	1965	1971	1965	1971	1965	1971
Berat	1,066	1,026	104,390	118,000	98	115	363·1	513·8	34·8	43·4
Dibër	1,569	1,569	93,812	101,500	60	65	76·8	112·2	8·2	11·0
Durrës	861	859	166,780	173,500	181	202	618·8	885·7	39·7	51·0
Elbasan	1,505	1,466	130,430	145,500	87	99	402·7	548·5	30·9	37·7
Fier	1,191	1,190	139,175	162,600	117	137	410·0	744·6	29·4	45·8
Gramsh	699	695	24,095	27,800	34	40	10·6	24·4	4·4	8·8
Gjirokastër	1,137	Same	49,170	52,200	43	46	124·4	181·4	25·3	34·7
Kolonjë	804	,,	18,685	18,800	23	23	17·0	26·1	9·1	13·9
Korçë	2,181	,,	159,115	170,100	73	78	435·4	608·7	27·4	35·8
Krujë	611	607	55,325	70,700	90	116	131·4	204·7	23·7	28·9
Kukes	1,564	Same	58,880	67,300	37	43	99·3	121·5	16·9	18·0
Lezhë	472	479	33,225	38,000	70	79	30·0	53·8	9·0	14·2
Librazhd	1,013	Same	42,730	45,700	42	45	58·0	61·2	13·6	13·4
Lushnjë	712	,,	81,595	93,000	115	131	82·1	136·7	10·1	14·7

Table 14—*continued*

| | Area (sq. km.) | | Population | | | | Gross Industrial Product | | | |
| | | | Total | | Per sq. km. | | (millions of leks) | | (per capita in 100 leks) | |
	1965	1971	1965	1971	1965	1971	1965	1971	1965	1971
Mat	1,028	,,	45,340	50,900	44	49	61·7	89·3	13·6	17·5
Mirditë	698	,,	22,465	27,500	32	39	119·4	163·6	53·2	59·5
Përmet	938	930	30,340	31,000	32	33	25·8	29·0	8·5	9·3
Pogradec	725	Same	42,775	47,100	59	65	63·2	99·0	14·8	21·0
Pukë	969	,,	27,568	30,500	28	32	47·3	63·2	17·1	20·7
Sarandë	1,097	,,	58,135	63,700	53	58	135·1	183·9	23·2	28·9
Skrapar	720	775	23,035	28,600	32	37	11·5	90·1	5·0	3·1
Shkodër	2,533	2,528	150,350	171,500	59	68	391·0	668·4	26·0	38·9
Tepelenë	817	Same	30,850	36,000	38	44	49·4	70·9	16·0	19·7
Tiranë	1,186	1,226	241,900	259,500	204	212	1,109·4	1,662·0	45·8	64·0
Tropojë	1,043	Same	25,570	28,800	24	28	8·7	20·0	0·3	0·7
Vlorë	1,609	,,	119,995	128,200	75	80	378·0	518·1	31·5	40·4
Albania	28,748	Same	1,964,730	2,188,000	68	76	5,200·2	7,924·2	26·8	36·2

Source: Vjetari statistikor.

Table 15

INDUSTRIAL AND AGRICULTURAL OUTPUT
(at 1971 prices, '000 leks)

	1960		*1965*		*1970*	
Industrial and agricultural output	5,230·3	100·0	7,190	100·0	11,507	100·0
Industrial output	2,781·3	53·0	3,864	53·8	7,104	61·74
Agricultural output	2,449·0	47·0	3,321	46·2	4,403	38·26

Source: Vjetari statistikor.

Table 16

PRODUCTION OF LEADING CROPS
(base index)

Year	*1937–8*	*1949–50*	*1959–60*	*1963–4*
Total	100	119	172	243
Grains	100	108	104	170
Rice	100	471	729	1,286
Industrial crops	100	313	856	1,508
Fruit	100	110	274	370
Livestock	100	100	146	161

Source: Pernack, op. cit.

Table 17

COMPOSITION OF INVESTMENT BY FIVE-YEAR PLANS (%)

	1951–5	*1956–60*	*1961–5*	*1966–70*	*1971–5*
Total government investments	100·0	100·0	100·0	100·0	100·0
Total investment in production	83·1	81·6	81·8	81·0	
Total investment in other sectors	16·9	18·4	18·2	19·0	

Source: Republika popullore e Shqipërisë, op. cit.

Appendix 169

Table 18

NATIONAL INCOME EXPENDITURE BY FIVE-YEAR PLANS (%)

	1951–5	1956–60	1961–5	1966–70	1971–5
Total national income[a]	100·0	100·0	100·0	100·0	100·0
Total capital accumulation	25·6	26·9	28·7	33·9	37·0
Total expenditure	74·4	74·1	71·3	66·1	63·0

(a) Foreign loans and assistance are included in the national income.

Source: Studime historike, Tiranë 1971, No. 3, p. 10.

Table 19

INCREASES IN LAND UNDER CULTIVATION 1938–1970

	1938	1964	1970
	(hectares)		
Total land area	2,874,800	2,874,800	2,875,000
1. Agricultural land	1,180,000	1,230,100	1,230,000
(a) Crop farming	276,000	442,700	599,000
(b) Truck farming	2,000	22,600	30,000
(c) Vineyards	4,100	12,600	12,000
(d) Olive plantations	10,000	22,900	36,000
(e) Meadows	39,400	17,400	8,000
(f) Pastureland	848,500	717,900	623,000
2. Forest	1,307,700	1,255,500	1,233,000
3. Unproductive land	387,100	389,200	412,000

Source: For 1938 and 1964, *L'Evolution politique et économique de la République populaire d'Albanie (1945–68)*, Secretariat-général du gouvernement, Paris 1969; for 1970, *Republika popullore e Shqipërisë*, op. cit.

BIBLIOGRAPHY

Books

Avramov, Smilja, *Medjunarodno javno pravo, Savremena administracija,* Beograd, 1963.

Amery, Julian, *Sons of the Eagle,* London: Macmillan, 1948.

——, *Approach March: a Venture in Autobiography,* London: Hutchinson, 1973.

Chloros, A. G., *Yugoslav Civil Law,* Oxford University Press, 1970.

Churchill, Winston, *The Second World War,* Vols. I–VI, London, 1948–54.

Conte, Arthur, *Jalta, delitev sveta,* 'Borec', Ljubljana 1969.

Dedijer, Vladimir, *Izgubljeni boj J. V. Stalina 1948–53,* ZGP Delo, Ljubljana, 1969.

——, *Jugoslovensko-albanski odnosi,* 'Borba', Beograd, 1949.

Djilas, Milovan, *Conversations with Stalin,* London: Penguin, 1969.

Dokumenta Kryesore të partisë së punës së Shqipërisë, Vols. I, II, Tiranë, 1960.

Durham, M. Edith, *The Burden of the Balkans,* London, 1905.

——, *High Albania,* London, 1914.

——, *The Struggle for Scutari,* London, 1914.

——, *Twenty Years of Balkan Tangle,* London, 1920.

Edwards, Lovett F., *Yugoslavia,* London: Batsford, 1971.

'L'Evolution Politique et, Économique de la République Populaire D'Albanie (1944–1968)', *La documentation française,* Paris, 1967.

Feis, Herbert, *Churchill Roosevelt Stalin,* Zavod 'Borec', Ljubljana, 1968.

Frashëri, Mehdi, *Liga e Prizrenit edhe efektet diplomatike te saj,* Tiranë, 1927.

Gjeqovi, Shtjefen, *Kanuni i Lekë Dukagjinit, përmbledhur dhe kodifikuar, ribotim sipas botimit të vitit 1933,* Prishtinë, 1972.

Goodwin, Geoffrey L., *Britain and the United Nations,* New York, 1957.

Griffith, William E., *Albania and the Sino-Soviet Rift,* Cambridge, Mass.: M.I.T. Press, 1963.

Grupa Autora, *Ekonomija politike e socijalizmit,* Univerziteti Shtetëror i Tiranës, Tiranë, 1972.

——, *Mbi Lëvizjen kombëtare shqiptare,* Univerziteti Shtetëror i Tiranës, Tiranë, 1962.

——, *Jugoslavia u medjunarodnom radničkom pokretu,* Institut za medjunarodni radnički pokret, Beogard, 1973.

——, *Iz istorije Albanaca,* Zavod za izdavanje udžbenika SR Srbije, Beograd, 1969.

Hamm, Harry, *Albania: China's Beachhead in Europe*, New York: Praeger, 1963.

Hadri, Dr Ali, Lëvizja nacionalçlirimtare në Kosovë 1941–1945, Rilindja, Prishtinë, 1971.

Historia e popullit shqiptar, Vols. I, II, Prishtinë, 1969.

Hoxha, Enver, *Vepra*, Vols. 1–12, Instituti i studimeve Marksiste-Leniniste pranë KQ të PPSH, Tiranë, 1968–72.

Ivanaj, Nikollë, *Historija e shqipëniës së ré*, Shkodër, 1937.

Jankovic, Prof. dr. Branimir, *Medjunarodno javno pravo*, 'Naučna knjiga', Beograd, 1970.

Kessle, G., and Myrdal, J., *Die albanische Herausforderung*, Frankfurt Main, 1971.

Khrushchev, N. I., *Khrushchev Remembers*, London, 1971.

Kodifikimi i Përgjitheshëm i legjislacionit në fuqi të Republikës Popullore të Shqipërisë, Kodet, vellimi I, botim i Kryeministrisë, Tiranë, 1961.

Kongresi VI i PPSH, Tiranë, 1972.

Lah, Dr. Avguštin, *Naše sosedne države*, Prešernova družba, Ljubljana, 1969.

Lendvai, Paul, *L'Europe des Balkans après Stalin*, Paris: Fayard, 1972.

Luarasi, Skender, *Isa Boletini*, Rilindja, Prishtinë, 1972.

Mihajlović, Kosta, *Regionalni razvoj socijalističkih zemalja*, Sprska akademija nauka i umetnosti, Beograd, 1972.

Milanov, Marko, *Život i običaji Arbanasa*, Titograd, 1967.

Mury, Gilbert, *Albanie terre de l'homme nouveau*, Paris: Maspéro, 1970.

Noli, Fan S., *Historia e Skënderbeut*, ribotim simbas botimit të federates pan-shqiptare 'Vatra', Boston, 1950.

Pano, Nicholas C., *The People's Republic of Albania*, Baltimore, 1968.

Pernack, Hans-Joachim, *Probleme der Wirtschaftlichen Entwicklung Albaniens*, München, 1972.

Plomer, William, *The Diamond of Janina: Ali Pasha 1741–1822*, New York: Taplinger, 1970.

Pokreti Otpora u Evropi 1939–1945, 'Mladost', Beograd, 1968.

Pupovci, Dr. Surja, *Gradjanski odnosi u Zakonu Leke Dukadjinija*, Prishtinë, 1968.

Samardjić, Radovan, *Mehmed Sokolovic*, Srpska književna zadruga, Beograd, 1971.

Selmanaj, Selman, Uslovi i koncepcije privrednog razvoja NR Albanije (magistarski rad), Ekonomski fakultet Beograd, januar, 1973.

Senkevic, I. G., Smirnova, N. D., Arsh, G. L., *Histori e shkurtë e Shqipnisë*, Rilindja, Prishtinë, 1967.

Shehu, Mehmet, *Lufta për Çlirimin e Tiranës*, (2nd imp.) Tiranë, 1959.

——, *Kujtime nga jeta e brigades parë sulmuesë*, (2nd imp.) Tiranë, 1959.

Shufflay, Dr. Milan, *Serbët dhe Shqiptarët*, Rilindja, Prishtinë, 1968.

Skendi, Stavro, *Albania*, New York: Praeger, Second Printing, 2nd ed.,
    1958.
———, *The Albanian National Awaking 1878–1912*, Princeton, N.J., 1967.
Smodlaka, Josip, *Partizanski dnevnik*, 'Nolit', Beograd, 1972.
Stipceviq, Aleksandar, *Ilirët*, Rilindja, Prishtinë, 1967.
Stojnić, Veljo, *Današnja Albanija* – članci iz 'Borbe' – knjižara
    'Budućnost', Novi Sad, 1945.
Tucović, Dimitrije, *Srbija i Arbanija*, 'Kultura', Beograd–Zagreb, 1945.
Vukadinović, Dr. Radovan, *Odnosi medju evropskim socijalističkim
    zemljama*, Školska knjiga, Zagreb, 1970.
Wilkinson, H. R., *Maps and Politics*, Liverpool, 1951.

Newspapers and Periodicals
Zeri i Popullit, Tiranë
Rruga e Partisë, Tiranë
Ekonomija Popullore, Tiranë
Nentori, Tiranë
Gjurmime Albanologjike, Prishtinë
Perparimi, Prishtinë
Rilindja, Prishtinë
Godisnjak Instituta za Medjunarodnu Politiku i Privredu, Beograd
Medjunarodna Politika, Beograd
ABSEES, University of Glasgow
Osteuropa, Stuttgart
Le Monde, Paris
Delo, Ljubljana
Politika, Beograd
Nin, Beograd
The Times, London
Nova Makedonija, Skopje
Vjetari Statistikor i RPSH
RPSH Në Jubileun e 30 Vjetorit të PPSH, Tiranë, 1971

INDEX

Essad Pasha, 40
European Security Conference, 126

FAMILY LIFE, 82–91
Fan Noli, 35, 44, 45, 115, 129
Ferrero, Gen., 32
Flag, national, 150
Folklore, 79
Foreign policy, 114–29, 126–9
France, 32, 33
Franciscans, 17
Frontier lines, 30, 31–2, 34

GREECE: CIVIL WAR, 118–9
relations with, 117–9, 128, 154
Grey, Sir Edward, 30

HAMID, SULTAN ABDUL, 26
History, 5–9, 135–7
Housing, 107, 138
Hoxha, Enver, 46, 65, 66, 142; political Commissar, 49; and Anti-Fascist Council, 53; Supreme Commander, 54; Commandant N.L.A., 56; correspondence with Gen. Wilson, 59; career, 66–71; relations with King Zog, 67–8; General Secretary Nat. Conference 1943, 69; founds *Zeri i Popullit*, 69; and Peace Conference 1946, 69, 115; relations with Russia, 70–1, 95, 120; speech on the economy 1970, 110; speech in Tiranë 1944, 117–8; visit to Yugoslavia, 120; pro-Stalin stand, 122; and VII Congress of APL, 125–7
Hoxha, Fadil, 141
Hoxha, Mehmet, 143

ILLITERACY, 78, 139, 148
Independence Proclamation 1912, 28
Industrialization, 4, 94–9, 100–2
International Control Commission 1914, 137
International Court of Justice, 116, 128 (*and see* Corfu incident)
Islamic influence, 16–17, 22, 76
Ismail Qemal Vlora, 27, 28, 137

taly: 32, 33; withdrawal from Albania, 33–4; influence with King Zog, 34, 36; Pact with Albania, 36; occupation 1939, 39, 41, 140; capitulation, 51

JANINA, 18, 19, 21, 25
Janissaries, 11, 12
Jubani, Zef, 22

KAÇANIK, 26
KANC, 53–4, 55–6
Kelmendi, Ali, 45
Krushchev, N., 70, 71, 95, 122, 1623, 12
Kosovë, 24, 45, 58, 138; battle of, 10, 11, 25; General Insurgent Committee of, 27, 28; uprising 1913, 137; and National Liberation struggle, 139–45; autonomous province, 146–51; development of, 146
Krujë, 12, 13, 14

LABINOT CONFERENCE, 49, 51, 142
Labour, Party of (see Communist Party)
Land tenure, 17–18, 102, 138
Language, 4, 5, 7, 17, 22, 25, 148
League of Nations, 34
League of Prizren, 23–5
Legality Party, 52, 55, 69
Legal systems, 63–4, 85
Lenin, V. I., 111
Lleshi, Haxhi, 4, 66, 73
Lloyd George, D., 32, 33
London Conference 1913, 34
London, Treaty of, 31–2
Lushnjë National Congress, 1920, 33, 34

MALINOVSKY, Marshal, 71
Marx, K., 111
Medical care, 107, 139, 148
Mehmet Shehu, 49, 56; biography, 71–3; and Spanish Civil War 72; disagreement with Russia 73; meeting with Chou En-lai, 124
Mihajlović, D., 143
Military missions, 116

Index 177

Mohammed II, Sultan, 13, 14
Molotov, V., 48
Manastir, 25
Montenegro Memorandum 1911, 26
Moscow Conference, 144
Mount Athos, 17
Mukjë Agreement, 51
Munich Conference 1938, 39
Muslim Peza, 44, 46, 59, 68
Mussolini, Benito, 33-4, 39; assistance from Nazis, 43; fall from power, 49

NAPOLEON I, 18
National Bank, 38
National Conference 1943, 69
National Liberation Army (NLA), 51-3
National Liberation Front (NLF), 46; and dispute with Balli Kombëtar, 50
NATO, 126
Nazi invasion, 41, 140
Nelson, Admiral, 18
Nitti, 32
Nixon, President, 125

OIL INDUSTRY, 99, 100

PARTISANS, 46ff., general offensive, 54-5; and Kosovë, 144
Peace Conference 1919, 32, 33, 137; of 1946, 115, 116, 118
Peza Conference, 1942, 69
Philby, H. A. R., 117
Plans, Five-Year (see Economic aspects)
Political organisations, 64-6; systems, 4, 63ff.
Pope Clement XI, 17
Pope Pius II, 14
Population statistics, 3, 138, 146, 147
Professional classes, 108
Progressive Party, 35-6
Prishtinë Memorandum, 28
Purges, 65

QUISLINGS, 52, 140

RANKOVIÇ, A., 149, 151
Rastatt, Treaty of, 22
Rebellions, 12-15, 21, 23, 36, 135, 136, 137 (and see Uprisings)
Regional development, 105-7
Religion, 75-8; suppression of, 77-8
Republic of 1925, 36
Reshad, Sultan Mehmed, 26
Resistance movement, 43-4, 46, 59
Roosevelt, President, 48
Rumelia province, 11, 15, 22
Russo-Albanian relations, 4, 73, 74, 94-6, 122-3
Russo-Austrian Convention (1877), 22
Russo-Turkish War (1877), 23
Rustemi, Avni, 44

SAN STEFANO TREATY, 23, 24, 29
Sarandë operation, 55
Saseno, Italian occupation of, 31, 34
Serbo-Turkish War (1876), 23-4
Shevchet bey Vrlaci, 36, 42
Shkodër, 18, 19, 21, 25, 26, 32, 39
Skenderberg, G., 10, 12-15
Social Security, 78
Social statistics, 38-9
Stalin, 108, 120, 121
Students, 79 (and see Education)

tanzimat, 19, 20
Teheran Conference, 144
Television, as foreign influence, 80
Tepelena, Ali Pasha, 18-19, 21
Tiranë, 33, 117; Agreement, 48; Treaty of, 34; liberation by partisans 1944, 56, 58
Tito, Marshal, 58, 120, 140, 143, 145, 150
Tittoni, Tommaso, 32; and Venizelos Treaty, 32-3
Toptani, Essad Pasha, 31
Tourism industry, 105
Trade, 4, 104-5, 140
Tribal organisation, 82-91, 147; systems, 10, 15-16
Truman, President, 116; 'Truman Doctrine', 117
Turkhan Pasha, 32, 33

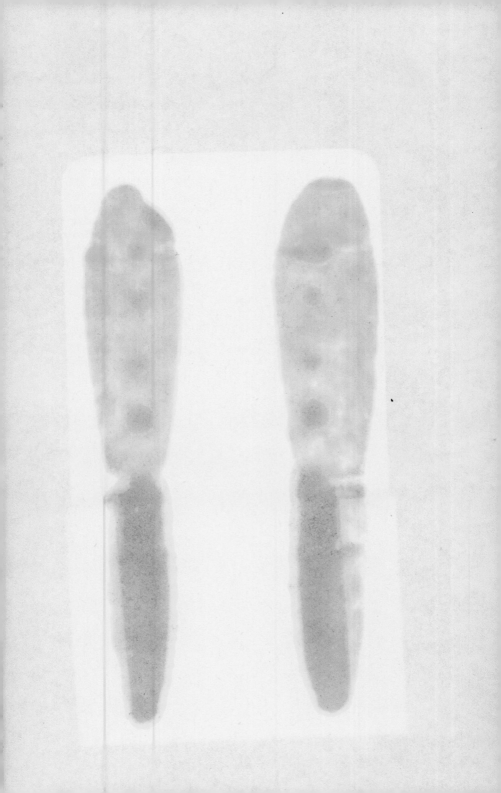

DATE DUE

GAYLORD

PRINTED IN U.S.A.